Women, Islam and Everyday Life

This book examines Islam and women's everyday life, focusing in particular on the highly controversial issue of polygamy. It discusses the competing interpretations of the Qur'anic verses that are at the heart of Muslim controversies over polygamy, with some groups believing that Islam enshrines polygamy as a male right, others seeing it as permitted but discouraged in favour of monogamy and other groups arguing that Islam implicitly prohibits polygamy. Based on detailed fieldwork conducted in Indonesia, it provides an empirically-based account of women's lived experiences in polygamous marriages, describing the different perceptions of the practice and strategies in dealing with it. It also considers the impact of changing public policy, in particular Indonesia's 1974 Marriage Law which restricted the practice of polygamy. It shows that, in fact, this law has not resulted in widespread adherence, and considers how public policy could be modified to increase its effectiveness in affecting behaviour in everyday life. Overall, the book argues that polygamy has been a source of injustice towards women and children, that this is against Islamic teaching and that a just Islamic law would need to call for the abolition of polygamy.

Nina Nurmila is a lecturer at the Faculty of Islamic Education and Teaching at the State Islamic University (UIN) Bandung, Indonesia. She is currently a Fulbright Visiting Professor of Islamic Studies at the University of Redlands, USA. She was previously an Endeavour Postdoctoral Fellow at the University of Technology, Sydney, Australia. Her research interest is Gender and Islam in Muslim Societies, especially Indonesia.

Women in Asia Series
Edited by Louise Edwards
University of Technology Sydney

Editorial Board
Susan Blackburn (Monash University)
Vera Mackie (Melbourne University)
Anne McLaren (Melbourne University)
Mina Roces (University of New South Wales)
Andrea Whittaker (Melbourne University)

Mukkuvar Women
Gender, hegemony and capitalist transformation in a south Indian fishing community
Kalpana Ram

A World of Difference
Islam and gender hierarchy in Turkey
Julie Marcus

Purity and Communal Boundaries
Women and social change in a Bangladeshi village
Santi Rozario

Madonnas and Martyrs
Militarism and violence in the Philippines
Anne-Marie Hilsdon

Masters and Managers
A study of gender relations in urban Java
Norma Sullivan

Matriliny and Modernity
Sexual politics and social change in rural Malaysia
Maila Stivens

Intimate Knowledge
Women and their health in north-east Thailand
Andrea Whittaker

Women in Asia
Tradition, modernity and globalisation
Louise Edwards and Mina Roces (eds)

Violence against Women in Asian Societies
Gender inequality and technologies of violence
Lenore Manderson and Linda Rae Bennett (eds)

Women's Employment in Japan
The experience of part-time workers
Kaye Broadbent

Chinese Women Living and Working
Anne McLaren (ed)

Abortion, Sin and the State in Thailand
Andrea Whittaker

Sexual Violence and the Law in Japan
Catherine Burns

Women, Islam and Modernity
Single women, sexuality and reproductive health in contemporary Indonesia
Linda Rae Bennett

The Women's Movement in Post-Colonial Indonesia
Elizabeth Martyn

Women and Work in Indonesia
Michele Ford and Lyn Parker (eds)

Women and Union Activism in Asia
Kaye Broadbent and Michele Ford (eds)

Gender, Household, and State in Post-Revolutionary Vietnam
Jayne Werner

Gender, Nation and State in Modern Japan
Vera Mackie, Ulrike Woehr and Andrea Germer (eds)

Cambodian Women
Childbirth and maternity in rural south east Asia
Elizabeth Hoban

Gender, Islam, and Democracy in Indonesia
Kathryn Robinson

Gender Diversity in Indonesia
Beyond gender binaries
Sharyn Leanne Graham

Young Women in Japan
Transitions to adulthood
Kaori Okano

Sex, Love and Feminism in the Asia Pacific
A cross-cultural study of young people's attitudes
Chilla Bulbeck

Gender, State and Social Power
Divorce in contemporary Indonesia
Kate O'Shaughnessy

Feminist Movements in Contemporary Japan
Laura Dales

Women, Islam and Everyday Life
Renegotiating polygamy in Indonesia
Nina Nurmila

Women, Islam and Everyday Life
Renegotiating polygamy in Indonesia

Nina Nurmila

LONDON AND NEW YORK

First published 2009
by Routledge
2 Park Square, Milton Park, Abingdon, Oxon, OX14 4RN

Simultaneously published in the USA and Canada
by Routledge
270 Madison Avenue, New York, NY 10016

Routledge is an imprint of the Taylor & Francis Group, an informa business

© 2009 Nina Nurmila

Typeset in Times New Roman by Swales & Willis Ltd, Exeter, Devon

All rights reserved. No part of this book may be reprinted
or reproduced or utilised in any form or by any electronic,
mechanical, or other means, now known or hereafter invented,
including photocopying and recording, or in any information
storage or retrieval system, without permission in writing
from the publishers.

British Library Cataloguing in Publication Data
A catalogue record for this book is available from the British Library

Library of Congress Cataloging in Publication Data
A catalog record for this book has been requested
Women, Islam and everyday life : renegotiating polygamy in Indonesia /
Nina Nurmila.
p. cm.—(Asian studies association of Australia women in Asia series)
Includes bibliographical references and index.
1. Muslim women—Indonesia—Social conditions. 2. Women in Islam—
Indonesia 3. Polygamy—Indonesia. I. Title.
HQ1170.N97 2009
306.84'2308829709598—dc22
2008046102

ISBN 10: 0–415–46802–7 (hbk)
ISBN 10: 0–203–87854–X (ebk)

ISBN 13: 978–0–415–46802–2 (hbk)
ISBN 13: 978–0–203–87854–5 (ebk)

This book is dedicated to my parents
Gholib Rohandi and Eutik Turinah for their
continued support, love and prayers.

Contents

List of illustrations   xi
Series editor's foreword   xii
Acknowledgments   xiii
Glossary   xvii

1 Introduction   1

   Muslim feminist as researcher 11
   Brief outline of chapters 19

2 Polygamy in context: family and kinship   21

   Women's situation in Java 22
   Changing patterns of marriage and family structure in Indonesia 28
   Feminist critiques of the family 33
   Conclusion 37

3 Muslim discourses on polygamy in Indonesia   39

   What is sharī'a? 40
   Muslim interpretations of polygamy 42
   The history of the 1974 Marriage Law 45
   The New Order government regulations on marriage and divorce for civil servants 58
   The promotion of polygamy in the post-Soeharto period 64
   Conclusion 77

4 Reactions to and negotiation around polygamous marriages   78

   Accommodating polygamy (the Textualists) 81
   Resisting polygamy (the Semi-textualists) 92
   Rejecting polygamy (the Contextualists) 103

  Varying degrees of women's acceptance of and resistance
   to polygamy 108

5 Polygamous households   115

  Relationship between wives in polygamous marriages 116
  Polygamous husbands' treatments of their wives 120
  The celebration of important days 131
  Attending wedding ceremonies and official parties 132
  Economic management in polygamous households 133
  The influence of polygamy on children's emotional and
   economic well-being 138
  A bargain with patriarchy and settling for polygamy 143

6 Conclusion   146

  Qur'an is divine, while its interpretation is human 146
  The need for a contextual approach in reading the Qur'an 148

Notes   155
References   174
Index   195

Illustrations

Maps

Map of Indonesia	xii
Map of Java	xiii

Tables

1.1	Bandung participants' origins	14
1.2	Jakarta, Depok and Bogor participants' origins	15
1.3	Participants' educational level in Bandung (as parents)	15
1.4	Participants' educational level in Bandung (as children or adult children of polygamous parents)	15
1.5	Participants' educational level in Jakarta, Depok and Bogor (as parents)	16
1.6	Participants' educational level in Jakarta, Depok and Bogor (as children of polygamous parents)	16
1.7	Household economic level in Bandung	16
1.8	Household economic level in Jakarta, Depok and Bogor	17
4.1	List of informants (*dramatis personae*)	79
5.1	Short reference list of informants (*dramatis personae*)	121

Figure

Book cover: Protest against polygamy on the Polygamy Award night of 25 July 2003 (Photo courtesy of Maman, Rahima). Description of banners: 'Polygamy bukan bersumber dari Islam tapi dari tradisi Masy. Jahiliyah' (Polygamy is not rooted from Islam but from the tradition of Ignorance Society); 'Polygame yes, polygamy no!' (Multiple games yes, polygamy no); 'Poligami adalah bentuk kekerasan terhadap perempuan' (Polygamy is violence against women); 'Jangan kasih izin suami kawin lagi …' (Do not give your husband permission to marry another woman …).

Series Editor's Foreword

The contributions of women to the social, political and economic transformations occurring in the Asian region are legion. Women have served as leaders of nations, communities, workplaces, activist groups and families. Asian women have joined with others to participate in fomenting change at micro and macro levels. They have been both agents and targets of national and international interventions in social policy. In the performance of these myriad roles women have forged new and modern gendered identities that are recognisably global and local. Their experiences are rich, diverse and instructive. The books in this series testify to the central role women play in creating the new Asia and re-creating Asian womanhood. Moreover, these books reveal the resilience and inventiveness of women around the Asian region in the face of entrenched and evolving patriarchal social norms.

Scholars publishing in this series demonstrate a commitment to promoting the productive conversation between Women's Studies and Asian Studies. The need to understand the diversity of experiences of femininity and womanhood around the world increases inexorably as globalisation proceeds apace. Lessons from the experiences of Asian women present us with fresh opportunities for building new possibilities for women's progress the world over.

The Asian Studies Association of Australia (ASAA) sponsors this publication series as part of its on-going commitment to promoting knowledge about women in Asia. In particular, the ASAA Women's Forum provides the intellectual vigour and enthusiasm that maintains the Women in Asia Series (WIAS). The aim of the series, since its inception in 1990, is to promote knowledge about women in Asia to both academic and general audiences. To this end, WIAS books draw on a wide range of disciplines including anthropology, sociology, political science, cultural studies and history.

The Series could not function without the generous professional advice provided by many anonymous readers. Moreover, the wise counsel provided by Peter Sowden and Tom Bates at Routledge is invaluable. WIAS, its authors and the ASAA are very grateful to these people for their expert work.

Louise Edwards
University of Technology Sydney
Series Editor

Acknowledgments

Alhamdulillahi rabbi-'l 'aalamiin. I thank God for making it possible for me to complete this book. This book is based on my PhD thesis in the Gender and Islamic Studies program, University of Melbourne, which I submitted on 12 February 2007. I am grateful to Routledge, London, for publishing this book and making it accessible to wider audience.

I would like to thank many people who have supported me during my PhD studies and the writing of this book. Throughout my studies, I have benefited from the range of expertise of a number of scholars in the University of Melbourne. I would like to express my special gratitude to my principal supervisor, Associate Professor Maila Stivens, for her enormous support, commitment and professional advice during my process of thesis writing. I would also thank Dr. Antonia Finnane, who was my associate supervisor in the first semester of my studies. I am also grateful to Professor Abdullah Saeed, who has been able to offer his expertise in Islamic studies as my associate supervisor after my conversion to PhD in mid 2003. I thank Dr. Kate McGregor for her extensive feedback on my thesis. She took over the principal supervision for a year when Maila was a visiting fellow at National University of Singapore, in 2004, and continued as my associate supervisor from early 2005.

Associate Professor Susan Blackburn from Monash University has also played an important role in this book. It was she who suggested that I publish my thesis as a book and put me in contact with Professor Louise Edwards, an editor of Asian Studies Association of Australia (ASAA), Women in Asia series. Professor Edwards has been working efficiently to supervise me from the early stage of writing a book proposal to turning my thesis into this book. I am very grateful for her supervision and her enormous support, such as providing me with office facilities and library access during my postdoctoral fellowship at the Institute for International Studies (IIS), University of Technology, Sydney (UTS), to prepare this book.

I would also like to thank several funding sources that have supported me throughout my studies and in preparing this book. First, I thank Australian Aid (AusAID) for providing me with an Australian Development Scholarship (ADS) to undertake my PhD in Australia with my family. Second, I am grateful to the Department of Education, Employment and Workplace Relations (DEEWR), Australia, for granting me an Endeavour Postdoctoral Award, which allowed me to prepare for the publication of this book at IIS, UTS, under direct supervision of my publisher's editor.

I acknowledge the help of Dr. Robert Cribb (Australian National University), who provided me with the maps of Indonesia and Java island. I really appreciate Ciciek Farha's help in introducing me to Maman at Rahima, who was able to provide me with photographs of Indonesian feminist protests against polygamy for the cover of this book.

I would also like to express my gratitude to many postgraduate students for their friendship and support while I was studying in Melbourne. They are, among others, Amelia Fauzia, Arskal Salim, Emi Emilia and their families, Dina Sona Laila and Cirila Limpangog. I also thank many friends who have supported me during my postdoctoral fellowship in Sydney. I am grateful to Maimunah and Nur Wulan's family for their warm welcome and for helping me to adjust and survive in Sydney; Dr. Nadirsyah Hosen's family for their hospitality and lovely conversation during our visit to Wollongong; and Jamila Hussain for sharing her experience in teaching Islamic Law and having a lunch together in her lovely house.

I would also like to acknowledge the support of my employers, Prof. Dr. H. Endang Soetari, Ad. M.Si and Prof. Dr. H. Ahmad Tafsir, the former rector and the dean of Islamic Education Faculty, State Institute of Islamic Studies (IAIN), Bandung, respectively, who gave me permission to study abroad. I also thank Prof. Dr. H. Nanat Fatah Natsir, the current rector of IAIN Bandung, which became UIN (State Islamic University) in 2005, and Dr. H. Afifuddin, MM, the current dean of Islamic Education and Teaching Faculty, for supporting me and giving me permission to undertake a postdoctoral fellowship in Sydney. I thank also Prof. Dr. H. Juhaya S. Praja, a professor of Islamic law, UIN Bandung, for being my external supervisor during my PhD fieldwork in Indonesia.

I am grateful to my sisters Irma Riyani, M.Ag, MA, and Nunung Nurdianah, S.Ag, and my brother, Irfan Nugraha, S.Ag, for their support during my fieldwork in Indonesia. I also thank my other sisters, Dra. Yanti Nuriyah, M.Ag, and Lilis Rahmi, S.Sos, for helping me with many non-academic matters that I could not handle when I was away. I would also like to thank my parents, Drs. H.O. Gholib Rohandi and Hj. E. Turinah, BA, who have always encouraged and supported me to pursue my higher education and prayed for my success. My father passed away on 9 July 2007 not long after we received the news that I had successfully completed my PhD. I felt very sorry that he did not have the opportunity to see the progress of my career after the completion of my PhD.

I devote my sincerest gratitude to my beloved husband, Drs. Sirajudin, MM, for his enormous support, patience, understanding and encouragement. The company of my husband and children, Ardhia Razna Ramadhan (14) and Afrizal Razna Rahman (4), during both my PhD studies in Melbourne and my postdoctoral fellowship in Sydney, has made my life more colourful. Without them, I would be very lonely and miserable.

My deepest thanks are directed to all my research participants, but for reasons of confidentiality, I cannot mention their names. I hope this book will fulfill some of their expectations: to uncover discomfort, violence and betrayal under the guise of male religious piety.

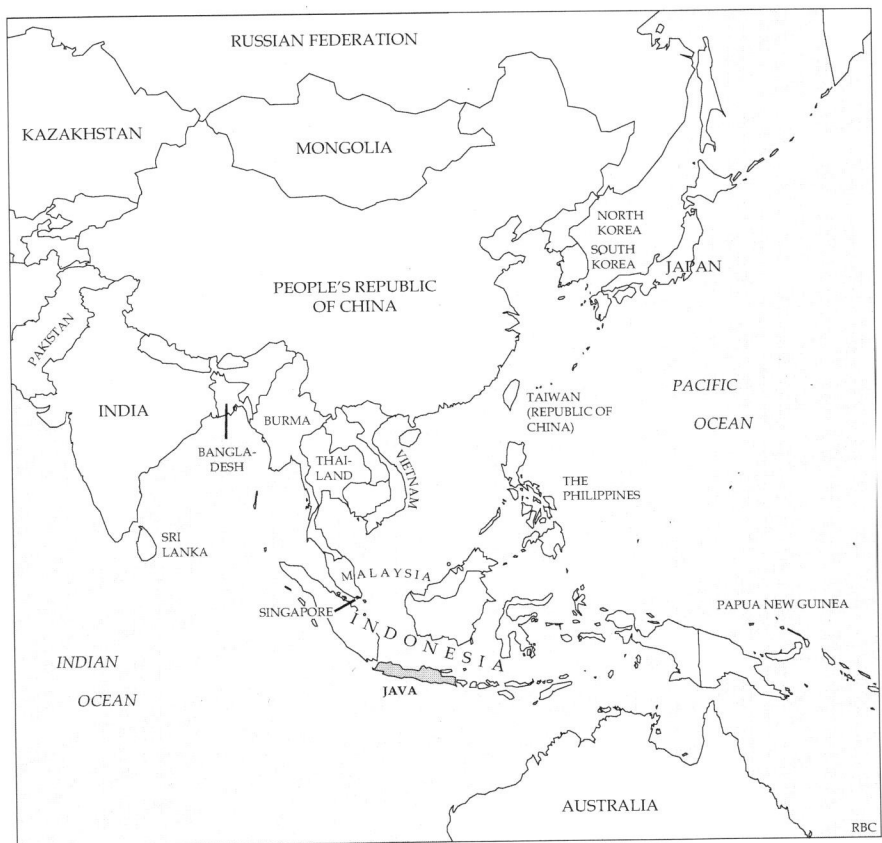

Map of Indonesia

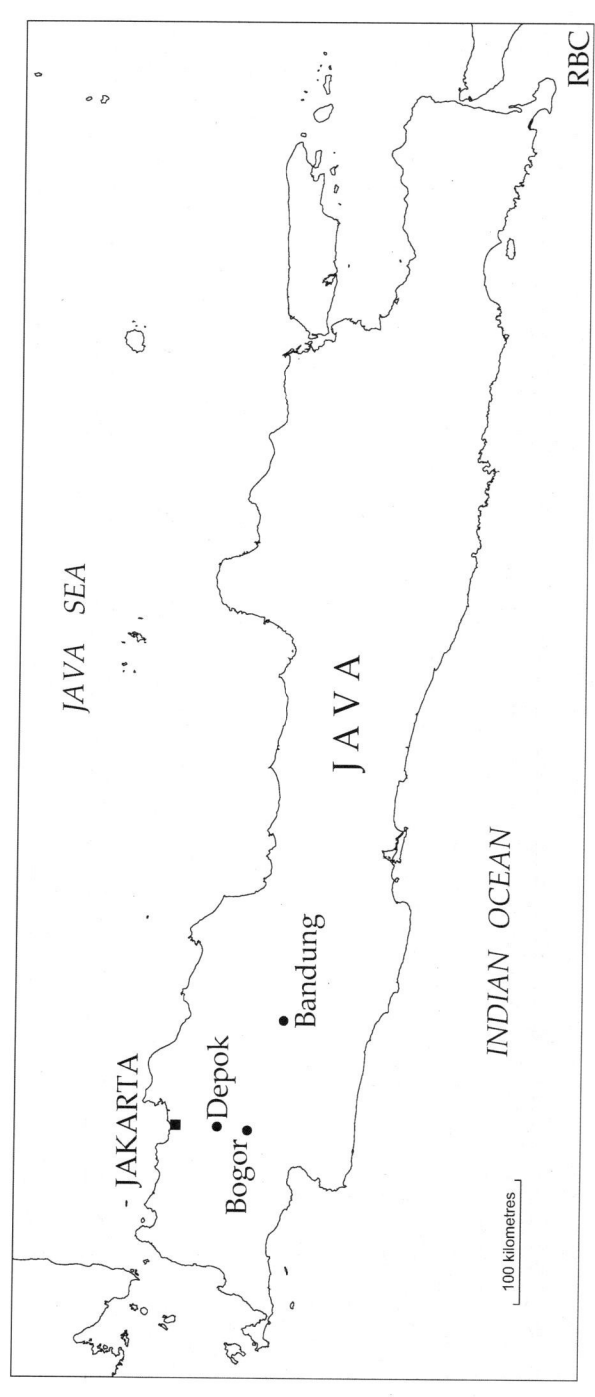

Map of Java

Glossary

Adat   customary systems
Fiqh   Islamic jurisprudence
Idul Fitri   Muslim feast after the end of the fasting month. In Indonesia, it is commonly called *lebaran*
Hadith   prophetic tradition
Ijtihad   Muslim's effort to understand the meaning of the Qur'anic verses
Idul Adha   Muslim feast after the end of Muslim pilgrimage to Mecca
Kiayi   Muslim religious leader
Mahar   a gift, usually gold or money, paid to the bride herself by the bridegroom. In Indonesia, it is commonly called *mas kawin*
Ojek   a motorcycle that carries public passenger
Pesantren   Muslim boarding school
Polygamy   derived from the Greek words 'poly' (many) and 'gamy' (marriage). It refers to marriage in which a spouse of either sex has more than one mate at the same time. The term 'polygamy' encompasses polyandry and polygyny. Polyandry ('andr' is the Greek stem for 'man') refers to marriage between one woman and two or more men, while polygyny ('gyn' is the Greek stem for 'woman') refers to marriage between a man and two or more women (Jones, 1994: 268; Bretschneider, 1995: 50). For the purpose of this book, the term polygamy will be used to refer to a man who has more than one wife at the same time.
Tafsir   Qur'anic exegesis
Ulama   religious scholars
Zina   an illicit sexual relationship.

Note on currency conventer: Australian dollars (A$) 1 = Rp. 7000 (IDR) in 2004 (the time of my field research).

On the age of participants: stated ages are participants' ages in 2004.

1 Introduction

> I disagree with polygamy that is practiced these days because it is based only on lust. One example is my husband, who entered into polygamy, even though he is not yet economically capable [of supporting his wife]. ... Several months after his second marriage, he had large debts and his children's tuition was unpaid. With that large debt, I thought that I had to ask my husband to divorce his second wife before our economic position further deteriorated.[1]
>
> (Interview with Tuti, 23 February 2004)[2]

This book explores Muslim women's perspectives on and experiences with polygamous marriages in Java, Indonesia, during the post-Soeharto period (after 1998). The quote above is the perception of one of my female interviewees about her experience of living in a polygamous marriage. It reflects Tuti's disapproval of her husband's second marriage and the resulting economic problems. These affected not only his own well-being but also that of his wives and children. However, Indonesian laws regulating polygamy appear more concerned with meeting men's interests in having subservient wives and less concerned with women's interests. Women who are unable to bear children or are sick are particularly vulnerable.

In Indonesia, polygamy is legal, but the law discourages and restricts its practice. The present Marriage Law, which was enacted in 1974, states that a man can take additional wives if his established wife is unable to fulfill her duties as a wife, is unable to bear children, or has an incurable illness. Before taking another wife, he must obtain permission from a Religious Court. This permission can be granted if the husband can demonstrate that he is financially capable of supporting more than one wife and capable of being just to his wives, and if he obtains the consent of the established wife/wives (Department of Information, 1979: 10–11).

In practice, it is not easy to know the actual number of incidences of polygamy in Indonesia because of the high prevalence of unregistered marriages. But overall, prior to the enactment of the 1974 Marriage Law, about 5 percent of all marriages were polygamous (Azra, 2003: 89; Bowen, 2003: 202). Vreede-de Stuers (1960: 128) and Geertz (1961: 131) reported, respectively, that in 1939 and 1953 the prevalence of polygamy in Java was 2 percent of all marriages. At a glance, this seems to be low, but when we look at the actual number of polygamous marriages it is quite large (163,362 out of 8,230,788 marriages). That is why polygamy has become one of the burning concerns of Indonesian women's organizations, since their first congress in 1928.

Jones also reported the incidence of polygamy in the Netherland Indies (now Indonesia) in earlier times, which varied from region to region. For instance, the 1920 Population Census showed that 1.5 percent of Javanese husbands were polygamous. The 1930 Census showed that 1.9 percent of Javanese husbands had more than one wife, while the rate of polygamy in the Outer Islands was about double that in Java (4.4 percent). The highest incidence of polygamy in 1930 was in Nusa Tenggara (Sumba 13 percent and Flores 12 percent), where traditional beliefs were more prevalent than Islamic influence. In more Islamized regions, the highest incidence of polygamy was in West Sumatra (9 percent) and then Lampung (5.9 percent) (Jones, 1994: 269–70). The practice of polygamy among rulers was an exception to the majority of monogamous marriages. For rulers, having many wives not only fulfilled their sexual desire but also indicated their high status and could be used as a diplomatic weapon (Reid, 1988: 151 and Lubis, 2000: 217–20). For instance, Sutherland (cited in Jones 1994: 270) reported that almost all Javanese Regents in the nineteenth century had more than one wife. The practice of polygamy among aristocratic men seems to continue until the early twentieth century.

Azra suggests that the percentage of polygamous marriages was probably lower after the 1974 Marriage Law, which made polygamy more difficult (2003: 89). Indeed, it might be officially lower than before the enactment of the Marriage Law, but the official figures should be accepted with caution owing to many cases of unregistered secret polygamy during the Soeharto period, as Suryakusuma (1996) suggested. In addition, as this book will show, in the post-Soeharto period polygamy has been promoted mainly among Islamists or Islamist political party members.

Despite the widespread and growing occurrence of polygamous households in Indonesia, there is a surprising dearth of detailed scholarship. In two recent studies, Susan Blackburn (2004) and Anita Rahman (2005) both noted the paucity of analysis on Indonesian polygamy.[3] Blackburn stated:

> In researching this book, I have been struck by the lack of documentation on women's experience of some of the important issues discussed, notably in relation to polygamy. Considering how crucial this issue has been within the women's movement and in its relation with the state, it is surprising how little evidence there is of the impact of polygamy on women's lives and how this changed over time.
>
> (Blackburn, 2004a: 226)

By providing detailed data from an empirical study of 39 households in Bandung, Bogor, Depok and Jakarta, the book fills the gaps in the existing literature on polygamy. In particular it explores polygamy in Islam, which has mainly centred on men's normative views of polygamy, as the discussion below reveals. This book sheds light on women's agency within polygamy, countering the existing view of women as passive and helpless victims of male subordination. As pointed out by Moghadam (2003a: 26–7), much feminist scholarship over the past 20 years shows that women are not merely passive recipients of social change, but are active agents of such change. Women and men are 'makers of history and builders of movements and societies'. Like women in the Middle East and North Africa (Moghadam, 2003a: 27), Indonesian women are also agents and have also been actively involved in social movements.[4] As will be demonstrated in Chapter 3, since the early twentieth century, Indonesian women have organized themselves and actively resisted various forms of injustice toward women such as child marriage, forced marriage, unilateral divorce and arbitrary polygamy by continually campaigning for marriage law reform (Vreede-de Stuers, 1960; KOWANI, 1978; Blackburn and Bessell, 1997; Martyn, 2005).

As a work of feminist scholarship, this book is not merely a collection of data about polygamy in Indonesia. 'It is a directly political and discursive *practice* in that it is purposeful and ideological' (her emphasis) (Mohanty, 1991: 53). This research is also intended as a significant intervention into the mainstream hegemonic interpretation of polygamy as it is written into Indonesian Marriage Law and government regulations. This study aims to be a political praxis that counters and resists the state's 'legitimate' interpretation of polygamy. The results of my research should have important implications for policy makers in relation to possible amendments of the Marriage Law on the issue of polygamy, especially with recent moves to prohibit the practice.

However, while this book is not a study of law *per se*, nonetheless, I am necessarily concerned with the social construction of law in Indonesia, and with the ways in which men and women interpret laws on an everyday basis. I am not a lawyer, but in order to understand the gap between the written law and the everyday practice of the law in relation to polygamy, I have read a great deal of legal material. I have also researched the historical and political background of marriage laws in Indonesia, focusing particularly on the 1974 Marriage Law and its related government regulations such as PP 10 and *Kompilasi Hukum Islam* (the Compilation of Muslim Family Law).[5] My research has delved into the complex world of Islamic law and its interpretations by Muslim scholars, religious leaders, community elders and lawyers. In addition, it has explored the manner in which ordinary people interpret and put into practice the advice these community leaders have provided.

In everyday life, even though codified laws such as the Marriage Law and the Compilation exist, many Indonesian Muslims prefer to follow the classical *fiqh*. *Fiqh*, which literally means 'understanding', is the result of Muslim scholars' understandings of the Qur'an and Hadith (prophetic tradition) in law-related issues (*ijtihad*). It is commonly called Islamic jurisprudence, or Islamic law, and is mainly written by male medieval *ulama* (religious scholars). Codified Muslim family/personal laws are derived from *fiqh* works, and modified to reflect the situation of the country at the time of the codification. Thus, they are like a national *ijtihad*. Many Indonesian literalist Muslims consider the stipulations of the Marriage Law and the Compilation, which are not found in the *fiqh* works, as 'secular'[6] and 'un-Islamic'.[7]

Therefore, they regard stipulations such as marriage registration and court intervention in cases of divorce and polygamy as unnecessary.

Following Abdullah Saeed's discussion of Muslims in Australia, I define 'Islamic law' as any law which does not contradict one's fundamental beliefs as a Muslim, and which is based on basic principles common to Islamic law, such as equity, justice and fairness.

> There are hundreds of thousands of laws that actually govern our lives, our relationships to others and various institutions in the country. All these become acceptable laws for the purpose of practice, but because these do not seem to be in conflict with one's beliefs as a Muslim, they are also seen as Islamic. So they're not actually in contradiction with my core beliefs as a Muslim and I take them as acceptable and Islamic for the purpose of practice. For a Muslim, the principles on which many of these laws are based are Islamic, such as equity, justice, and fairness. For this Muslim, these laws are not burdensome, so-called secular laws, they are Islamic. The Muslim has Islamized them in practice by considering them to be not in conflict with his or her beliefs:
>
> (Saeed, 2002: 3)

Saeed's view on the constituent elements of Islamic law is more inclusive, as it includes even secular laws (such as traffic laws, company law and taxation law) as long as they do not contradict one's basic Muslim beliefs and principles. Based on this definition, I shall argue that marriage registration and court intervention in cases of divorce and polygamy – as stipulated under Indonesian Marriage Law and the Compilation – *are* Islamic, because they aim to prevent injustice toward women and to reduce the incidence of divorce and polygamy, which many Indonesian Muslims believe to be discouraged under Islam: this belief derives from a *hadith*, narrated by Abdullah ibn Umar: '*The Prophet (peace be upon him) said: Of all the lawful acts the most detestable to Allah is divorce*' (Abu-Dawud, 2007).

My acceptance of Saeed's inclusive definition of Islamic law also affects my attitudes toward secular concepts such as feminism, which I consider to be in harmony with Islamic principles because it aims to achieve justice and equality.[8] I see feminism as *an awareness of the existing oppression or subordination of women because of their sex and as working to eliminate such oppression or subordination and to achieve equal gender relations between men and women.*[9] I am aware, however, that at a practical level western feminists' actions may differ from those of Indonesian feminists, because of a different context and different assumptions regarding the sources of injustice toward women and how to eliminate such injustice. For instance, Indonesian feminists in the first half of the twentieth century were very active in the national struggles for independence, unlike European or American feminists. In addition, many Indonesian women stressed harmony with their male counterpart, supporting 'companionate feminism' (Locher-Scholten, 2003) – an approach not shared by all sectors of western feminism, which the former saw as often too confrontational. I also agree with Sears (1996: 12), who sees 'all feminisms conditioned by questions of class, ethnicity, sexual orientation, religion, seniority, and ideology'. Thus, diverse groups of feminists exist, and their struggles may take different forms depending on what they identify as the cause of their injustice.

Drawing on my intensive research in four locations in Java, this study aims to answer the following research questions:

1 What are the characteristics of Indonesian Muslim discourses on polygamy?
2 What are Muslim women's perspectives on polygamy, and what are their experiences in polygamous marriages in Java, Indonesia, during the post-Soeharto period (after 1998)?
3 What is Indonesian society's response to polygamous marriages?
4 How does polygamy affect the well-being of women and their children?

The post-Soeharto period, in terms of practices relating to polygamy, is distinctively different from the time that preceded this era. On coming to power, it was clear that the Soeharto government (1966–98) saw polygamy and divorce as social problems. Polygamy and divorce were not only discouraged by the Law and government regulations, but also by the president's obvious disapproval of polygamy. During this period, polygamous marriages were considered to be deviant from the 'normal' heterosexual monogamous marriage advocated by the Soeharto government. President Soeharto and especially his wife expressed negative attitudes toward divorce and polygamy. They not only provided a role model for the rest of Indonesian society, but also played a significant role in 'punishing' high-ranking officials who disobeyed the Government Regulations on marriage and divorce. Any high-ranking officials who were known to have extramarital relationships or to have divorced or committed polygamy were relieved from their position. For instance, Widjojo Nitisastro, who divorced his wife to marry his secretary, was relieved from his position as Minister for National Development, even though he still held the position of Economic Advisor to former President Soeharto (Suryakusuma, 1996).

During these years, women's media, such as the magazine *Femina*, and numerous women's organizations also expressed their opposition to polygamy. In the 1980s two moderate Muslim women's organizations, Muslimat NU (*Nahdlatul Ulama*, the largest moderate Muslim organization founded in 1926) and Aisyiyah, promoted the ideal family under the concept of *keluarga maslahah* (virtuous and prosperous family) and *keluarga sakinah* (peaceful family), respectively (Candland and Nurjanah, 2004). In 1985, the Indonesian government adopted the latter concept to promote a family planning program, in which the ideal family consists of two monogamous parents, a breadwinner husband and a housewife and two children – similar to the idealized western concept of the nuclear family.

As a result, many proponents of polygamy kept silent about their views on polygamy. Many Indonesians regarded polygamy as a shameful act that needed to be kept secret. But sooner or later, the secret practice of polygamy usually became public, and invited negative reactions. These negative reactions were usually directed to polygamous husbands and to their first or additional wives. First wives were usually blamed for not being able to 'serve' (*melayani*) their husband well – which is considered their duty – or suspected of having an incurable illness or of being barren if they did not bear children. Additional wives are often spoken of as bees that take honey from flowers and fly away when the honey is gone. This construction of a 'good wife' (*istri yang baik*) who has to be healthy, to 'serve' or support her husband and to bear children, is written in the Marriage Law and the Compilation, which 'allow' a husband to take another wife if his first wife is not 'good'. In addition, this construction of a 'good wife' was also promoted by two government-created women's organizations: *PKK* (*Pembinaan Kesejahteraan Keluarga*/Family Welfare Movement) and *Dharma Wanita*. The latter is an organization of the wives of civil servants designed to facilitate women's support of their husbands' careers in service of the nation and the state.[10] The *PKK* is a rural-based organization led by the wife of the village head. Every village in Indonesia has a branch of this organization, and its program is displayed in front of the village head office. Both of these organizations promote state ideology stated in *Panca Dharma Wanita* (Five Responsibilities of Women): A wife is to (1) support her husband's career and duties; (2) provide offspring; (3) care for and rear the children; (4) be a good housekeeper; and (5) be a guardian of the community (Sunindyo, 1996: 125).[11]

After the Soeharto period, proponents of polygamy became increasingly outspoken in their support for polygamy, especially during the presidency of Megawati (2001–4). One possible explanation is that her Vice President's practice of polygamy contributed to more relaxed attitudes toward polygamy, allowing for its public promotion. This promotion was mainly sponsored by Puspo Wardoyo, a prominent successful restaurateur who had four wives. Given the influence of this promotion on the increasing openness of some men about their polygamous marriages, I shall examine it more closely in Chapter 3: my research took place in this context of intense public debates surrounding Wardoyo's polygamy. Wardoyo even sponsored a Polygamy Award night in July 2003. Several months after that, I commenced my field research in December 2003. As I shall describe, some of my research subjects participated in this Award night, and appeared to be proud of their practice. But others disagreed with Wardoyo, and tried to counter his representation that 'polygamy is nice or beautiful (*poligami itu indah*)'.

In addition, the post-Soeharto period was also characterized by a more visible 'popular re-Islamization' (Robinson, 2001: 18), or Islamic 'resurgence' or revival (Brenner, 1996: 679) led by Islamist groups. Islamism, according to Roy (2002: 58), is:

> the brand of modern political Islamic fundamentalism that claims to re-create a true Islamic society, not simply by imposing *sharia*, but by establishing first an Islamic state through political action. Islamists see Islam not as a mere religion, but as a political ideology that should reshape all aspects of society (politics, law, economy, social justice, foreign policy, and so on).

Similarly, Tibi (2002: xxv) sees Islamism as 'an aggressive politicization of religion undertaken in the pursuit of nonreligious ends'. In addition, according to

Saeed (2006a: 144), Islamists or political Islamists are strongly against 'westernization' and modern ideologies such as nationalism, secularism and communism. For the purpose of this book, I shall expand this definition of Islamists to include literalist 'conservative' Muslims who are concerned with the implementation of *shari'a*, not necessarily interested in establishing an Islamic state such as members of organizations like *Hizbut Tahrir Indonesia* (HTI), *Majlis Mujahidin Indonesia* (MMI), *Jamaah Islamiyah* (JI) and *Front Pembela Islam*/FPI (Islamic Defence Front). These groups are often called conservative, revivalist, fundamentalist or hard-line Muslims (Azra, 2005b: 203). Within this group, as with Islamist groups in other countries where the majority of citizens are Muslims, such as Egypt (Mahmood, 2005) and Turkey (Göle, 1996, 2000), Islam is seen as an alternative, perhaps as a mode of resistance to western, capitalist modernity (Brenner, 1996).

This popular re-Islamization is partly evidenced by the demands made by Islamist political parties (such as *Partai Bulan Bintang*/PBB, The Moon and the Star Party, and *Partai Keadilan Sejahtera*/PKS, the Prosperous Justice Party) in 2000 to return to the Jakarta Charter by formally re-including the implementation of *shari'a* in the Indonesian Constitution.[12] This demand, however, was unsuccessful owing to an absence of support from mainstream parties such as Golkar, PPP and PKB (Salim, 2006). But these Islamist parties did not seem to give up on their efforts. They continued their attempt to formally implement *shari'a* at the regional level by taking advantage of decentralization. They tried to enact PERDA (*Peraturan Daerah*/Regional Regulation) on the implementation of *shari'a*. In 2006, several regional governments such as Cianjur, Banten (both are located in West Java), Aceh, and Bulukumba in South Sulawesi have enacted this PERDA. This has threatened women's rights because the implementation of *shari'a* in Indonesia was mainly based on a literal interpretation of the Qur'an, which tends to marginalize women and restrict their movement (Noerdin, 2002).[13] In addition, decentralization tends to revive local 'traditional' culture, which in many regions often means the return of patriarchy (Budianta, 2006).

The anti-pornographic materials and actions draft law (*Rancangan Undang-Undang Anti Pornografi dan Pornoaksi*/RUU APP) widely discussed in 2006 shows further government efforts to control women's dress and behavior, mainly supported by Islamist parties. The law was drafted in 2003 by the parliament members of the Committee VI, but was not discussed in the parliament until 2006 owing to many other important work priorities. The draft was publicly discussed in response to the increasing spread of pornographic media (both electronic and printed media such as the publication of the Indonesian version of *Playboy* magazine) and porno-action (such as the erotic dance of Inul Daratista). This draft was mainly debated by its proponents such as MUI (religious scholars council of Indonesia), ICMI (the association of Indonesian Muslim scholars), Hizbut Tahrir, FPI (defenders front of Islam), MMI (council of Indonesian Muslim fighters) and PKS (Prosperous Justice Party) on one side, and the opponents of the draft such as women's activists (feminists), artists, Liberal Muslims (JIL) and academicians on the other (Hakim, 2006). The proponents of this draft argue that pornography is against religious teaching and destroys the morality of the society, and can lead to sexual harassment and rape of women and under-aged girls, even by their family members. Therefore, the government has to regulate it (Hakim, 2006). The opponents of the draft also argue against pornography but they disagree with the law. They see the draft to be ambiguous in defining pornography and argue instead that the focus should be on women as the subject of pornography, in order to protect them from exploitation within male hegemonic culture. They propose that the government regulate the availability of pornographic movies, picture and so on, rather than regulate women's proper dress and behavior (*Indonesia Matters*, 2008). Because of the controversial nature of this draft, it was in legal deadlock until 30 October 2008, when it was finally passed into law despite of the controversy.

Furthermore, many Islamists understand polygamy to be permitted in Islam and part of *shariʿa*.[14] They support the promotion of polygamy as the promotion of an 'Islamic value', to counter and even resist western culture, which they regard as against polygamy but allowing sex without marriage. Many Islamists suggest that polygamy is far better than 'western permissive sexual freedom' or extramarital relationships (*selingkuh*).[15] This constitutes a shift from the dominant and mainstream discourse of polygamy, wherein a first wife is blamed when her husband takes another wife, to outright admiration by Islamists of the first wife who allows her husband to take another wife (e.g. Dodik, 2006; Majelis Muda Muslim Bandung (M3B), 2006; Tim Detikcom, 2006; *The Australian*, 2006).[16]

However, it is surprising that in this context of popular re-Islamization, Indonesian feminists were successful in their lobbies against domestic violence. After years of efforts, in September 2004 the Indonesian government enacted Law No. 23/2004 on the Eradication of Domestic Violence (*Undang-undang Penghapusan Kekerasan dalam Rumah Tangga/UU PKDRT*). This Law is radical for bringing violence occurring in the domestic sphere, which has usually been regarded as private, into the public arena and regarding it as a criminal act, making the perpetrators of the violence subject to punishment such as fines and imprisonment. This Law also broadly define domestic violence to include physical, psychological, sexual and economic neglect. It also covers all members of household: extended-family members and domestic servants also come under its protection – not just the husband, wife and their children (Bataramunti, 2006; Republik Indonesia, 2006).[17] My research, therefore, will provide unique insights into women's and men's experiences of polygamous marriage in the changing political situation of post-Soeharto Indonesia.

There is a significant body of writing on polygamy beyond the Indonesian case study in the scholarly literature. Outside the Muslim world, social research on polygamy has mainly focused on Mormon fundamentalists in the United States of America (USA) during the nineteenth century and more recently (e.g. Altman and Ginat, 1996; Iversen, 1997; Peck, 2006; Ostling and Ostling, 1999). There has also been significant writing on polygamy in Africa (e.g. Gage-Brandon, 1992; Grossbard-Shechman, 1993; Jacoby, 1995; Schoellman and Tertilt, 2006; Spencer, 1998).[18] In the Muslim world, almost all *fiqh* (Islamic jurisprudence) and *tafsir* (Qur'anic exegesis) works have a section discussing Muslim interpretations of the Qur'anic verse 4: 3 on polygamy (e.g. Averroes, 1995; al-Zamakhsharī, 1995;

al-Zuḥaylī, 1991). Other than *tafsir* and *fiqh* works, there are many books on women in Islam that also include discussions of polygamy. These books are mainly written by men and offer their normative perspectives on polygamy (e.g. Khan, 1995a, 1995b; Muṭahharī, 1981).

Since the mid 1970s, and especially since the early 1990s, there has been an increasing body of literature on women in Islam written by Muslim women scholars (e.g. Afshar, 1998; Ahmed, 1992; Al-Hibri, 1982; Barlas, 2002; Hassan, 1999, 2002; Jawad, 1998; Mernissi, 1975, 1991, 1994, 1996; Wadud, 1992, 1999, 2006).[19] They have offered critical feminist points of views on various women's issues in Islam, such as veiling, female circumcision, the story of the creation of the first humankind, leadership, inheritance, marriage, divorce and polygamy. On polygamy, they mainly argue that Islam prefers monogamy and discourages polygamy (Afshar, 1998; Jawad, 1998). They emphasize that the main import of Qur'anic verses 4: 2–3 and 129 is not about polygamy but about justice, especially just treatment of orphans and women (Wadud, 1999; Barlas, 2002). These Muslim feminist points of view provide a counterbalance to the views of conservative male Muslims, who tend to see polygamy as a male right. Their feminist scholarship has also influenced many Indonesian Muslim scholars both men (e.g. Abdul Kodir, 2001, 2002, 2004, 2005, 2007; Alimi, 2002, 2004; Alimi *et al.*, 1999; Mas'udi, 1997; Umar, 1999a, 2002a, 2002b; Umar *et al.*, 2004;) and women (e.g. Dzuhayatin *et al.*, 2002; Ismail, 2003; Mulia, 1999, 2005a, 2005b, 2006, 2007, 2008; Subhan, 1999) in writing about gender equality in Islam including the issue of polygamy. These Indonesian feminist works have been very useful in countering the existing patriarchal culture and the increasing widespread of Islamism in Indonesia.

There are many books published in Indonesia which particularly focus on polygamy: before Puspo Wardoyo's campaign of polygamy (e.g. Ja'afar, 1995; Mulia, 1999);[20] and after his campaign of polygamy (e.g. Abdul Kodir, 2005a); and even more after the practice of polygamy of Aa Gym, a famous Indonesian preacher, known to the public (e.g. Aedy, 2007; Amarudin, 2007; Basyir, 2007; Faridl, 2007; Gusmian, 2007; Mustofa, 2007; Takariawan, 2007). These books can be categorized into three groups.[21] The first group are the books that argue against the abuse of polygamy to fulfill male sexual desire and try to emphasize that Islam prefers monogamy because it can prevent men from despotic and unjust treatment of women (e.g. Abdul Kodir, 2005a; Gusmian, 2007; Mursalin, 2007; Mustofa, 2007; Takariawan, 2007). These books also try to critically evaluate and counter the argument made by the proponents of polygamy, such as 'polygamy is part of *shari'a* or *ibadah* [worship] or *sunnah* [recommended act]' and '*lebih baik polygamy daripada zina* [polygamy is better than adultery]'. Even though men are the authors of all of these books, they argue for equality and justice for both men and women. The second group are the books that try to take the middle or neutral position, such as that by Faridl (2007). However, his book cannot hide its male-biased position in repeatedly stating that polygamy is permitted by Islam in certain circumstances such as when a wife cannot sexually 'serve' her husband, when he wants to have children and to fulfill his high sexual desire. In these circumstances, the book argues, polygamy is a solution that is better than *zina,* an argument commonly quoted by the proponents of polygamy. The third group includes the books written in response to the Indonesian feminist call to ban polygamy. They argue that polygamy is permitted by Islam and describe the 'benefit' of polygamy for both men and women from their male perspective (e.g. Aedy, 2007; Amarudin, 2007; Basyir, 2007). Most of these books are written by Islamists or members of Islamist parties such as PKS (Prosperous Justice Party).

There is an exception to the majority of Islamists who mostly argue for polygamy or promote polygamy as part of Islam. Cahyadi Takariawan (2007), one of the founders and members of the consultative council of PKS, shows his disagreement with the practice of polygamy, which is commonly recommended and practiced by PKS members. His disagreement with the practice of polygamy, which he wrote about in his book, was based on his observation as a family consultant among PKS members, which led him to conclude that polygamy could destroy the family institution, especially for women and children. Unlike his fellow members of PKS who argue that polygamy can smoothen their *dakwah* (missionary activities), he argues that polygamy can become obstacles of *dakwah*. Some PKS members and leaders who practice polygamy reportedly show their upset and disagreement with his book and try to stop its distribution for fear of preventing PKS women from entering polygamous marriage (Jawa Pos, 2007). Didin Amarudin, vice treasurer of PKS, who has three wives, even wrote a book specifically to criticize Takariawan's book, which he believes to be misleading (Amarudin, 2007).

However, most of these books and the Muslim feminist works discussed earlier are mainly concerned with the legal views of polygamy, or with the interpretation of the Qur'an. None of them focuses on the experience of living in a polygamous marriage. Thus, their approach tends to be normative rather than anthropological.

Many anthropological studies of marriage and kinship in Indonesia include some discussions of polygamy, but most do not discuss it at length (e.g. Djamour, 1965; Firth, 1966; Geertz, 1961; Reenen, 1996). I will discuss those studies that do focus on the practice of polygamy in Indonesia in my discussion below. Krulfeld's study (1986) among Sasak peasant communities in Lombok, Nusa Tenggara Barat, is a useful starting point. It shows that women had a relatively higher status in 'traditional' villages than in modern and 'Islamized' villages.[22] They demonstrated a correlation between women's social status and the incidence of polygyny: that there was more incidence of polygyny in a village where women's status was low, than in the traditional village where women's status was relatively high. Krulfeld reports that women in traditional villages tended to be more outspoken in their opposition to polygamy than women in modern and Islamized villages, who tended to tolerate polygamy and avoid discussing it. Grace (2004) conducted a more recent study in the same location in 1991, exploring the varying degrees of autonomy that Muslim women are able to exercise in negotiating marriage, polygyny and divorce. Another example is Jennaway's (2000) study of polygamous Hindu households in North Bali in 1992 and 1993. This study revealed the importance of female agency, especially the agency of junior wives, in initiating a polygamous marriage – often owing to the limited choices these women faced in their lives. Therefore, despite the risk of conflict with the senior co-wives and the bitterness of sharing a husband, this study reports that a position as junior wife could provide women with better economic prospects and improve their self-image.

None of these studies, however, focuses on Muslim polygamous marriage in Java in the post-Soeharto period. Of the existing studies, Krulfeld's study (1986) was conducted in the Soekarno era (1945–66), when polygamy might have been more frequent than it was in the Soeharto era (1966–98), partly because of President Soekarno's own practice of polygamy and the absence of codified marriage law. In contrast, Grace's and Jennaway's studies were conducted in the Soeharto era, when polygamy was mostly kept secret owing to Soeharto's negative attitude toward polygamy, and the Marriage Law, which restricts polygamy. In addition, Jennaway's study focused on Hindus, not on Muslims. In contrast with the previous studies, this book will provide information on Muslim discourses around polygamy, and on the lived experiences of Muslim women who have been involved in polygamous marriages in Java during the post-Soeharto period.

Muslim feminist as researcher

This study mirrors and is influenced by my own subjectivity and experiences. Critical theory argues that knowledge is not value-free. The production of knowledge is influenced by the background, experiences, interests and the values of its producers (Agger, 1991). This book is also not free from the influence of my background, experiences, interest and values. Brenner's article (Brenner, 2005) has been useful to me in understanding more about the context in which I live and my position as a researcher. As a Muslim woman who grew up during the transition from the tradition of parentally arranged marriage to marriage by personal choice, my mother – even though she successfully resisted the marriage her parents wished to arrange for her – did arrange her oldest daughter's marriage. But because of my sister's successful resistance to the arrangement, she stopped the tradition.

Educated and devout Muslims both, my parents sent all their children away to Muslim boarding schools (*pesantren*) after we graduated from primary school. At the *pesantren,* we studied Arabic and other Islamic Studies subjects such as *Usul al-Fiqh* (Principles of Islamic Jurisprudence), *Fiqh* (Islamic Jurisprudence) and *Tafsir* (Qur'anic exegesis).[23] After six years studying at boarding school, I completed my undergraduate degree at the State Institute for Islamic Studies, (IAIN) Bandung (1988–92), where I am currently employed as a lecturer. During my undergraduate studies, I was involved in an Islamist student organization and was an admirer of Islamist ideas, including the concept of complementary roles of men and women. My marriage and my encounter with feminisms, however, made me critical of these Islamist ideas. The problematic nature of Islamist ideas when I put them into practice, especially those regarding complementary roles of men and women, changed me from a supporter of Islamist ideas to a supporter of Muslim feminism. My encounter with western feminism began in 1994, when I prepared to undertake my Masters degree in Gender and Development, Development Studies Program, in the School of Arts and Humanities, Murdoch University, Western Australia (1995–7).

I believe that inequalities between men and women, and injustice toward women in Muslim societies, result in part from a literal reading of the Qur'an. Thus, in Karam's categorization of feminisms, I am a 'Muslim feminist' (Karam, 1998); in Rinaldo's categorization, I am 'an Islamic Reformist' (Rinaldo, 2006) who believes in the importance of reinterpretation of the Qur'an. I believe that for equality and justice to be achieved, the Qur'an needs to be read contextually, not literally. Within the discourse of liberal or progressive versus Islamist or literalist Muslims in Indonesia, I tend to agree with liberal Muslim thought, which makes political space for arguments for the emancipation of women. I am against Islamist or 'conservative' thought, which I see as unduly perceiving women as sexual beings who exist only to breed for and 'serve' men, rather than as full human beings who are capable of producing knowledge.

This study will aim to work within the standpoint feminist framework by trying to reconstruct knowledge from the perspective of women.[24] Muslim laws have almost always been formulated based on men's experiences and relationships, and have also been regarded as deriving from men's 'authority'. As a result, these laws tend not to take into account women's perspectives and experiences. Nevertheless, like Harding (1987: 11–12) and Scheman, I am aware that it is neither necessary nor sufficient to be a woman in order to undertake research within a standpoint feminist framework or to formulate law that takes into account women's perspectives and experiences. The male-biased nature of laws is not a matter of *biology* but of *culture*. Men subordinate women, not because they have certain chromosomes and bodily characteristics, but because they have learned certain norms of thought, feeling and behavior (1993: 1–2). Thus, some men may contribute to the formulation of law that takes into account women's perspectives, and some women may contribute to the perpetuation of male-biased law.

My research concentrates on the practice of polygamy in particular locations in Java, within the very diverse country of Indonesia. Indonesia is the world's largest archipelago, located between the Indian Ocean and the Pacific Ocean and consisting of 17,508 islands. Its land area is around 2 million square kilometers, with territorial waters nearly four times that size. Its climate is tropical: hot, humid and more moderate in the highlands. In religious terms, its population of 246,448,336 (GeoHive, 2006), consists of Muslims (88 percent), Protestants (5 percent), Roman Catholics (3 percent), Hindus (2 percent), Buddhists (1 percent) and others (1 percent) (Centre for Intercultural Learning, 2006). Indonesia is the world's most populous Muslim nation and the majority of the population lives in Java.

Initially, I planned to undertake fieldwork in three main cities in Java: Jakarta, Bandung and Yogyakarta. I chose these cities because I had lived in each place before and I had useful contacts there. In addition, these three cities reflect Indonesia's ethnic diversity. The population of Bandung is largely Sundanese; Yogyakarta is more Javanese; and residents of Jakarta are made up of both the indigenous Batavians and other people from all over Indonesia. People migrate to Jakarta because of the employment opportunities, educational institutions and facilities that the metropolitan city offers. At the beginning of my research, I found it difficult to find a contact person in Yogyakarta who could help me find research participants, even though I had contacted one of the NGOs there well before my fieldwork. Therefore, I replaced my choice of Yogyakarta with Depok and Bogor, because of their geographical proximity to Jakarta and the availability of participants who were willing to be interviewed. The population of Bandung in 2005 is 2,270,970 (BPS Bandung, 2005: 33); Bogor is 855,085 (BPS Bogor, 2006: 19) and Depok is 1,374,522 (BPS Depok, 2005: 27).

I conducted fieldwork for four months (December 2003–April 2004), in these four cities in Java, Indonesia. It was not easy to find polygamous men to interview because generally they hoped to keep their marriages secret. I was fortunate that I could find research participants in Jakarta, Bogor and Depok through a publication that advocated polygamy – it listed the names and addresses of men practicing polygamy. In contrast to the common assumption that polygamous men are rich, the list of names showed that the men in fact came from various economic backgrounds, the majority being lower-income earners (see Table 1.8). This was probably due to the greater willingness of lower-income polygamous men to be publicly listed when they were offered a financial reward by the publisher, compared to men from middle- and upper-income groups. In addition, while middle-class polygamous men seemed to be more concerned with their reputation when their practice of polygamy was publicized, lower-class polygamous men seemed to be less concerned with the impact of the publicity of their practice of polygamy on their career or their daily lives. As my fieldwork experiences show, the lower-income polygamous men tended to be more open and friendly and more generous in giving time and information than those of the middle- and upper-income group. I also made contacts through an economic empowerment program conducted by LBH APIK (*Lembaga Bantuan Hukum Asosiasi Perempuan Indonesia untuk Keadilan*/Legal Aid for Indonesian Women's Association for Justice) in Jakarta. This program aims to empower women who had been victims of domestic violence, especially after their divorces. Many of the participants in this program were previously first wives in a polygamous marriage, some of whom were willing to be interviewed.

To find research participants in Bandung, I relied on my friends and acquaintances for information about possible polygamous families. Even though I am more familiar with Bandung than Jakarta, Bogor and Depok, it was harder for me to find research participants in Bandung for at least three reasons. First, residents of Bandung generally kept their polygamous marriages secret or unregistered, because they seemed to be aware of their neighbors' negative attitudes toward polygamous marriage.[25] Second, no one from Bandung participated in the Polygamy Award held in Jakarta, even though Bandung is geographically close to Jakarta. After I found some research participants in Bandung, I also used the snowball sampling method by asking them whether they knew friends or relatives who were involved in polygamous marriages. As most of my friends and acquaintances are middle class and educated, most of the Bandung participants whom they recruited were also middle class and educated.

Given the nature of the recruitment of my informants, it is possible that in Bandung educated and middle-class polygamous participants were overrepresented. In addition, it might be assumed that my recruitment of participants from LBH APIK, who had been victims of domestic violence in their polygamous marriages, could result in overrepresentation of female victims of domestic violence. In total, they formed five cases of the 39 marriages. Their cases form part of my study statistics and data, although none of the cases appear in my chosen cases studies presented below. In fact their experiences did not appear to differ substantially from those of other informants. As discussed later, the case studies from my other informants will show that polygamy is associated consistently with significant degrees of emotional and physical violence.

To investigate the impact of polygamy on the well-being of women and children, I used in-depth interviews as my method of data collection. I interviewed all of those who are involved in polygamous marriages: the husband, his wives, and their children, if the children were aged 11 years old or older. I also interviewed several participants who were in monogamous marriages, to contrast their situation with that of those in polygamous marriages. Altman and Ginat's book on polygamy in the USA (1996) has been a useful guide for conducting research among polygamous families, how to deal with ethical issues and how to eliminate hierarchy between researcher and research participants.

Overall, I interviewed 74 participants, male and female, involved in a total of 39 marriages. The sample consisted of three women who had left polygamous marriages because they preferred divorce to polygamous marriage, one first wife who was divorced by her husband, who then took another wife, and the rest were in current marriages: five women and four men involved in monogamous marriage, 20 polygamous husbands, 16 first wives, nine second wives, two third wives and one fourth wife. As well, I interviewed 11 children from polygamous families and two committee members of the Polygamy Award, one of whom is also a polygamous husband. As a researcher, I rely mostly on my informants' narratives, but I do not know whether or not my informants have told the 'truth' about their lives, a factor beyond my control. But I tried to interview members of a relationship in separate interviews, to understand their possibly varying versions of 'reality'.

Owing to the different nature of the participants in Bandung and in Jakarta, Depok and Bogor, especially with regard to the societal attitudes toward polygamy discussed above, I shall present their backgrounds in separate tables. Tables 1.1–1.8 reflect the diversity in ethnic, educational and income levels of my respondents:

Table 1.1 Bandung participants' origins*

No.	Origins	Male	Female	Total
1.	West Java	9	23	32
2.	Padang	2	—	2
3.	Riau	1	—	1
	Total	12	23	35

Notes
* All descriptions in the tables in this book are only a valid description of the participants of the research and not representative of the whole population of Jakarta, Depok and Bogor.

Table 1.2 Jakarta, Depok and Bogor participants' origins

No.	Origins	Male	Female	Total
1.	Jakarta	3	10	13
2.	Central Java	6	6	12
3.	West Java	3	5	8
4.	Padang	2	1	3
5.	Palembang	—	1	1
6.	Medan	—	1	1
7.	Kupang	1	—	1
	Total	15	24	39

The male and female participants represented a broad range in educational background, from illiteracy (those who did not attend or did not finish primary school) to doctoral-level education. The educational level of participants in all of the cities is divided into two groups, based on their positions as either parent/married participants or as children of polygamous marriages. Overall, most participants in Bandung were more highly educated than those in Jakarta, Depok and Bogor. This can be seen from the Tables 1.3–1.6:

Table 1.3 Participants' educational level in Bandung (as parents)

No.	Educational level	Male	Female	Total
1.	Doctoral degree	2	—	2
2.	Master's degree	4	2	6
3.	Undergraduate degree	5	10	15
4.	Diploma	—	1	1
5.	Senior high school	—	3	3
6.	Junior high school	—	1	1
7.	Primary school	—	—	—
	Total	11	17	28

Table 1.4 Participants' educational level in Bandung (as children or adult children of polygamous parents)

No.	Educational level	Male	Female	Total
1.	Undergraduate degree	—	1	1
2.	Senior high school	1	1	2
3.	Junior high school	—	3	3
4.	Primary school	—	1	1
	Total	1	6	7

16 Introduction

Table 1.5 Participants' educational level in Jakarta, Depok and Bogor (as parents)

No.	Educational level	Male	Female	Total
1.	Doctoral degree	—	—	—
2.	Master's degree	1	—	1
3.	Undergraduate degree	1	2	3
4.	Diploma	1	4	5
5.	Senior high school	4	6	10
6.	Junior high school	2	4	6
7.	Primary school	3	4	7
8.	Unfinished primary school	2	—	2
9.	No school at all	—	2	2
	Total	14	24	36

Table 1.6 Participants' educational level in Jakarta, Depok and Bogor (as children of polygamous parents)

No.	Educational level	Male	Female	Total
1.	Undergraduate degree	1	—	1
2.	Senior high school	—	1	1
3.	Junior high school	—	—	—
4.	Primary school	—	2	2
	Total	1	3	4

It is not easy to categorize the economic level of all participants. I can, however, roughly divide their economic level into three groups based on their income, creating a lower, middle and upper group.[26] The monthly income of the lower group is less than Rp. 3,000,000 (about A$300),[27] the monthly income of the middle group is between Rp. 3,000,000 to Rp. 7,000,000 (about A$300 to A$1000) and the monthly income of the upper group is above Rp. 5,000,000 (above A$1000). The economic levels of the participants can be seen in Tables 1.7–1.8:

Table 1.7 Household economic level in Bandung

No.	Economic level	No. of households
1.	Upper group (monthly income above Rp. 7,000,000/above A$1000)	6
2.	Middle group (monthly income between Rp. 3,000,000 and Rp. 7,000,000/between A$300 and A$1,000)	12
3.	Lower group (monthly income up to Rp. 3,000,000/up to A$300)	1
	Total	19

Table 1.8 Household economic level in Jakarta, Depok and Bogor

No.	Economic level	No. of households
1.	Upper group (monthly income above Rp. 5,000,000/above A$800)	4
2.	Middle group (monthly income between Rp. 1,000,000 and Rp. 5,000,000/between A$160 and A$800)	5
3.	Lower group (monthly income up to Rp. 1,000,000/up to A$160)	11
	Total	20

This study has a flexible research design. I prepared guidelines (*aides-mémoires*) for the open-ended interviews, but allowed the topics to expand after meeting the research participants. Even though I asked similar questions to each participant in the hope of getting comparable data, I found that each case of polygamous marriage was unique. At the same time, I did not limit interviews by stopping informants who were willing to share experiences outside of the interview questions. Some participants were very enthusiastic in expressing their views about and experiences in polygamous marriages. Others needed to be encouraged to provide even small amounts of information.

The length of interviews varied from at least two hours to four hours. About half of the interviews were conducted in the participants' homes. The rest took place in cafés or restaurants, in participants' workplaces and in the home of the participants' relatives, depending on the participants' requests. Most of the interviews in Bandung, Bogor and Depok were conducted in the participants' homes and workplaces. In Jakarta, I mostly interviewed lower-income participants in their homes, while the middle-income participants mostly asked to be interviewed in a café or restaurant. I paid for all the food and drinks consumed during the interviews.

The middle-income participants' preference for a café or a restaurant possibly resulted from their awareness of personal privacy (from others in their household) compared to those from the lower-income group. Therefore, they seemed to wish to avoid being interviewed by a 'stranger' in their home. For many of them, home seemed to be one of the symbols of economic status; therefore some of them may have been ashamed to be visited in a home that they might have felt was 'inappropriate' to display to a stranger; or they might feel that they could speak more freely outside their home. On the other hand, most of the lower-income group did not have a telephone number through which I could contact them. Therefore, I did not have any choice about visiting their home directly.

The lower-income group participants in Jakarta were mostly friendly and happy to talk to me. They initially provided me with a tea bottle that they bought in the shop near their home after I was there for a few minutes. Compared to the upper-middle-class participants, the lower-class participants seemed to be more generous in giving their time and hospitality when I visited their homes.[28] They tended to treat me as a respected guest, even though I was just a 'stranger' to them. In exchange for their time and hospitality, I gave them some money to buy food when I left. I had not promised to give them money before the interview, because it is considered rude and unethical. I usually sat on the floor, as they mostly did not have any chairs. Some of their rented homes consisted of just one room of around 4 × 4 meters in size.

In undertaking this research, I encountered both physical and psychological difficulties. This research requires a high level of mobility in order to reach research participants who live in a wide range of geographical locations.[29] The average traveling time was six hours daily. In a day, I could sometimes interview two people if they lived close to each other. After traveling a long distance, I needed to be mentally ready to listen to the women's stories – often detailing their marriage grievances for at least two hours in each interview. But sometimes, even though I had traveled a long way, the person I intended to interview refused to participate.

Unlike the procedures commonly found in natural science research, I regarded the people in my samples as participants or informants, not as 'objects'. I attempted to maintain an egalitarian relationship with the participants by giving them as much space as they wished to ask about my research, and by underlining the voluntary nature of their participation, as per the usual ethics protocol. Thus, they could withdraw from their participation in my research whenever they wished. Before conducting the in-depth interview, I asked them to fill in the consent form. Several informants were illiterate, and therefore I explained the content of the consent form. I also told the participants that I would protect their confidentiality by not using their real names. In addition, I offered them the opportunity to check the results of my interviews with them, if they wished to confirm the validity of my reporting of the information they had given to me. Thus, I met most of my participants twice, once for the interview and once to confirm the interview results. However, some of the participants did not want to check the results, saying that they believed that I had written a valid account of the interview.

I found many upper-middle-class participants were more concerned with the issues of confidentiality of the interviews and were more critical of my research than the lower-class participants. While the former usually asked me many questions, such as about the aims and the possible benefits of my research, and also about my personal and professional background, such as my marital status, education and workplace, the latter barely asked any questions and tended to take for granted what I explained and asked. Some female participants from the upper middle class, such as Lina and Dahlia, were really eager to participate in my research, with higher expectations than others. Both of them expected and hoped that when my research was published many people would learn from their bitter experiences of living polygamously that there is nothing good in the practice of polygamy.

I am aware, however, that no matter how hard I tried to maintain an egalitarian relationship with my participants, this did not necessarily occur. Even though I represented myself as an Insider or Self, as someone who was born and grew up in the same country as they did, the fact that the research that I was undertaking was part of my overseas education seemed to make many of the participants aware that I was not a 'wholie', but a 'halfie'.[30] It is important, however, to note that I was not always in the position of being seen as 'superior' to my participants. Among upper-class and highly educated male participants who were mostly older than me, such as Syamsul and Suhadi, I felt that I was just seen as a young female student who needed information from them. They might even have regarded me as no different from a salesperson asking for their time and help. Regardless of the power relation during the interview, however, I was aware that I alone had the power to decide how I would present the results of my interviews.

Ideally, I wanted to interview both husband and wife (in separate interviews) to get a balanced view of their marriage. From the 39 marriages, however, I could only interview both husband and wife in 16 cases in total. In the other 23 marriages, I could only interview either the wife or the husband. From the 16 cases, I could only interview four polygamous families along with all their family members (the husband, his first and second wives and, where relevant, their children): these were the families of Jajang, Suhadi, Fahmi and Maman.

There are some barriers to interviewing both husband and wife. First, some husbands/wives did not want their spouses to be interviewed. Some said that their spouse was too busy to participate. Some of them said, 'My spouse is very quiet and I think s/he will be ashamed to talk with you.' This response is understandable because, as noted earlier, the wife's failure to 'serve' her husband is often viewed as the cause of a husband's polygamy. Some of the husbands also seem to be afraid that my interviews would endanger their marriages, because their second marriages were still secret from their first wives. Even though I convinced them that I would not tell their first wife about their second marriage, they politely refused. The second obstacle was geographical. Some husbands lived with one of their wives in one of the cities under my study, while the other wife or wives lived far away.

Brief outline of chapters

In the following chapters, I shall present the results of this research process. Chapter 2 will discuss the context of polygamy, in relation to family and kinship. This will consist of the discussion of women's situation in Java, changing patterns of marriage and family structure in Indonesia and feminist critiques of the family. It sets the background for a deeper understanding the context in which polygamy is currently practiced. Because many proponents of polygamy often claim that 'polygamy is part of *shari'a*', Chapter 3 will begin with a discussion of the dimensions of *shari'a*. This chapter will also emphasize the difference between the Qur'an, which is divine, and its interpretation, which is human, and will discuss various Muslim interpretations of the Qur'anic verse on polygamy. After that, this chapter will look at the historical background prior to the enactment of the 1974 Marriage Law, in which polygamy was hotly debated. Prior to its enactment, women were active in pressing the government to reform the marriage law. However, because of the limited representation of women in Parliament just prior to the enactment of the Law, and the conflicting interest between Muslim parties and secular government, women's desires to better their position within marriage were largely overruled by the interests of Muslim parties and the government. This chapter will also discuss government restrictions on polygamy and divorce, and how this regulation was implemented during the Soeharto presidency and during the post-Soeharto period. In addition, this chapter will describe the more recent promotion of polygamy that took place in the context of more relaxed attitudes toward polygamy among Indonesian leaders.

Chapters 4 and 5 present the results of my field research. Chapter 4 explores Indonesian societal attitudes toward polygamy, which I shall, with Jones (1994), argue are generally negative. These negative attitudes will be seen in the reactions from other people experienced by those who practice polygamy, which I shall describe. This chapter will report how first wives, their relatives and neighbors responded to polygamous marriages. The first wives' responses to their husbands' additional marriages will be categorized into three groups, depending on their approach to the Qur'an and the degree of their acceptance/resistance to polygamy. This chapter also explores the possible impact of polygamy on the emotional well-being of the first wives. Chapter 5 discusses the living arrangements of polygamous marriages. This will consist of a discussion of relationships between wives in polygamous marriages and of the husbands' 'rosters' of contact with their wives. It is important to include the information on rosters, because promoters of polygamy emphasize the supposedly harmonious relationships between co-wives, and the supposedly 'just' arrangements instituted. Just treatment is also measured by the husband's income distribution between or among his wives. Therefore, this chapter will also discuss the economic management of polygamous households. As children were also involved in these polygamous households, the chapter will explore the possible impact of polygamy on the economic and emotional well-being of these children. Chapter 6 will provide a concluding discussion and suggest future research directions.

2 Polygamy in context
Family and kinship

Polygamy is a highly controversial issue, not only among Muslims but also among non-Muslims. Polygamy has been legally prohibited throughout western countries, including the USA. This does not mean, however, that it is not practiced in those countries. Some men may legally have only one wife, but they may have extramarital relationships or keep one or more mistresses in different places (*de-facto* polygamy). In addition, even though the majority of western people seem to oppose polygamy, some writers such as Altman and Ginat (1996), Kilbride (1994, 1997) and Cairncross (1974) suggest that a polygamous family is a viable alternative to the existing household arrangements such as extended, blended, nuclear, single-parent and gay/lesbian family structures. Kilbride (1994, 1997), an African American Roman Catholic, proposes plural marriage as an option to save neglected American children in cases of their parents' divorce within monogamous marriage.

Among Muslims, even though polygamy has often been widely discussed, it is not commonly practiced (Jones, 1994: 27). In Indonesia, as discussed earlier, Azra suggests that prior to the enactment of the 1974 Marriage Law about 5 percent of all marriages were polygamous, but this percentage was probably lower after the 1974 Marriage Law, which made polygamy more difficult (2003: 89). Indeed, petitions regarding polygamy were among the most rare cases heard before the Religious Courts. This can be seen, for instance, in the data I collected from two Religious Courts in West Java. In the Religious Court of Kodya Bandung, there was no application for permission for polygamous marriage in 2003, while in the same year the Court tried 1,871 cases including applications for divorce, child custody and inheritance division. Unfortunately, the staff there could not find the 2002 yearly records for me (Pengadilan Agama Bandung, 2003). In another Court, the Religious Court of Cimahi, there were five applications for polygamy out of 2,001 total cases received in 2002. This compared to 1,046 cases of divorce initiated by women, and 627 cases of divorce initiated by men. In 2003, the Court received two applications for polygamy out of 1,788 total cases. This compared to 1,015 cases of divorce initiated by women and 484 cases of divorce initiated by men (Pengadilan Agama Cimahi, 2002 and 2003). These official figures should be accepted with caution, owing to some cases of unregistered secret polygamy, as my case studies will show. But overall, polygamy is not a common practice among contemporary Indonesians.

In other Muslim countries, Jones (1994: 272) reported that Huzayyin's studies in 1979 found that 1 percent of marriages in Damascus, 2 percent of marriages in Cairo and 7 percent of marriages in Bangladesh were polygamous. Other studies show that rates of polygamous marriages were around 3 to 6 percent in North Africa and the Middle East, but that rates of polygamy were higher (11.7 percent) among Kuwait Muslim marriages in 1975.[1] Rates were also higher in Sudan in 1956: 15.9 percent, which constituted half of all marriages. According to Jones (1994: 272), this high incidence of polygamy is more to do with African 'culture' [sic] – in which 20 to 30 percent of Sub-Saharan African marriages were reportedly polygamous – than with Islamic influence.

In Indonesia, polygamy has been mostly associated with Islam – even though it had been practiced in the Indonesian archipelago before the coming of Islam in the thirteenth century. For instance, it was permitted by several customary systems (*adat*) such as the *adat* of Hindu Bali and Chinese Indonesians, and was practiced by Javanese aristocrats who usually had many *selir* (secondary wives) (Blackburn, 2004a: 113). Hindus in Bali also practiced polygamy (Jennaway, 2000).

The rate of polygamy in Indonesia is far lower than the divorce rate, which in the 1950s in West Java appeared to be one of the highest in the world (Jones, 1994: 96).[2] Many Indonesian Muslims consider both polygamy and divorce to be against the spirit of Islam, but they are more tolerant of divorce than of polygamy. According to Jones, polygamy is not only rare among Indonesians but also generally not fully approved socially. For example, Javanese people of both sexes view polygamy very negatively. Acehnese women also have a negative attitude toward polygamy, even though men there reportedly view it positively (1994: 283–4). These negative attitudes toward people practicing polygamy will be discussed in Chapter 4.

According to Jones (1994: 277), there is a correlation between the incidence of divorce and polygamy, in which divorce could be an escape route for women from the practice of polygamy or from the threat of it. Since the divorce rate in Indonesia and the Malay world was very high, the incidence of polygamy itself, according to Jones (1994: 210, 277), could not be a major cause of divorce. The *threat* of polygamy – such as when a wife knew of her husband's intention to take another wife – could become a reason for divorce. But reports given by parliamentary members (local councils) at Jakarta and Bandung in 1954 and 1955, and some figures reported by Ibu Mangunpuspito (cited in Vreede-de Stuers, 1960: 133) in her speech in the 1959 parliamentary debates, show a belief that polygamy was a significant underlying cause of divorce (32 percent and 29 percent of divorces in Bandung and Jakarta respectively in 1955 and 24.9 percent in Jakarta in 1957 were caused by polygamy, the second highest cause cited after economic causes).

Women's situation in Java

As discussed in Chapter 1, Krulfeld's study (1986) shows a correlation between women's low status and the incidence of polygyny: there was more polygamy in villages where women's status was low, as compared to those villages where women's status was relatively high. Lestari and Munti (2003) make a similar argument: that when women are seen as subordinate, the practice of polygamy tends to flourish, but when women's status is seen as high, its practice tends to decrease. This section will discuss the situation of Indonesian women within marriage and society, to explore the question of Javanese women's 'status' and vulnerability to polygamous marriage.

'Status' is a contested term. In the modern era, it is usually equated with and measured by education, occupation and income, which allow women to access and control economic resources within and outside their household through paid employment (Widayatun, 1991). But Dube (1997) also argues that the kinship system plays an important role in determining women's status.[3] Given the importance of the kinship system in determining women's position in society, I shall briefly describe the kinship system in Indonesia.

Indonesia in general has a bilateral or cognatic kinship system (Djamour, 1965: 23; Geertz, 1961: 76; Hüsken and Kemp, 1991; Koentjaraningrat, 1957: 91; Sairin, 1982: 15; Surjadi, 1974: 129–30; 132–3; Wolf, 1992: 56). The main exceptions are Minangkabau, which has a matrilineal kinship system, and Bali and northern Sumatra (Batak society), which have patrilineal kinship systems. In bilateral kinship systems, both paternal and maternal kin are important; descent from either the mother's or the father's side is equally recognized; and sons and daughters have equal rights of inheritance from either maternal or paternal lines (e.g. Brenner, 1998: 138). Therefore, within this system, there is no preference for sons over daughters – both are highly valued (Hirschman and Edwards, 2006: 6). Within matrilineal kinship systems, like that of Minangkabau, descent follows the female line (Reenen, 1996: 23) and residence after marriage is uxorilocal. This means that a husband generally moves to his wife's natal household (Blackwood, 2005: 10) after their marriage. He is often regarded as an outsider or 'guest' in his wife's family (Blackburn, 2004a: 8; Blackwood, 2005: 12) and does not become 'incorporated into his wife's group' (Reenen, 1996: 29).[4] As a 'guest', he does not have authority and is structurally marginal to the affairs of his wife's kin group (Blackwood, 2005: 10). This marginal position of a husband in his wife's *matrihouse* is described in a famous saying 'the husband is like ashes on the fireplace: one blow and he is gone' (Reenen, 1996: 3).[5] As matrilineal kinship governs the local social relations of Minangkabau, and families and lineages are oriented around the mother and her daughters and sons, this form of matriliny empowers women as controllers of land and houses (Blackwood, 2000: 1).[6]

In contrast, under the patrilineal kinship system – for example, that of Bali and northern Sumatra – descent is traced through the father's line, as is inheritance of property, titles, group membership and so on (Geertz and Geertz, 1975: 161). Women within this kinship system do not have rights to inheritance of money or property, and are economically dependent on their husbands (Blackburn, 2004a: 8).[7] Residence after marriage is virilocal. After marriage, a woman leaves her parents' household to live in her husband's family household and becomes part of it if she is marrying endogamously. Even if when marrying endogamously she does not leave her natal household, she symbolically belongs to her husband's ambit (Geertz and Geertz, 1975: 161). In the event of divorce, women have no right to custody of their children, because children are seen as primarily a part of their father's family (Jennaway, 2000).

Many historians and anthropologists, including Firth (1966), Stoler (1977), Strange (1981), Reid (1988: 146), Burling (1992: 2), Andaya (2001) and Gonsoulin (2005), claim that women in Southeast Asian countries with bilateral kinship systems and shared common historical and cultural roots have high status.[8] For instance, Aletta H. Jacobs (1854–1929), a Dutch suffragist who visited Dutch East Indies in 1912, was impressed by the Indies (Indonesian) women's valuable independence and status in their society: 'she considered Indonesian women far in advance of those she had met in India' (Blackburn, 1997: 12). Similarly, Andaya points out a number of Southeast Asian cultural features that have often been cited as demonstrative of gender equality in these regions:

> the importance of women in food production, especially rice cultivation; their prominence in marketing and other economic activities; complementary gender roles in ritual, and female prominence as healers and spirit mediums; the prevalence of bilateral kinship patterns, matrilocal residence and bride wealth; the fact that women commonly inherit family property and maintain their own source of income; low population densities prior to the nineteenth century, which place a high value on women's work and female fertility; the absence of strong state structure and a low level of urbanization.
>
> (Andaya, 2001: 14677)

In addition, Reid (1988: 146) argues that despite the gradual increase of the influence of Islam, Christianity, Buddhism and Confucianism over the last four centuries, Southeast Asian women in the years 1450 to 1680 possessed relatively high levels of autonomy and economic importance.

This generalization about the high status of women in Southeast Asia, particularly in Java has, however, been criticized by a number of female scholars. For instance, Sears argues that Reid's impression was based mainly on the perspective of male European observers, who seemed most impressed by sexual freedom of some women, especially those who lived in the port cities. These women reportedly negotiated the terms of their sexual union with male travelers while the men waited for the winds to change so their boat could return home (Sears, 1996: 31). Stoler (1977) also challenges this generalization. She argues that such simplification conceals fundamental differences in women's access to and control over productive resources. Indeed, Southeast Asian women in general are not homogeneous. In the past, peasant women might have been more economically active in supporting their family than the higher-class women. But, as Vreede-de Stuers argues (1960: 47–8), colonial exploitation in the nineteenth century undermined the position of Indonesians in general and women in particular. Also, the development process in the postcolonial era may have reduced women's access to and control over productive resources, as Boserup (1970) and Roger (1980) have argued. In addition, Soeharto's New Order ideology of state motherhood or state *Ibuism* has further subordinated and domesticated Indonesian women (Suryakusuma, 1996, 2004).⁹

As my research was conducted in Java, I shall discuss Javanese kinship in somewhat more detail. Two important features of Javanese kinship are the structural autonomy of the nuclear family, and the absence of extended kin groups (Geertz, 1961: 77; Koentjaraningrat, 1967: 262; Surjadi, 1974: 131; Jones, 1995: 189).¹⁰ This means that soon after marriage, a couple are expected to establish their own separate nuclear family. The value placed on the autonomy of the nuclear family, according to Geertz (1961: 77–8), can be seen in the Javanese preference for conjugal ties over consanguinal ties, and the Javanese tendency to avoid conflict by minimizing close contact with certain relatives who may disrupt their conjugal ties. But the wife tends to see her kin as less threatening to conjugal ties. Kinswomen, in fact, tend to help each other. This female-centered network of kinship among women, which is often termed 'matrifocal', becomes a secondary, supplementary structure to the primary structure of the nuclear family (Geertz, 1961: 78). This is supported by Stivens (2003a: 351), who argues that it is clear that the everyday kinship practices of most Muslim social groups in the Malay world are often strongly female-centered (matrifocal).¹¹

Hildred Geertz's strong emphasis on women's autonomy and matrifocality in her work in Java has been criticized by a number of female scholars who worked in Java, such as Wolf (1992) and Sullivan (1994). For instance, Wolf sees it as overemphasizing Javanese women's autonomy or their independence. She argues that Geertz fails to take into account key points of tension in Javanese women's lives, such as women's lack of control over sexuality, their lack of power inside or outside their household, the poverty that may constrain their lives, the very small amount of financial resources that they might control and the contradictory nature of expectations regarding women's economic behavior and 'feminine' behavior (Wolf, 1992: 56). Wolf's criticism appears to be strongly influenced by her work among poor Javanese rural women. But middle- and upper-class women may have access to larger financial resources. The above criticism about Geertz's overemphasis on Javanese women's autonomy within the household may also apply to Jay's strong emphasis on Javanese women's autonomy within the household (e.g. Jay, 1969: 44–5, 61, 87, 92).

In contrast to Geertz (1961), Sullivan argues that Javanese women are subordinate to men (1991, 1994). Citing White and Hastuti (1980), she suggests that the relationship between men and women in Java is like the relationship between masters (men) and managers (women). A manager, no matter how senior her position, only obtains authority to manage her household from her real master, in this case the male of the family (her husband, or adult son or father, for young women). Women are exercising 'derived authority' from 'the real power holders' (Sullivan, 1994: 8). Her argument is supported by Djajadiningrat-Nieuwenhuis (1992: 50) who affirms that 'real power remains the prerogative of men; women achieve only a derivative form of power'. Similarly, Berninghausen and Kerstan (1992) suggest that Javanese women's control and access to the household finances, which in the West may be interpreted as a sign of autonomy or power, do not necessarily mean that these women have more autonomy or authority than men. These authors explain that Javanese women are expected to spend money and manage household finances in order to take care of their husband and children. They argue that the dominant patriarchal system has often made these Javanese women act against their own interest in managing family finance (Berninghausen and Kerstan, 1992: 163). In addition, within Javanese culture, dealing with money is often considered a sign of low status (Brenner, 1998). As a woman born and brought up in Java (West Java and Central Java), I find that Sullivan's analysis rings true. Although my evidence is anecdotal, like Geertz (1961) and Jay (1969) I see many Javanese households as matrifocal and many Javanese women as dominant within their household. But I agree with Sullivan that these Javanese women's high status and power is 'itself part of the subordinate familial-private sphere' (Sullivan, 1994: 9–10). This subordinate position of women, according to White and Hastuti (1980), is '*hidden* by the dominant gender ideologies espousing [the idea] that Javanese men and women are separate but equal' (cited in Sullivan, 1994: 191).

There are other important studies in relation to economic management and power relations within households that will be useful when examining power relations within polygamous marriages. For instance, Pahl's study on patterns of money management within marriage in Britain shows the relationship between unequal distribution of household resources and marital problems (Pahl, 1980: 316). In this study, Pahl also categorizes income management within households into three categories: the *whole wage* system, the *allowance* system and the *pooling* system, in which each system has different consequences for either a symmetrical or an asymmetrical relationship between a couple (Pahl, 1980: 319, 322, 330).

Pahl's finding of the unequal distribution of resources within households is supported by Whitehead in a classic argument about the UK and West Africa (1981). She argues that women lose control over their own income when it is brought to the household. This, in her view, clearly reveals the existing hierarchies of super-subordination in the household. According to her, most women's income is spent to cover the family's basic material needs. The conjugal contract, including the ideology of maternal altruism, often prevents women from freely spending their income on themselves (Whitehead, 1981: 107–8). Whitehead's argument is similar to that of Berninghausen and Kerstan (1992), Djajadiningrat-Nieuwenhuis (1992) and Sullivan (1994), all of whom studied Javanese women. They argue that women's role in managing money is not necessarily a sign of their power within their household, because women do not tend to spend money in accordance with their own interests (Berninghausen and Kerstan, 1992); dealing with money is considered as a sign of low status (Djajadiningrat-Nieuwenhuis, 1992); and the power that women have in managing money is not 'genuine' but 'derived' from their husbands, who control the ultimate direction of the household (Sullivan, 1994: 9).

Brenner (1998) provides another interesting discussion on the relationship between control over money and sexual desire in Java. She notes two contradictory Javanese representations of women and men in managing money. On the one hand, within Javanese *priyayi* culture, excessive attention to financial matters is viewed as a sign of low status. Therefore, to maintain their high status, men tend to hand over the management of financial matters to their wives (Brenner, 1998: 140). On the other hand, while both women and men can be tempted by their own innate passions and desires (*nafsu*), women are believed to have greater control over their desires. To understand these contradictory beliefs on women and men, Brenner suggests seeing them as alternative paradigms that can be used to justify or interpret the actions of men and women in different contexts: male potency and self-control tend to be more emphasized in *formal* discourse, while the belief that men have less self-control than women often appears in *informal* discourse when there is no ideological risk (Brenner, 1998: 149–50, my emphasis).[12]

In addition, she notes that many Javanese men believe that men by nature have greater sexual desire and that this desire is very hard to suppress, even though this belief contradicts the Islamist ideology that men have greater control of their instincts and emotions than women. This belief leads Javanese people in Solo to assume that women are 'naturally' better suited to managing household finances, the family firm or the marketplace, drawing a clear connection between controlling money and controlling one's passions. It is believed that when men control the money, they will spend it to fulfill their desire for women (Brenner, 1998: 150).

One can also argue that women's power to influence their husbands is often limited to minor economic decisions in Indonesia. Larger decisions such as buying a car or children's schooling is usually either decided by both husband and wife, or by the husband alone. Similarly, Munir (2002) supports Wolf's argument on Javanese women's lack of control over their sexuality. She argues that Javanese culture is hierarchical, with women placed in a subordinate position to their husband within marriage. 'Women are perceived as passive sexual agents whose major task is to fulfill the needs of the male' (Munir, 2002: 198). According to Munir (2002), this is perpetuated by a male-biased interpretation of the Qur'anic verses and state gender ideology, which emphasize women's domestic roles as wives and mothers. Furthermore, the growing influence of Islamist ideas concerning ideal gender relations may further domesticate women, as many conservative Islamists share a belief that women's appropriate place is at home (Shehadeh, 2003).

Shehadeh (2003) argues that fundamentalists, whom I prefer to call Islamists, believe that men are biologically, physically, physiologically and psychologically stronger/superior to women, but that men and women are spiritually equal. Therefore, they believe that men are destined to undertake public duties and to provide for and protect women. As providers and protectors, men are believed to have the right to a larger share of inheritances, unilateral divorce and the absolute obedience of their wives. On the other hand, women are believed biologically destined to undertake domestic roles such as doing housework, taking care of children and supporting their husbands. Many Islamists believe that women's capability to undertake public roles is limited, owing to the burdens of menstruation, childbearing and child rearing. Among fundamentalists, women are seen as sexual beings, who need to be sexually segregated and confined to the home. Otherwise, they believe, women's seductive powers would cause *fitnah* (social anarchy and chaos) because men are believed to have unappeasable sexual desire. Seeing, smelling and hearing women distracts men and hinders their productivity. Because women are supposedly the source of all sexual temptation, they are required to cover all of their body except the hands and face (Al-Mawdudi and al-Turabi, the leading fundamentalist ideologues, require even the hands and face to be covered) (Shehadeh, 2003).

Not all Islamists adhere to such a rigid sexual division of labor. As Yakan (2002: 164–5) noted, women within Ikhwanul Muslimin, one of the Islamist organizations in Egypt, are permitted to work outside home when it is necessary, and may be politically active. However, the provisions for women within this organization still tend to be restrictive: for example, women can contribute and participate in social activities only if all the participants are women. In addition, even though it is stated that they have the right to an education, the organization suggests that women should prioritize their duties as housewives over self-development (Yakan, 2002: 165).

From the above discussion, it can be concluded that although many Javanese women have some autonomy, this autonomy is often limited to minor economic decisions and only located within their household. Within society, women are often seen to be subordinate to men and therefore may be vulnerable to polygamous marriage.

Changing patterns of marriage and family structure in Indonesia

There have been changing patterns of marriage and family structure in Indonesia, and Southeast Asia in general, since the 1970s.[13] To better understand these changing patterns, I shall first describe the pattern of marriage and divorce from the 1950s to the 1970s. Prior to the 1970s, marriage in Indonesia was considered very important and was almost universal (Wolf, 1992: 60; Hirschman, 1994: 407; Dube, 1997: 124), representing a critical rite of passage from childhood to adulthood (Geertz, 1961: 69). Although there has been a gradual increase in the number of unmarried women over 30, the unmarried woman is often considered 'not fully adult' and often stigmatized as being undesirable, perhaps lesbian or not virginal (Porter and Hasan, 2003: 164–5). Muslims in Indonesia believe that sexual desire is a natural human need, the fulfillment of which must be confined to marriage (Dube, 1997: 109; Smith-Hefner, 2005: 454). Even though there are cases of couples who have sexual relationships and have children outside marriage, these cases are religiously and socially unacceptable.

Some anthropologists reported that in Java in the 1950s parents mostly arranged marriages at an early age and often without the couple's consent (e.g. Geertz, 1961: 56; Koentjaraningrat, 1985: 125; Jaspan and Hill, 1987: 2). Parentally arranged marriage served to fulfill many interests of the parents. For instance, many Muslim parents did not let their daughters choose their own marriage partner, because they were afraid the girls might not make the right choice and might become the victim of a womanizer (Blackburn and Bessel, 1997: 109, 111). They tended to protect family honor by marrying off their daughters soon after they reached puberty, to prevent sexual misconduct and pregnancy outside marriage (Jones, 1997). Some parents were motivated by economic interest, holding elaborate wedding feasts in which they would receive contribution from their neighbors in return for donations they had made in the past (Blackburn and Bessel, 1997: 113; Geertz, 1961: 70). Wedding feasts also served to confirm parents' social status in their communities. In her first marriage, a girl could have an elaborate wedding feast and perhaps also receive expensive engagement presents. For many parents, arranged marriage served as a ritual celebration of their daughter's entry to adulthood, when she would be free to make her own choice, either to stay or to leave her arranged marriage (Geertz, 1961: 69–70).[14]

Many Indonesian Muslims believe that Islam stipulates that marriage is to be celebrated (*dirayakan/walimah*). They usually invite neighbors, friends, relatives and colleagues to wedding celebrations. The invited guests usually come to congratulate the newly married couple, who sit side by side in a decorated room, give presents and are then provided with meals served by the host. It is unusual for a Muslim marriage not to be celebrated, and marriages that take place without ceremony usually become a topic of gossip. Neighbors of the bride or the groom may wonder why the marriage took place in secret, perhaps suspecting that the bride might already be pregnant before the marriage, which is considered shameful.

Hildred Geertz reported that in the 1950s and 1960s, most Javanese girls had been married by the age of 16 or 17 (1961: 56).[15] Many Javanese parents in the 1950s would be embarrassed if they had a 16-year-old unmarried daughter, and the girl would be considered a spinster. To avoid such embarrassment, some parents would find a man who could marry her temporarily and then divorce her after a week or so. After divorce, it would be easier for the girl to find a husband, who might previously have been embarrassed to be involved in an elaborate first wedding (Geertz, 1961: 70).

Arranged marriage at an early age was vulnerable to divorce, owing to immaturity and incompatibility (Jones, 1997; Firth, 1966: 44; Heaton *et al.*, 2001). According to Wolf (1992: 62), though, this high divorce rate was generally observed among *abangan*,[16] who did not see divorce as morally wrong. In contrast, she reports that *santri* and *priyayi* (upper-middle-class people) tended to see divorce as morally wrong and shameful. In addition, she states that *priyayi* women tended to avoid divorce owing to their economic dependence on their husbands.

There was no stigma attached to the divorced state, for either men or women, because the first marriage was considered a probation or experiment (Firth, 1966: 44). As a result, Geertz (1961: 56, 69) reported that in 1950s in Java nearly half of all marriages ended in divorce and that divorce occurred most often in a couple's first, parentally arranged marriage. After divorce, the girl usually returned to her parents and had more freedom to choose her own husband. If she was too young, her parents might still arrange her marriage, with her consent (Firth, 1966: 46). However, it is important to note that it is not easy for a woman to be *janda*, a divorced woman, especially if she has no kin to rely on for financial support.[17]

Hirschman and Teerawichitchainan (2003: 243–4) emphasize how different kinship systems had different effects on divorce rates. They argue that under the bilateral kinship system, which features matrilocal residence, divorce was high, while within the patrilineal kinship with patrilocal residence, divorce was lower.

They argued that under the bilateral kinship system, women generally could rely on the network of their natal kinship and more easily escape their unhappy marriages. Under the patrilineal kinship system, however, women were generally cut off from their natal kinship network and had no right to custody of children after divorce. Given the negative consequences of divorce, they might be more willing to stay in unhappy marriages. But while some scholars argue that the processes of urbanization and modernization do not necessarily undermine kinship ties (e.g. Brunner, 1961; Djajadiningrat-Nieuwenhuis, 1992; Stivens, 1985, 1991, 1996), others argue that the process of urbanization/industrialization/modernization has broken down or lessened kinship ties because people have become more individualistic and secularized (e.g. Goode, 1970; Heaton et al., 2001; Redfield, 1941, 1947; Wirth, 1939).

Since the 1970s, there has been a significant change in patterns of marriage in Southeast Asia. The age of marriage rose sharply in the 1960s, and continued to rise until 1990. The average age of marriage increased from less than 19.5 in 1980 to 20.9 by 1990 (Jones, 1994: 108 and 131). In Indonesia, for instance, the average age at first marriage rose to over 20 in 1985 (Hull, 1994: 136). This increase continued throughout the Malay world. Currently it is not uncommon to find unmarried Malay men or women in their thirties. Jones even points out the growing tendency to leave 'the tradition of universal marriage' (Jones, 1995: 191),[18] with an increasing number of women in most Southeast Asian populations remaining unmarried at 30 to 40 or even throughout their lives (Jones, 1995: 191; 2004: 7, 51).[19]

Jones (1995: 190) argues that this trend is closely related to the increasing autonomy of young women in choosing their marriage partners. The long interval between puberty and marriage provides them with many chances to interact with their opposite sex, engaging in courtship (*pacaran*) or self-initiated romance beyond parental oversight (Smith-Hefner, 2005: 451). Thus, marriage in Indonesia has clearly shifted from being a parental arrangement to being a personal choice based on romantic love.[20] Although their efforts became increasingly visible in the 1970s, Indonesians' struggles to end arranged marriage began in the early twentieth century. During this time, many western-educated men and women such as Kartini (1879–1904), who has become an important symbol of emancipation for Indonesian feminists, and many members of women's organizations, opposed and criticized arranged marriage. Vreede-de Stuers (1960: 75) noted that many novels published between 1920 and 1940, such as *Siti Nurbaja* (1922) and *Azab dan Sengsara* (1927), some of which were written by western-educated men in Minangkabau, argued in opposition to the local *adat* of the arranged marriage by contrasting it with marriage based on mutual affection.[21]

The lengthening period of adolescence and the new freedoms young women have gained have also caused societal and familial concerns about sexual promiscuity. Many parents often admonish their daughters to safeguard their sexual 'purity' or virginity prior to marriage. They believe that girls carry their family name and reputation, which can be safeguarded by virginity or ruined by pregnancy out of wedlock, often a great source of shame and humiliation for the family. Sons can also safeguard family honor, but male transgression is considered to have less serious consequences. Because of such anxieties, parents usually arrange for the pregnant girl to marry as soon as possible. Premarital pregnancy is the subject of much gossip and joking, for example by using the term MBA (Married By Accident).[22] Smith-Hefner describes parents' embarrassment over a daughter's premarital pregnancy:

> For her parents then, what should be the final testimony to their skill and accomplishment, and a joyous public display of their social status and prestige within the community, is instead a painful, hurried ordeal which becomes the focus of malicious community gossip.
>
> (Smith-Hefner, 2005: 453)

However, as Bennett (2005) pointed out, marriage was not always the solution for unmarried pregnant women because not all their sexual partners were willing to be responsible for their partner's pregnancy and some of the pregnancies might be concealed from their parents for shame and fear of destroying family reputation. Consequently, some of these women abort their pregnancies using various means, which may be unsafe for their reproductive health. Some of them go to medical doctors for their abortion. However, because of their unmarried status, they are vulnerable to discriminatory treatment from health service providers.

'Lengthened' adolescence has also created ambivalence among young unmarried women who live and study away from their parents. They have more freedom and autonomy to interact with the opposite sex, but are still expected to safeguard their chastity. With the Muslim revivalism since the early 1980s, many young Muslim women chose to wear the veil (*jilbab*) to protect them in their interactions with the opposite sex.[23] Smith-Hefner (2005: 454), for instance, found that 60 percent of female students at the University of Gadjah Mada (UGM) in Yogyakarta wear the veil. (This is a dramatic change from their previous style of dress, which in the 1970s consisted of western style knee-length skirts and short-sleeved blouses.) Some of them also join campus organizations such as KAMMI (Action Group of Indonesian Muslim Students), which is a supporter of a version of Islamism. This organization provides a set of clear guidelines regarding courtship and marriage. Many members of this organization believe that having a boyfriend or a girlfriend (*pacaran*) is sinful, or can create the opportunity for sin. They discourage premarital *pacaran,* and encourage marriage for those unable to restrain their sexual desire. This organization facilitates marriage without premarital *pacaran.* When some members of this organization feel ready to get married, they can submit their 'bio data' to a committee who will help them find their match. The committee also provides a chaperone, to accompany the couple while they get to know each other so that they can avoid being alone together (Smith-Hefner, 2005: 456).

The long interval between puberty and marriage has also become a concern for many Islamists. In the post-Soeharto period, many Islamists have been vocal in promoting early marriage and polygamy to solve what they called the 'moral crisis' among young Muslims.[24] For instance, Mohammad Fauzil Adhim, in his speeches among university students and in his popular book *The Beauty of Early Marriage (Indahnya pernikahan dini)* has encouraged young Muslims to marry early to avoid *zina* (fornication) and not to postpone marriage until they graduate or find a job (Smith-Hefner, 2005: 455).

The rising age at marriage and the increasing number of free-choice marriages are seen as contributing to the decline of the divorce rate in Southeast Asia. Marriages made by choice at an older age tend to be longer-lasting and more durable, owing to maturity and the marriage being based on romantic love and attraction (Hull, 1994: 136; Jones, 1995: 192, 1997: 105; Wolf, 1992: 213). These two major factors are interrelated with socioeconomic development, increasing levels of education for both sexes and women's participation in the labor force. Strict official regulation of marriage and parents' changing preferences toward supporting their daughters' education and career give young women both economic and social benefits (Jones, 1995, 1997). For instance, increasing economic opportunity reduces poverty-related causes of divorce. In addition, the enactment of the 1974 Marriage Law in Indonesia has made the process of divorce difficult (Jones, 1997: 107). Before 1974, a husband could simply divorce to his wife, even without the wife's knowledge. Now a husband must take his case for divorce to the Religious Court and pay all legal expenses. To obtain a divorce, a couple need to attend at least three hearings. The first hearing aims at reconciliation. The second is to find out the result of the reconciliation effort. If the effort has no result, the third hearing legalizes the divorce procedure (Jones, 1994: 247).

During the 1970s and 1980s, the New Order improved roads and transportation and expanded schools. This made it easier for girls to attend school closer to home, without parents being concerned about their daughters traveling long distances. Consequently, a larger number of girls completed the first nine years of schooling. Some of their parents could support their girls' further education, even when this required the girls' leaving home. Changing attitudes toward the upbringing of girls were partly due to a view about the clear benefit of education. Parents now see that education provides their daughters with employment opportunities and economic security, and social status (Smith-Hefner, 2005: 450). Unlike in the 1950s, when a sixteen- or seventeen-year-old unmarried girl was considered unmarketable (*tidak laku*) or an 'old maid' (*perawan tua*), women who marry at a young age are now ridiculed and looked down upon, especially if the marriage is brought about by pregnancy: '*kok kawin, masih muda!*' (how come she is married, she is so young!) (Smith-Hefner, 2005: 451).

In addition, unlike in the 1950s when there was little or no stigma attached to divorce, 'modernity', according to Hirschman and Teerawichitchainan (2003: 245), stigmatizes divorce, which was previously associated with social and economic backwardness.[25] They predict that the decline in 'traditional divorce' in the 1960s and 1970s will be followed by a rise in 'modern divorce'. This is supported by Jones, who points out that not all regions of Southeast Asia had declining divorce rates during this period. Many major cities had a rising divorce rate which paralleled that of many other parts of the world. This, according to Jones (1995: 192), may be due to more individualistic attitudes that emerge in the fast industrializing and urbanizing societies, pressures arising from women's double roles, and more opportunities to interact with the opposite sex in the workplace. Similarly, data from two Religious Courts in West Java show high rates of divorce, with most divorces initiated by women (Pengadilan Agama Bandung, 2003; Pengadilan Agama Cimahi, 2002, 2003). This can mean that contemporary Indonesian marriage is more like what Giddens has called a 'pure relationship' in which a couple only stay together as long as the relationship satisfies both sides and makes the couple happy (Giddens, 1992).[26] It can also mean that the educational opportunities that women gain give them economic independence, so they are free to choose divorce when they are unhappy with their marriage, for example when their husband is unfaithful or attempts to take another wife. In sum, if women have better choices such as kin networks or their own economic independence to rely on, they tend to prefer divorce in order to escape from unhappy marriages, which can be caused by, among other factors, polygamy.

There has also been a changing construction of parenthood in Indonesia. Since the early twentieth century, there had been more emphasis on the woman's role as mother and educator of her children (Kartini, 1992; KOWANI, 1978; Tiwon, 1996). But since 1999, there has been a campaign to promote men's involvement in the process of childbearing and child rearing. For instance, during Habibie's presidency, the Indonesian government launched *Gerakan Sayang Ibu* (the movement to love mothers) and *Gerakan Bina Keluarga Balita* (the movement to nurture families with a baby under five years old). These movements aimed to decrease the maternal mortality rate during pregnancy and childbirth and to provide children under five with improved healthcare. These movements were promoted on television and radio and in newspapers and advertisements distributed throughout Indonesia using the slogan *Suami Siaga*. *Suami Siaga* stands for *Suami Siap Antar Jaga,* which means that a husband is expected to be ready to accompany his wife when she gives birth (Nurdin, 2003: 107). Before the campaign, pregnancy and childbirth were often regarded as only 'women's business'. After the campaign, however, husbands have been not just encouraged but expected to attend their wife's labor. This campaign seemed to change many Indonesian women's expectations of their husbands, especially regarding their involvement in pregnancy and childbirth. Expectations of marriage have also changed. A man seems to expect his wife to be his companion, not just a housewife and mother to his children. Similarly, a woman seems to expect her husband to be a partner or companion instead of just a breadwinner.

Feminist critiques of the family

There has been an extensive body of work by western feminists critiquing the family.[27] These western feminists have been critical of the normalization or idealization of 'the family' (VanEvery, 1999), a normalization that glosses over the diversity and complexity of family life in contemporary societies (Zinn, 1992). Some western feminists, especially radical feminists, have challenged the idealized vision of the family as domestic haven and marriage as 'an arrangement of love between equals', or 'the companionate' or 'egalitarian' marriage (Thorne, 1992: 20). Collier *et al.* (1992) argue that the assumption that 'the family' is a loving place has led to a more tolerant attitude toward violence, abuse or homicide committed by family members than toward that committed by strangers. In addition, Rayna Rapp (1992: 56) points to the contradiction between the norm of the family as a place where people should be loving, sharing and protective, and the reality of domestic violence. Even without violence, she argues, 'the family' does not necessarily provide a peaceful environment when there are, for instance, alcoholic parents, parental desertion and divorce. Feminists have also challenged the tendency of sociologists and historians to see the family as a single unit and to assume that all of its members share similar resources and opportunities in life (Gittins, 1985: 2).

The idealization of the nuclear family can also be seen in the emergence of the 'pro family' movement first established in the USA in the 1970s (Segal, 1999: 209) and in the Christian Right's call for a return to the nuclear family consisting of breadwinner husband, housewife and their children (Buss and Herman, 2003) in response to what they see as the weakening of family values. The proponents of family values blame this weakening for 'social problems' (Allan and Crow, 2001). They also often blame feminists for causing the shift from the nuclear family and for the problems in women's lives, ignoring other factors such as social and economic changes that facilitated such changes (Allan and Crow, 2001; Walby, 1997: 157; Jagger and Wright, 1999). In their efforts to restore and promote family values, Christian fundamentalists globally, Orthodox Jews in the USA, anticommunists in Eastern Europe and the former Soviet Union in the late 1980s and Islamists in the Middle East united and created global alliances (Moghadam, 2003a: 114). Malaysia together with other Muslim countries has joined these global alliances to 'defend' and 'strengthen' the family (Stivens, 2006: 8–9) as well as to oppose abortion and homosexuality.

Feminisms are not only diverse, but also fluid and contextual. Feminist struggles can take different forms from time to time and from one place to another, based on the changing circumstances they face. As argued by Segal (1995), feminist critique of and contribution toward understanding family life is changing, from the intense attacks on the institution of the family in the 1960s to the celebration of women's role within it in the 1980s.[28] She also notes the tendency of men influenced by feminists to reclaim and celebrate 'fathering' in the home and in the academy, at the end of 1970s (1995: 306).

In the 1980s, western feminists changed the focus of their writing, from women's subordination within the family to women's agency. They observed the ways in which women had actively negotiated and resisted the structures that subordinated them (Thorne, 1992: 7). For instance, Deniz Kandiyoti (1988) argues that within the patriarchal system of the traditional nuclear family, women passively resisted the system by being submissive in exchange for men's economic support and protection. In addition, feminist writings, even though still focused on their critique of the monolithic family, have shifted their attention to various meanings and experiences of 'family'.[29] These writings show that there are diverse experiences of 'family' and household across social class, race and ethnicity (Thorne, 1992: 8). The shift in feminist discourse can also be seen in the emergence of third-wave feminism in the 1990s, which among other things is characterized by the celebration of heterosexuality and a women's right to pleasure (Henry, 2004).[30]

Western scholarship, including western feminism, has been criticized for being Euro/America-centric (e.g. Oyewumi, 2002; Stivens, 1990: 103, 1991, 1996: 4–5); or western-centric (Lazreg, 1988, 1994); for seeing the non-western as the 'Other' (Said, 1978); and for universalizing/homogenizing third-world women as a group subordinated by men, ignoring issues such as race, class and local/global stratification (Freeman and Murdock, 2001; Lazreg, 1988; Mohanty, 1988, 1991). For instance, Lazreg (1988), resisting what she sees as western feminist hegemony on Algerian feminism, argues that the problems faced by Algerian feminists are different from those of western feminists. This seems to imply that feminisms are culturally based, contextual and local, but at the same time also global. Global feminisms, in which feminists from various countries participated at the United Nations women's conferences (Stivens, 2000) and built international networking and cooperation (Moghadam, 2003b), do have significant influence on local feminisms.

Even though western scholarship has been criticized for being Euro/America-centric, this scholarship is useful in bringing about a critical awareness among feminists in the non-western world of the existing gender inequalities and women's subordination within marriage and family. For instance, as I shall argue, I have found western feminist scholarship useful in helping me to uncover unequal power and gender relations in the polygamous marriages of my informants, where husbands marry polygamously without consulting the first wife. In addition, a number of Indonesian feminists, who seem to be influenced by western feminist critiques of the family and the international women's movement, have set up non-governmental organizations (NGOs) concerned with domestic violence against women (Blackburn, 2001: 276). As in the West, this domestic violence has been regarded as a private matter and is not seen as criminal. These NGOs, such as Rifka Annisa and Yasanti in Yogyakarta, Flower of Aceh in Aceh, Institut Perempuan Bandung in Bandung and Mitra Perempuan and LBH APIK in Jakarta, provide shelters, advocacy and legal aid for female victims of domestic violence.[31] Other Indonesian feminists, mainly western-educated, are also critical of 'the family' in Indonesia (see, for instance, Koning *et al.*, 2000 and Sears, 1996; both published their findings abroad).[32] The relative absence of critiques of the Indonesian family in the national media may be due partly to the prolonged period of Soeharto's presidency, which is commonly characterized as a militaristic authoritarian regime. During this period (1966–98), freedom of the press was highly suppressed. People who dared to express opinions contrary to state ideology could be accused of being communist party members and find their lives endangered (Sen 2000; Suryakusuma, 2004; Wieringa, 1995). Therefore, it is understandable that during the Soeharto era, most published writings were supportive of the state gender ideology.[33]

Julia Suryakusuma is one among the few western-educated Indonesian feminists who overtly criticize the New Order state ideology of *ibuism*.[34] She suggests that this housewifely state *ibuism,* has been spread throughout Indonesia by non-political women's organizations: *Dharma Wanita* and PKK (*Pembinaan*

Kesejahteraan Keluarga/ Family Welfare Guidance). Suryakusuma argues that this ideology tends to be urban and upper-middle class- (*kelas menegah ke atas*) oriented, because it promotes activities and values that are irrelevant to the lives of poor rural women who mostly must work for their survival and do not have time to join in such activities such as cooking, knitting and sewing classes. She also criticizes this ideology for overlooking many aspects of rural life such as a large number of female-headed households, the high rate of divorce, desertion, migration and unemployed husbands. This ideology, she argues, views women merely as male dependants and therefore denies their autonomy as widows, divorcées and single women. In line with western critiques of the family, Suryakusuma also criticizes the New Order government's tendency to normalize the nuclear family, and its failure to acknowledge family arrangements other than the nuclear family. She notes that the sexual division of labor among the poor is more egalitarian than within the the upper-class family, partly owing to necessity. She asserts that upper-middle-class women are better off economically but are more subordinate to men. Influenced by Mies (1982), she highlights the negative effects of this state *ibuism*, such as the assumption that women are housewives: this has led women to be regarded as the 'secondary income earner', an assumption which is then used to justify lower wages and salaries for women. In addition, the view that men are the heads of households, she argues, has excluded women from certain beneficial programs such as credit extensions and income-generating programs (Suryakusuma, 2004: 161–88).

Suryakusuma's assertion that upper-middle-class women are more subordinate to men may have been true within aristocratic families during the colonial era. According to Brenner, gender relations among Javanese women in the colonial era were constructed differently in different classes. Within merchant communities, women were valued for their economic productivity through their ability and willingness to engage in trade. In contrast, within the aristocratic family, women were valued for their domestic roles and for their sexuality and fertility (which were under men's control). Within this community, the role of wives was to 'serve' their husbands, to bear their children and to maintain their household (Brenner, 1998: 76). It seems to me that the state ideology of *ibuism* is based on just such Javanese aristocratic ideology. Suryakusuma's assertion may also be true among contemporary upper-class women who are economically dependent on their husbands and follow this aristocratic construction of femininity. But this is unlikely to be true among contemporary women who are highly educated and have professional jobs such as lawyers, doctors and lecturers. Coming from an upper-class background, and as an educated woman with resources, Suryakusuma may have had a more egalitarian relationship with her husband than the lower-class women described by Hilmy (2005). Hilmy reports the case of a female factory worker who often refused to have sex with her husband, because of tiredness after a long day of factory work and domestic labor at night. Rather than sharing the housework, her husband used her refusal to have sex with him as an excuse to take another wife.

Another Indonesian feminist critical of the state ideology is Sita Aripurnami. She argues that the image of domesticated, 'dependent, emotional, passive, weak and incapable women subject to the leadership of men' has been promoted through *sinetron* (TV series like soap operas) with national viewers (Aripurnami, 1996). According to her, these programs carry government messages suggesting that no matter how extensive women's responsibilities outside the home, they must be still be responsible for domestic work, including cooking, cleaning and child care. This state ideology seems to be part of Soeharto's own ideology about the role of women. Thus, in one chapter of his biography entitled 'Concerning Our Women', Soeharto emphasized the role of women as the mother in a household (*ibu rumah tangga*) and simultaneously as the motor of development. He also outlined women's *kodrat* (nature) 'as beings who must provide for the continuation of a life that is healthy, good and pleasurable' (cited in Tiwon, 1996: 59). This insistence on *ibu* as the core of women's nature, according to Tiwon (1996: 59), denies a woman's social identity as 'a person in her own right'.

Some scholars have suggested that this construction of femininity, which emphasizes women's domestic roles, derived from western influences. According to Gouda, indigenous Indonesian custom did not set boundaries between public and private spheres, and most indigenous women were actively involved in what is considered the public sphere, working in plantations and factories, cultivating crops and trading in markets. However, in the late nineteenth century some colonial voices began to reorient definitions of women's proper place to a western pattern by incorporating *all* women, whether white or indigenous, into the domestic realm (Gouda, 1995: 178).[35] This view is supported by Kipp (1998: 231–3), who explains that the role of housewife (a function under the sexual division of labor in which men were assigned with paid work, while women performed unpaid work) was invented in Europe in the nineteenth century and was promoted by the western missionaries in the archipelago in the 1930s. This incorporation of women into the domestic realm seemed to be more appropriate for upper-middle-class women, who did not need to earn a living owing to the support of their rich husbands, than for poor rural women.

However, Lev argues that the New Order leaders' conservative attitudes may be rooted in their lower-middle-class background and nouveau riche achievements. In addition, Lev points out that compared to the intellectuals who led the early nationalist movement, many New Order leaders were less well-educated, less well-read, less influenced by ideals of reform and change and politically suspicious of popular movements and social mobilization as sources of 'instability' (Lev, 1996: 197–8).

Conclusion

This chapter has described the Indonesian kinship system, which could affect women's status and their attitudes toward marriage and divorce. The presence/absence of financial support either from the women's kin or their own income is likely affect women's decision to either stay or escape from unhappy marriage, caused for instance by their husband's polygamous marriage. This chapter has also shown that significant changes occurred in Indonesia after the 1970s such as the rising age of marriage, the increasing number of free-choice marriages, the declining rate of divorce, and the changing expectation of men and women of the role of their marital spouse. However, the rising age of marriage, which means the lengthening period of adolescence, has become a great concern of some Islamists, who then encourage early marriage as a way to avoid *zina*. They also see the high number of unmarried women over 30 years old as a 'problem' which should be solved by encouraging polygamous marriages (encouraging married women to share their husbands with the unmarried women) as if all women need to be married. All of this context of Indonesia will be useful in understanding the cases of polygamous marriage, which is not commonly practiced but has attracted controversies, mainly between Indonesian feminists who argue against polygamy and Islamists who argue that polygamy is part of *shari'a*. Whether or not polygamy is part of *shari'a* and what it means by *shari'a* will be discussed in the next chapter.

3 Muslim discourses on polygamy in Indonesia

> Personally, I dislike and hate polygamy because it has many negative effects. Sometimes, I am wondering why this Islamic law is very hard for a woman to accept if it is implemented in the way that my husband did. ... Preventing polygamy is a big challenge for women because many people use the Qur'an to legitimize their practice of polygamy.[1]
>
> (Interview with Lina, 13 March 2004)

Lina (39) is the first wife of Hadi (49), who secretly took a second wife, Nani. Lina, who had a Bachelor's degree in Islamic Studies and was taking her Masters in one of the Islamic universities in Bandung, told me that her married life had been miserable since she discovered her husband's secret second marriage. Lina was not the only woman who assumed that polygamy is part of Islamic law. Many of my research participants believed that Islam permits polygamy, even though they personally disagreed with the practice. They believed that they had to accept polygamy as part of their acceptance of their religion and the Qur'anic verses, the main sources of *shari'a*. They were afraid of being seen as rejecting Islam through rejecting polygamy. In addition, many proponents of polygamy often used religious slogans to promote and defend the practice. These slogans include: 'polygamy is part of *shari'a*', 'polygamy is *Sunnah Rasul* [recommended by the Prophet]', 'polygamy is better than *zina* [illicit sexual relationship]' and 'polygamy is a solution for prostitution' (Suryono, 2003).

In this book I emphasize the difference between the Qur'an and its interpretation, because some Muslims, including my research participants, tend to equate human interpretation with the Qur'an itself and to regard this interpretation as divine and immutable. Thus, they are in danger of giving 'sacredness to mere human opinions' ('Ashmawy, 1998: 97). I argue that the belief that Islam permits polygamy is only one possible interpretation of the Qur'an. I shall begin this chapter by discussing *shari'a*, which is often used by proponents of polygamy to justify the practice. Second, I shall discuss various Muslim interpretations of the Qur'anic verses in relation to polygamy. Third, I shall discuss Indonesian feminist struggles over marriage law. I show that the prevalent discourse on Qur'anic-sanctioned polygamy in Indonesia throughout the twentieth century has been an abiding tension for women's organizations. In addition, the political tension between Islamist versus secular parties had forced the secular government to compromise with Islamist parties' interests, such as that allowing divorce and polygamy to be controlled by the Religious, not the Civil, Courts. Fourth, I discuss government restriction of divorce and polygamy through regulations that require civil servants to obtain permission from their superior before divorcing or taking additional wives. Fifth, I highlight the shifting discourse of polygamy in the last decades: from its restriction in the Soeharto period to its promotion in the post-Soeharto period. This promotion, as noted in the introduction, contributes to more relaxed attitudes toward polygamy among its proponents. However, I suggest that the opponents of polygamy remain in the majority and continue to express their opposition in various media.

What is *shari'a*?

Shari'a is a contested term. It is often narrowly understood as *fiqh* (Islamic jurisprudence). According to 'Ashmawy (1998: 97), *shari'a* in Qur'anic terminology and Arabic dictionaries means 'path, method, or way', not 'law in the sense of legal rules'. According to Schacht (1964: 1), *shari'a* is the religion of Islam itself. Similarly, Mohammad Hashim Kamali (1999: 108) argues that *shari'a* is a wider concept than *fiqh*. He affirms that *shari'a*:

> comprises the totality of guidance that God has revealed to the Prophet Muhammad relating to the dogma of Islam: its moral values and its practical legal rules. Shariah thus comprises in its scope not only law but also theology and moral teaching.

Therefore, Islamic *shari'a* means the Islamic way of life, and/or Islamic teaching. It is what is written in the Qur'an and Sunnah, the two main sources of *shari'a*.[2] From the above quotations, it is also clear that the legal aspect is only part of a broad and comprehensive set of meanings of *shari'a*. Therefore, stressing the legal aspect of *shari'a* unduly narrows its meaning. In contrast to *shari'a* (which is divine), *fiqh*, as discussed earlier, is a human interpretation of the Qur'an and the *Sunnah* in legal issues. Therefore, equating *shari'a* with *fiqh*, or translating *shari'a* as Islamic law 'is just another method of abusing the semantics of discourse in shaping its power and validity' (Wadud, 2006: 50).

Nathan J. Brown (1997) and Muhammad Sa'id 'Ashmawy (1998: 97) point out a major shift in the understanding of *shari'a*. They argue that the meaning of *shari'a* has been expanded over time, which tends to narrow down its meaning into fixed legal rules. 'Ashmawy (1998: 97) notes four phases in the expansion of the meaning of *shari'a*:

> The word Shari'a was initially used by the first generation of Muslims in its proper meaning. Then it was extended to include the legal rules in the Qur'an. This was expanded over time to cover the legal rules, either in the Qur'an or in

the prophetic traditions. Finally, the term incorporated legal rules in all Islamic history. Today, Islamic law or Shari'a refers to Islamic jurisprudence.[3]

Abdullahi An-Naim is one of the Muslim scholars who equate *shari'a* with *fiqh* for two reasons: first, human beings can only understand the purpose of divine revelation through their own limited human understanding and behavior and therefore, for him, '*Shari'ah* is always *fiqh*'; second, according to him, in normal Islamic political and legal discourse, no distinction is made between *shari'a* and *fiqh* and the two terms are used interchangeably, such as in relation to women's human rights, in order to defend human understanding with divine sanctity (An-Naim, 2000: 34). Even though I agree with his call for 'deconstruction of *shari'a*', which in my understanding is reinterpretation of the Qur'an and Sunnah, I tend to disagree with his equating *shari'a* with *fiqh*. In my opinion, what is divine (*shari'a*) is clearly written in the Qur'an and Sunnah, which cannot be changed over time, but their interpretations (human products) are written in *tafsir* and *fiqh* works and other human-written books that vary and can be re-written over time. His equating *shari'a* with *fiqh* could be confusing, especially when he identifies that some aspects of *shari'a* violate human rights: for example, *shari'a* treats various categories of human being as unequal; custody of children up to certain age is usually given to mothers, who will automatically lose their rights for custody after that. This could give a negative connotation to *shari'a* because it tends narrow the meaning of *shari'a* into human interpretation of the divine teaching in a particular time only. This also could lead to treating human understanding as divine. I tend to agree with scholars who differentiate between *shari'a* and *fiqh*, in that *shari'a* is Islam itself, the Islamic way of life that is written in the Qur'an and Sunnah, while *fiqh* is human interpretation of *shari'a*; or in Umar's definition, *shari'a* is the basic teaching that is universal and permanent, while *fiqh* is cultural understanding of *shari'a*, which is local, elastic and not permanent (Umar, 2002b: 98).

In addition to An-Naim, 'Ashmawy's elaboration of the expansion of the meaning of *shari'a* also seems to explain many contemporary Indonesian Muslims' understanding of *shari'a*. They mostly regard *shari'a* as all legal rules in all Muslim history, mainly written in *fiqh* works. Therefore, when they proposed 'the implementation of *shari'a*', what they meant was 'the formalization of what is written in medieval *fiqh* works'. In a contemporary Indonesian context, this is likely to create problems. Arskal Salim has undertaken one of the important current studies in this area. He argues that the understanding of *shari'a* as laws, rather than as a way of life or a set of principal values, is likely to create dissonance (Salim, 2006: 28). For example, a proposal for the formal implementation of *shari'a* would restrict the religious freedom of individuals. As a result, nationals of the Indonesian state, according to him, would be treated as a religious community, not as autonomous individual citizens. This would contradict the concept of a nation state, would be likely to coerce citizens to follow the dominant interpretation of *shari'a* and would foster political fractions among citizens of different religious affiliation (Salim, 2006: 222).

Furthermore, according to Hilmy (2006), in some regions such as Aceh, *shari'a* is often understood in a more narrow sense as *hudud* (punishment). Therefore, for them, the application of *shari'a* means the application of punishment such as the flogging of unmarried people and stoning to death of married people who commit *zina* (fornication) and cutting off the hand of someone found stealing. Many of those who understand *shari'a* in a narrow sense as *fiqh* cannot differentiate between the Qur'an and its interpretation, assuming *fiqh* to be divine. Therefore, many of them argue against 'reinterpretation' of the Qur'anic verses, or any effort to understand the Qur'an contextually.[4] Owing to their inability to differentiate between the Qur'an and its interpretations (written in *tafsir* and *fiqh* works), they often feel irritated by any criticism against these works, assuming that this criticism is directed at the Islamic religion itself. They appear to regard human works as divine.

The understanding of the term *shari'a* to include law throughout Islamic history also has implications for how Muslims understand polygamy. Those who understand *shari'a* according to the above definition usually regard *fiqh* as *shari'a*. The fact that all *fiqh* (and also *tafsir*) writers believe that polygamy is permitted and that none, apart from Muhammad Abduh (1849–1905), the nineteenth-century reformer from Egypt whose writings have been highly influential (Rida, 1973: 350), believes that it can be prohibited, leads many Indonesian Muslims, like my informants, to claim that 'Islam [equating *fiqh* or *tafsir* with Islamic religion itself] permits polygamy'. Therefore, as will be discussed later in this chapter, any move to prohibit polygamy is viewed as 'against the teaching of Islam', when it is actually 'against the interpretation of the dominant *fiqh* or *tafsir* works'.[5] Abduh's interpretation of polygamy tended to be ignored. This may be because Abduh was not among the medieval *ulama* (religious scholars), and the door of *ijtihad* was considered closed at the end of the medieval era.[6] It is surprising to me that even though Muhammadiyah, one of the biggest Muslim organizations in Indonesia, was founded based on Abduh's reformism (Koentjaraningrat, 1978: 188; Abdul-Samad, 1991), most of Muhammadiyah's followers do not adopt Abduh's standpoint on polygamy. Abduh's interpretation of polygamy seemed to influence only a minority of western-educated Indonesian Muslims, such as Bahder Djohan, whose view on polygamy will be discussed later.

Muslim interpretations of polygamy

The Muslim scholar Abdullah Saeed has categorized three approaches in interpreting the ethico-legal content of the Qur'an in the modern context: Textualist, Semi-textualist and Contextualist. This categorization is based on the degree of the interpreters' (1) reliance on linguistic criteria to understand the meaning of the text; (2) consideration of the socio-historical context of the Qur'an and the current context (Saeed, 2006b: 3). This section will discuss, using Saeed's classification, Muslim interpretations of the Qur'anic verse 4: 3, which is commonly quoted to justify polygamy:

> And if ye fear that ye will not deal fairly by the orphans, *marry of the women who seem good to you, two or three or four*; and if ye fear that ye cannot do

justice (to so many) then one (only) or (the captives) that your right hands possess. Thus it is more likely that ye will not do injustice. [my emphasis]
(Pickthall, 1979: 79)

The first group, the Textualists, based on their literal reading of the italic part of the verse – *marry women of your choice, two, or three, or four* – believe that Islam permits polygamy and justify their opinion by referring to the Prophet Muhammad's practice of polygamy. The second group, the Semi-textualists, believe that polygamy is only permitted under certain circumstances, when wives can be treated equally.[7] They base their opinion on a literal understanding of verse 4: 3, eliminating the context of the verse revelation that deals with orphans: *marry women of your choice, two, or three, or four; but if ye fear that ye shall not be able to deal justly (with them), then only one, or that which your right hands possess. That will be more suitable, to prevent you from doing injustice....* In addition, this group believe that unlike pre-Islamic polygamy, which had no limitation on the number of wives, in Islam the number of wives is limited to four. The third group, the Contextualists, believe that polygamy is prohibited. They interpret the verse comprehensively and contextually. They not only base their opinion on one segment of the verse 4: 3, but begin from the verse 4: 2 and continue their reading with the verse 4: 129. As one sympathetic to the views of the third group, I shall use Fazlur Rahman's approach of *double movement* in reading the verses on polygamy. Rahman (1919–88), a prominent Pakistani-American scholar whose writing has been influential, advocated reading the Qur'an, not piecemeal but comprehensively, and argued that there is 'no inner contradiction' in the Qur'an if it is read as a whole (Rahman, 1982: 6).

According to Rahman, to understand the Qur'anic message one must move from the present time to the Qur'anic time and then move back to the present. The aim of the first movement back to the Qur'anic time is to understand the intended message of the verses or to 'distil' the general moral–social objectives from specific texts. This is because, according to Rahman, the Qur'an was revealed in response to a specific historical context. After distilling the intended message of the texts, he argues, one has to move back to the present time. In order to apply the intended message of the text, one has to understand the situation at the present time in which the intended message will be applied. This, he asserts, may involve changing the rules of the past to adapt to the present situation, provided that this change does not contradict the general principles and values derived from the past. It also aims at changing the present situation in order to conform to these general principles and values (Rahman, 1982: 5–7).

There are at least two versions of the socio-historical context of the revelation of the verse 4: 3. One version reports that this verse was revealed to the Prophet after the *Uhud* war, which killed 70 Muslim men and left others to care for their wives and children. This was an acute social problem that was solved by the revelation of the verse which asked male Muslims who could afford to take care of the orphans to marry the orphans' mothers so that the orphans had guardians (Doi, 1989: 5; Khan, 1995a: 185). Another version states that some male guardians wanted to marry the orphans because they were interested in their beauty and wealth, but did not want to give them the appropriate amount of *mahar*.[8] They thought that they could treat their orphaned wives as they wished, because the orphans had no one to protect them (Mawdudi, 1989: 6; Rida, 1973: 344; Tabari, 1903: 144).[9]

In the above context, the following verses were revealed to guide and prevent male guardians from being unjust towards the orphans:

> To orphans restore their property (when they reach their age), nor substitute (your) worthless things for (their) good ones; and devour not their substance (by mixing it up) with your own. For this is indeed a great sin. If ye fear that ye shall not be able to deal justly with the orphans, marry women of your choice, two, or three, or four; but if ye fear that ye shall not be able to deal justly (with them), then only one, or that which your right hands possess. That will be more suitable, to prevent you from doing injustice. (Qur'an verses 4: 2–3)
> (Ali, 1989: 184–5)

Amina Wadud, a contemporary Muslim feminist writer, interprets these verses as not about polygamy being permitted, but about the importance of being just toward powerless orphans (Wadud, 1999: 83). Justice, the primary requirement for marrying more than one wife, is stated in the Qur'anic verse 4: 129 to be impossible for men to achieve: *Ye are never able to do justice between wives even if it is your ardent desire* (Ali, 1989: 227). Therefore, the Contextualists interpret polygamy as prohibited. Muhammad Abduh is the leading proponent of this group.[10] His interpretation of polygamy spurred many Muslim scholars and reformers to legislate against polygamy, especially Tunisian scholars who decided to ban polygamy in 1956 (Jawad, 1998: 45). Abduh suggests that polygamy was permitted at the time of revelation, to meet special social, political, economic and military conditions of Muslim communities, but then it may no longer be appropriate. Also, irresponsible men have abused polygamy, leading to it becoming more harmful than beneficial. Thus, it is imperative to prohibit polygamy in order to protect public interest (Jawad, 1998: 45). Similarly, some Turkish scholars also believed that Qur'anic pronouncements about polygamy were a great improvement on the unlimited polygamy in pre-Islamic Arabia, but that the changing social and economic conditions in Turkey had made polygamy 'unrealizable' (Mahmood, 1972: 21).

The Contextualists present many other arguments against polygamy. For instance, Subandrio (1959), writing from Indonesia, regards polygamy as an outmoded form of marriage, which can only survive among societies in which women are less educated and are economically controlled by men. Subandrio believes that better-educated women can be better equipped to maintain monogamous marriage. Similarly, Mernissi (1975), a Moroccan scholar, regards polygamy as an outmoded form of marriage, which many Moroccans can no longer afford owing to their economic problems. Ave (1959) from Indonesia also believes that polygamous marriage cannot be the norm, because if the majority of men have more than one wife, some women might have to become polyandrous. In addition, Djohan (1959) from Indonesia believes that polygamy may actually lead to prostitution. The practice of some men who marry more than one woman will reduce the number of women that other men can marry, which may lead other men to turn to prostitutes as a form of sexual compensation.

There are also many other reasons raised to justify polygamy. These include the argument that women outnumber men, and that an established wife can no longer take care of her husband and cater to his high sexual drive (Jawad, 1998). Jawad agrees with some of the reasons, such as a wife's childlessness and illness as well as the unbalanced sex ratio. But Wadud (1999) and Barlas, a Pakistani-American Muslim feminist (2002), writing from North America, reject all of those reasons. They believe that polygamy in Islam is not a solution for women's economic problems, men's desire for children or male sexual satisfaction, but was a practice intended to ensure social justice for orphans. Koentjaraningrat (1959: 98–9), an anthropologist from Indonesia, also rejects the statistical reasons for polygamy. He argues that much of the Indonesian population data does not differentiate the age of the female population, which is important in understanding marriage patterns. The higher number of women than men may be caused by the greater life expectancy among women. This means that many old widows, rather than young women, may be the only ones available for men who want to practice polygamy.

In Indonesia, the Textualists mainly consist of Islamists who promote polygamy as part of Islamic values, and their view has gained media coverage in the post-Soeharto period. The Contextualists in the 1950s consisted of western-educated secular Muslims such as Subandrio, Ave and Djohan, whose views are presented above. In the post-Soeharto period, this group has mainly consisted of Muslim feminists, some of whom are lecturers and researchers in the Institutes for Islamic Studies (IAIN) or the State Islamic Universities (UIN) throughout Indonesia or employees of women's NGOs such as LBH APIK, Yasanti and Rifka Annisa. The most vocal group advocating the prohibition of polygamy has been Muslim feminists from LBH APIK and *Lembaga Kajian Agama dan Jender*/LKAJ (The Institute for Religious and Gender Research). In October 2004, a working group from LKAJ, led by Musdah Mulia, a Muslim scholar who actively advocates for women's rights, launched *Counter Legal Draft Kompilasi Hukum Islam*, a legal draft to counter the new draft of the Compilation of Islamic Law, which is slated to be passed into law. In this draft, polygamy is clearly prohibited. The draft invited reactions from the Textualists, who condemned it on the grounds that it contradicted Islamic *shari'a*. The Semi-textualists consisted mainly of *santri* Muslims. Most were members of the two largest mainstream Muslim organizations: Muhammadiyah and NU (*Nahdlatul 'Ulama*). Their interpretation of polygamy gained support and was adopted into Indonesian family law, which is written in the 1974 Marriage Law and the Compilation.[11] Conflict between the two groups existed prior to the enactment of the 1974 Marriage Law, which will be discussed next. Despite the constant efforts made by secular women's organizations to prohibit polygamy in marriage law, most mainstream Muslims were against such a prohibition.

The history of the 1974 Marriage Law

In this section, I first explain the historical background to the enactment of the Marriage Law to show the continuing struggles of Indonesian women's organizations against polygamy. Second, I discuss the ambiguity of the Law in relation to the validity of marriage, and its problematical practice in relation to the restriction of polygamy. Third, I look briefly at the implications of the enactment of the Law for Indonesian marriages. Even though women's organizations initially and continually pressured the government to reform marriage law, women's interests became submerged within the conflicts in the Parliament, especially conflicts between Muslim and secular parties. Therefore, some articles of the enacted Marriage Law tend to disadvantage women and are open to Indonesian feminist criticism.

This section will show that the pro-polygamy discourse in Indonesia was highly *political*, used by Muslim political leaders to demonstrate their resistance to the Dutch colonial government when the government issued the 1937 Marriage Ordinance, and to non-Muslim and secular groups prior to the enactment of the Marriage Law. The opposition of Muslim political leaders to the abolition of polygamy seemed to be caused by fear of secularism, which some equated with westernization or Christianization. They also believed that the abolition of polygamy was against *shari'a* – in Daniel Lev's words, the failure to abolish polygamy was due to 'the symbolic importance of the Qur'anic passage that allows it' (Lev, 1996: 193).

I argue that the failure to prohibit polygamy came about because of two additional factors. First, Muslim women's organizations at that time were not independent of their male organizations or political parties – like Aisyiyah, the women's wing of Muhammadiyah, and Muslimat, the women's section of Masyumi, one of the Muslim political parties. The women did not dare to openly oppose their male counterparts' views on polygamy. Second, Indonesian women's organizations were divided over polygamy, with secular and Christian women's organizations arguing against polygamy and Muslim women's organizations defending it. As a result, the former had to compromise for the sake of national interest and to maintain unity among all women's organizations (Locher-Scholten, 2003: 51).

Indonesian feminist calls for Marriage Law reform

The letters of Kartini (1879–1904) demonstrate an early Indonesian feminist critique of the family and marriage.[12] In writing to her Dutch friends, Kartini expressed her opposition to local Javanese aristocratic traditions of women's seclusion, parentally arranged marriage and polygamy. In her opinion, marriage existed only to fulfill male interests, and offered nothing to women. In her socially segregated aristocratic family, she said, there was no place for love. She also criticized the discriminatory treatment of girls and boys in education. She lobbied the government to provide education for girls, to allow for women to be economically independent and avoid sole reliance on marriage. In her time, only the male elite could access education. As a child of an aristocrat, she was allowed to study in a Dutch primary school – a most unusual practice – though she ended up being secluded when she reached the age of 12. Javanese aristocratic tradition secluded girls from the time that they reached puberty until they were married off to the man of their father's choice (Kartini, 1992). Raised in a polygamous family, Kartini could see directly the misery of a woman competing with a co-wife to gain their husband's attention. Despite her views, she ended up being married to a man who already had three wives and six children. She felt powerless to resist polygamy because she believed *Islamic law* protected it (Kartini, 1992), a perception shared by many Textualists and Semi-textualists.

Indonesian women's organizations in the early 1900s also expressed their objection to the uncodified Muslim marriage law, which they saw as resulting in uncertainties over Muslim women's rights and their protection. At that time, there were many cases of child marriage, forced marriage, arbitrary divorce and polygamy that were not approved by Islamic regulation (Katz and Katz, 1975: 656; Soewondo, 1977: 283–4). Indeed, Dewi Sartika, one of the advocates for women's education in West Java at that time, called polygamy 'a gangrene on society' (Vreede-de Stuers, 1960: 175; Wieringa, 1995: 58). A number of periodicals also debated the issue. For instance, in 1913, *Putri Mardika* (Independent Woman), one of the women's organizations that advocated women's education and women's involvement in public, published articles on child marriage and polygamy (Wieringa, 1995: 60). In addition, polygamy had become an issue of burning interest for women's organizations. For instance, Selegoeri, the outspoken writer, criticized polygamy in *Soeara Kaoum Iboe Soematra* (The Voice of Sumatran Women) in the 1930s. Selegoeri wrote that polygamy in Minangkabau had caused neglected children not to know their father, and that co-wives were unhappy (Hatley and Blackburn, 2000: 53). Many women who joined women's organizations to openly oppose polygamy were motivated by personal experience, including personal ties and sympathy with women who were suffering because of polygamous marriages or other marital problems (Blackburn, 2004a: 116; Wieringa 1995: 141).

Thirty women's organizations held an initial congress on 22–25 December 1928 in Yogyakarta (Soewondo-Soerasno, 1955: 128),[13] where they gave speeches about nationalism and against polygamy. Siti Soendari declared in a speech entitled 'The duties and ideals of the Indonesian woman':

> Cases of polygamy and child marriages ... of repudiation and divorce are without number ... . Once the woman's independence has been lost in marriage, once love has flown away, the home is broken and the emancipation of our people impeded.
> (Vreede-de Stuers, 1960: 106)

But differences around polygamy became apparent, with Muslim organizations such as Aisyiyah arguing that polygamy is literally permitted by the Qur'an, and others arguing for its abolition (Vreede-de Stuers, 1960: 104–5). They also discussed a wide range of issues such as women's education, the fate of orphans and widows, child marriage, the evils of forced marriages, marriage law reform and the importance of greater self-esteem among women (Wieringa, 1995: 77). In the following women's organization congresses of 1935, 1938, 1941, 1955, 1957, 1958 and 1961, the women continued to put pressure on the government to reform marriage law, with polygamy and arbitrary divorce remaining constant issues at the meetings (Katz & Katz, 1975: 657; Vreede-de Stuers, 1960; Wieringa, 1995).[14]

Not all Muslim men and women interpreted the Qur'anic verse on polygamy literally. Soepinah Isti Kasiati and Moehammad Sjafei, from Minangkabau, expressed progressive and contextual interpretations of polygamy in *El-Fadjar* (The Light), organ of the Young Muslim Association, in 1927 and 1929 respectively:

> If I had to reply to the question whether polygamy assures a happy marriage, I should without fear of being contradicted answer: No! Islam itself offers polygamy only as a variety of marriage permitted (but not obliged) .... I am therefore convinced that I am not opposing the spirit of Islam when I express the opinion that one should by all means combat polygamy as it is practiced in our country today .... There is no longer question of extenuating circumstances ... polygamy has become nothing other than disguised prostitution. The best way to contend polygamy lies in a more thorough study of Islam itself.
> (Kasiati cited in Vreede-de Stuers, 1960: 105)

> Polygamy is not prohibited by Islam, but it is distressing that many abuse their rights .... They practice a 'polygamy de luxe' ... and I mean by this that such polygamy is inspired entirely by man's passion.
> (Moehammad Sjafei cited in Vreede-de Stuers, 1960: 105)

At the individual level, not all members of Muslim women's organizations supported polygamy. Many shared concerns about polygamy, but were constrained by their association with male-dominated religious organizations (Wieringa, 1995: 141) and by ideas that the Qur'an sanctioned it (Wieringa, 1995: 81). Members of Muslim women's organizations and their leaders were thus in a difficult situation. For instance, Ibu Mangunpuspito, a member of Aisyiyah who attended the first Women's Congress of 1928, expressed her views on polygamy: 'Personally I have never agreed with polygamy. I would never have allowed it. But *it is a religious rule,* so what can we say against it?' (my emphasis) (Wieringa, 1995: 81).[15] Again, this shows the tendency toward literal reading of the Qur'anic verses or equating the position of the interpretation of the Qur'an with the Qur'an itself.

Some male figures in the nationalist movement, such as Bahder Djohan, later a President of the University of Indonesia, joined women in objecting to polygamy.[16] Djohan suggested that polygamy was an obstacle to achieving an equal partnership between a man and a woman and building a happy household. Agreeing with Muhammad Abduh (d. 1905), Djohan saw polygamy as only a temporary solution to the problems of widows and orphans who need male guardians, and argued that the provisions for polygamy could be changed (from being permitted to being prohibited) in changing times and situations (Djohan, 1977: 26–7; Vreede-de Stuers, 1960: 68).

In 1937, the Dutch government issued the Marriage Registration Ordinance (Soewondo-Soerasno, 1955). This Ordinance, according to Locher-Scholten

(2003: 47–8), was issued for two reasons: first, to protect European women who married Indonesian Muslim men from the miseries of polygamy;[17] second, in response to pressure from women's organizations for marriage law reform. This Ordinance was obligatory for marriage between European women and Indonesian men, while voluntary for others (Locher-Scholten, 2000: 196). Locher-Scholten (2003: 48) argues that the fact that this Ordinance was directed at urban elite European women in the Indies implied a 'construction of whiteness' because it created a different legal position for European women. As well, the fact that this Ordinance also targeted elite urban Dutch Indies women implied, according to Locher-Scholten (2003: 48), 'classed modernity' because it excluded rural women and did not offer protection to Indonesian women involved in concubinage (the *nyai*) with European and Chinese men.

The Ordinance offered voluntary marriage registration, and stipulated that marriage is basically monogamous and that non-monogamous marriage is invalid. It also stated that marriage might be dissolved by the death of a spouse, or if a spouse went missing without trace for two years. In the absence of either of these two conditions, divorce needed to take place in court. The Ordinance also stipulated that a husband was obliged to support his ex-wife, and it gave directions on dealing with custody of children after divorce. To consider public opinion, the government discussed a draft of the Ordinance with various men's and women's organizations. Leaders of secular women's organizations, including Maria Ulfah, a western-educated lawyer and one of the leading women in the Indonesian women's movement, expressed their support.[18] However, Muslim organizations mostly opposed the Ordinance (Soewondo-Soerasno, 1955: 150–4).

Locher-Scholten (2000: 200) reports that the Ordinance became a burning topic among the Dutch Indies Muslims at that time, causing a large number of protests all over the archipelago. The roots of this massive Indonesian Muslim protest against Dutch colonial interference in Muslim marriage law, according to Locher-Scholten (2000: 202), could be found in the political and religious context at that time. She explained that during the colonial period, Muslim law was restricted only to family matters. Therefore, the Ordinance was a further government intrusion into an already limited domain of Muslim law. In addition, this Ordinance interfered with what she sees as the private sphere, the core values of Muslim law and hence the very essence of Muslim identity. At the time, Indonesian Muslims believed that the private sphere ought to be governed by personal or Muslim law, as in other Muslim countries. This Muslim family law, and the position of women within it, were regarded as essential to Muslim identity, at a time when this identity was threatened by the forces of colonialism and secular nationalism. Therefore, the issue of the Ordinance gave Muslims an opportunity to unite against external challenges (Locher-Scholten, 2000: 202). In sum, it was the political context at that time, together with a belief that Islam permits polygamy, which prevented Indonesian Muslims from accepting the Ordinance.

After independence, in an attempt to improve women's rights within marriage, the Ministry of Religion issued the law No. 22 of 1946. This law required all Muslims to register their marriage, divorce and reconciliation (*rujuk*) with a local religious officer, who was appointed by the Minister of Religion. To implement law No. 22, the Ministry of Religion issued Instruction No. 4 of 1946, Law No. 32 of 1954, Instruction No. 1 of 1955 and a Decree No. 15 of 1955. These regulations gave advisory power to registrars in cases of forced marriage, divorce and polygamy. In addition to marriage procedures, the last two regulations contained a divorce stipulation (*taklik talak*), which gives a woman automatic right to a divorce if her husband broke one of the stipulations (Azra, 2003: 80–1; Mahmood, 1972: 193–4).[19]

Katz and Katz (1975: 658–9) argue that the regulations did not work effectively in reforming the existing practice of marriage for the following reasons. First, marriages did not have to be registered in order to be considered valid. Second, it was not obligatory for the groom to adopt *taklik talak*; therefore, it could not necessarily be used to protect women within marriage. Third, the marriage registrars only had advisory powers in dealing with forced child marriages, unilateral divorce and arbitrary polygamy. Therefore, they had little power to change these marriage practices. Accordingly, the regulations could not change these marriage practices, and the divorce rate especially remained high – in fact the highest in the world in the 1950s (Jones, 1997: 96). This situation motivated women activists to continue their struggles for marriage law reform. Activists argued that the high divorce rate caused social and family instability, led to problems for women and children, and was fundamentally unfair to women (Azra, 2003: 81). Vreede-de Stuers (1960: 136) has even termed polygamy and arbitrary divorce at that time a 'two-headed monster':

> There is general recognition of the insecurity of the woman in social life and, coupled with it, the growing disintegration of family life and neglect of children, resulting from the abuses of polygamy and arbitrary repudiation.
> (Vreede-de Stuers, 1960: 140)

Vreede-de Stuers also reported that to achieve reform, the women's movement and the Women's Front in Parliament established a Marriage Law Committee, known as *Panitia NTR (Nikah, Talak dan Rujuk)*, in 1950. This committee consisted of male religious leaders and various women's leaders such as Nani Suwondo, Maria Ulfah Santoso, Sujatin Kartowijono, Kwari Sosrosumarto (of *Wanita Katolik* – Catholic women) and Mahmudah Mawardi (representative of the NU). Two drafts of the marriage law were prepared: a general law for all Indonesians (*Rancangan Undang-undang Perkawinan Umum*/General Marriage Law draft, 1952) and another one for Muslims (*Rancangan Undang-undang Perkawinan Umat Islam*/Muslim Marriage Law draft, 1954), the latter permitting polygamy under strict conditions. (Catholic women expressed their opposition to polygamy under any circumstances.) After lengthy debate, the draft was submitted to the Ministry of Religious Affairs in 1954 (Nasution, 2002: 50–1; Vreede-de Stuers, 1960: 125–6; Wieringa, 1995: 142–3), but never introduced in Parliament, and the Women's Front demanded more comprehensive legislation (Wieringa, 1995: 147).

In 1952, many in the women's movement were shocked by Law 19/1952, which gave pensions to widows of polygamous husbands. Many members of women's organizations demonstrated against this government support for polygamy. Even though this demonstration was orderly and well publicized, the government did not respond (Vreede-de Stuers, 1960: 127–8; Wieringa, 1995: 143). In 1953, with the initiative of Perwari, one of the secular women's organizations, several women's organizations held a demonstration to urge the government to enact a marriage law (Soewondo, 1977: 284).

In 1954, President Soekarno's polygamous marriage posed a further obstacle to marriage reform. Only *Perwari*, one of the secular women's organizations led by Sujatin Kartowijono, bravely showed strong opposition to Soekarno's second marriage to Hartini. Kartowijono faced death threats, and many members of her organization withdrew after pressure was placed on their husbands. The Indonesian women's movement seemed to have reached a low point, and division within the movement became more apparent. The women's federation could do nothing for marriage law reform, and Muslim women's organizations accepted Law 19/1952 and Soekarno's polygamous marriage. Gerwani, which usually opposed polygamy, remained silent on the President's second marriage owing to its proximity to the communist party and Soekarno (Wieringa, 1995: 145–7).

In 1956, Nani Suwondo expressed her anxiety regarding the government's response to women's demands for marriage law reform, and her envy of the progress achieved in another Muslim country, Tunisia. Her comments were published in *Suara Perwari*:

> It is with envy that we read in the newspapers that Tunisia, a country which has only just obtained sovereignty and whose population, like ours, is chiefly Muslim, has passed a bill which aims at protecting the interests of the family by prohibiting polygamy, by depriving the husband of his power of repudiation, and by forbidding child marriages.
>
> (cited in Vreede-de Stuers, 1960: 137)

In 1958, Mrs Sumari, a parliamentary member from *PNI* (*Partai Nasional Indonesia*/Indonesian nationalist party), launched her personal draft of the marriage law. This draft stipulated monogamy for all Indonesians and equal rights to divorce for men and women (Wieringa, 1995: 147–8). Like other previous draft laws prohibiting polygamy, male Muslim representatives in the Parliament unsurprisingly opposed this draft. For instance, Tuan Sidi Mardjohan, a representative of *Perti*, one of the Muslim parties, spoke in the Parliament:

> Among other considerations [it had to be noted that] women age more quickly than men do sometimes even though they are of the same age when they marry, but when a woman has already borne two or three children, her figure has already declined one hundred to three hundred percent from the figure she used to have. It is very rare that women are like old Bugis' clothes, the more they are used, the more they shine; the majority of women generally fade quickly while

men are still strong and their lust still powerful and they are still boiling with sexual desire ...

(Soewondo cited in Wieringa, 1995: 148)

Wieringa argues that this quotation shows that male members of Muslim parties wanted to retain their 'right' to polygamy, while their female members did not dare to oppose them (Wieringa, 1995: 141). It also shows his view of women, which he shared with many proponents of polygamy: he saw them as sexual beings whose function is to satisfy male sexual desire. The questions of justice and protection of orphans, mentioned in the Qur'anic verse dealing with polygamy, were not mentioned at all.

Eleven women's organizations suggested a compromise, proposing that polygamy would be permitted for Muslims, while the Civil Marriage Law Code for non-Muslims would be based on monogamy. But the Ministry of Religion rejected this proposal. The women's movement then urged Prime Minister Juanda not to let this matter be handled by a Muslim-dominated Ministry of Religion. The Prime Minister promised to discuss the marriage law with all Cabinet members, but because of the introduction of Guided Democracy, the Parliament was dissolved before this could take place (Wieringa, 1995: 148).

The marriage law was discussed again by the Working Cabinet in 1960, but Nani Soewondo, a lawyer who was concerned with marriage law reform, felt that the government was not taking it seriously and that Indonesia was lagging behind other countries in Asia and Africa that had already codified marriage laws (Wieringa, 1995: 148). Between 1960 and 1973 the marriage law was continually discussed by the Parliament and by various women's organizations. Some argued for unification of the law (one law for all Indonesians); others argued for differentiation of the law (different laws for different religious groups) (Nasution, 2002; Soewondo, 1986).

The New Order's support for the Marriage Law reform

In the early 1970s, the Soeharto government supported the women's organizations' proposal to reform marriage law, because the government wanted to unify the law throughout Indonesia as a tool to homogenize gender ideology (Robinson, 2000) and to eliminate the influence of the Dutch colonial law (Azra, 2003). The government thought that colonial law was divisive and discriminatory (Azra, 2003; Katz and Katz, 1975).[20] Implementation took a long time. It was not easy to reconcile the conflicting interests of literalist Muslims, secularists, Christians and Chinese. The Muslims again feared 'veiled Christianization', while Christians and Chinese, who made up only a small percentage of the population, were afraid of the increased influence of Islam in Indonesia if a marriage law derived from Muslim law (*fiqh*) was enacted (Azra, 2003: 82). Some Indonesians were in favor of legal diversity, whereby different religious groups were governed by different marriage laws, while others preferred unification. And the issue of polygamy was also hotly debated by its proponents and opponents. Proponents of polygamy used the issue of polygamy as a weapon against secular groups who had rejected the inclusion of the implementation of *shari'a* in the Indonesian constitution.

Several important events preceded the enactment of the marriage law. On 31 July 1973 the government submitted the new draft law to the House of Representatives. It was clear, however, that the Ministry of Religion and Muslim political parties were not consulted during the drafting process. As a result, they not only felt that they had been pushed aside, but also objected to several articles that they considered contradictory to their religion (Katz and Katz, 1975: 660).[21] For instance, article 2 (1) of the draft stipulated that registration was necessary for a valid marriage. This was strongly opposed by the Muslim faction, who believed that Muslim marriage could only be valid if performed according to Muslim law (Gandhi-Lapian, 1979: 76). In addition, articles 3 and 40 required Muslims to ask the permission of the Civil Court before obtaining divorce and practicing polygamy. These provisions took away the authority of the Religious Court in handling Muslim family cases, and were therefore regarded as a threat to Muslim religious affairs in Indonesia. For many Indonesian Muslims, the Religious Court was regarded as a symbol of Muslim authority and a guarantor of the implementation of Muslim law (Katz and Katz, 1975: 660–2).[22]

Muslim leaders were reportedly unhappy with the degree of consultation (LBH-APIK, 2000: 17). Various segments of Indonesian society, including Muslim intellectuals, Muslim leaders, student associations, Muslim mass organizations and women's religious groups, became concerned at rumors that the law was a disguised attempt at Christianization and secularization. They organized mass demonstrations in many cities such as Yogyakarta, Bandung, Bogor, Surabaya and Ujung Pandang, with dissent reaching a peak on 27 September 1973 when mass student demonstrators invaded Parliament building and halted discussion. Some of the students were arrested, but these arrests only spurred on a larger demonstration (LBH-APIK, 2000: 20–1).

Within Parliament, only the United Development Faction (*Fraksi Persatuan Pembangunan*) opposed the draft, while the Armed Forces Faction, the government party (*Golkar*) and the Democratic Party principally supported it.[23] The United Development Faction were set to lose, and threatened to walk out. Because of the continuing controversies inside Parliament and a large number of demonstrations, to restore stability the government compromised to accommodate Muslim political interests. They formed a working committee to revise the draft, consisting of ten representatives from all parties, which deleted articles that were considered to be contradictory to Muslim law. For instance, civil registration would no longer be necessary for a valid marriage. To decrease the incidence of divorce and polygamy, the right to give permission was returned to the Religious Court (Katz and Katz, 1975: 662–6).

Bowen explores the possible causes of Muslim resistance to the marriage law draft. In his view, the historical moment was wrong. Muslim parties had not gained many votes in the 1971 election, and the government had recently instructed all Muslim parties to unite into a single new party without an Islamic name, *Partai Persatuan Pembangunan* (United Development Party). Muslims also feared

Christian missionaries' efforts, which were substantial at that point. As no Muslim groups had been involved in drafting the bill, they assumed that Catholic members of Golkar had drafted it (Bowen, 2003: 180–1).

Given the important role of women's organizations in urging marriage reform, how far were these women directly involved in the critical debates in 1973, prior to the enactment of the law? Only one unidentified woman from Golkar was among the ten members of the working committee, and this woman rarely acted on her right to speak. She was reportedly assigned the stereotypical role of secretary (LBH APIK, 2000: 14). There is no information on the part played by the most vocal women such as Maria Ulfah, Nani Soewondo and other women's representatives of *Istri Sedar* at this critical moment of the history of the marriage law. The lack of female representation seemed to contribute to the marginalization of women's issues, which were being set aside by the tensions between the secular and Muslim parties (LBH APIK, 2000: 14).

After a long, heated debate, the new marriage law was finally passed by the Parliament on 22 December 1973 and signed by President Soeharto on 2 January 1974 (Cammack, 1989: 53). Members of Muslim parties and organizations were generally happy with it, but Protestants and Catholics were unhappy about the requirement to apply religious law in marriage and, along with women's organizations, preferred the original draft. However, the provisions on divorce, polygamy and the position of women in the Marriage Law were closer to their expectations (Katz and Katz, 1975: 665–6) because the law required court intervention, to prevent easy divorce and arbitrary polygamy. But the enacted Law failed to eradicate discrimination against women in marriage, leaving women subject to religious codes that, for instance, obliged them to accept polygamy (Blackburn, 1999: 190).[24]

The validity of marriage and the restriction of polygamy

The 1974 Marriage Law stipulates that a marriage is valid if it has been performed according to the religious requirements of the parties involved, but it also requires registration of the marriage. It sets the minimum age of marriage at 16 for females and 19 for males. It also requires court intervention for divorce and polygamy. The following articles of the Marriage Law on the validity of marriage and court intervention on polygamy are very important to my research, because I explored in some depth my informants' understandings of practices in relation to and responses to these articles:

Article 2
(1) A marriage is legitimate, if it has been performed according to the laws of the respective religions and beliefs of the parties concerned.
(2) Every marriage shall be registered according to the regulations of the legislation in force.

Article 3
(1) In principle in a marriage a man shall be allowed to have one wife only. A woman shall be allowed to have one husband only.

(2) A Court of Law shall be capable of granting permission to a husband to have more than one wife, if all parties concerned so wish.[25]

Article 4

(1) If a husband desires to have more than one wife, as referred to in Article 3 paragraph (2) of this Law, he shall be required to submit a request to the Court of Law in the region in which he resides.

(2) The Court of Law referred to in paragraph (1) of this article shall grant permission to the husband wishing to have more than one wife if:

　　a. his wife is unable to perform her duties as wife;
　　b. his wife suffers from physical defects or an incurable disease;
　　c. his wife is incapable of having descendants.

Article 5

(1) In order for a request to be submitted to the Court of Law as referred to in Article 4 paragraph (1) of this Law, the following requirements shall be obtained:

　　a. the approval of the wife or wives;
　　b. the assurance that the husband will guarantee the necessities of life for his wives and their children;
　　c. the guarantee that the husband shall act justly in regard to his wives and their children.

(2) The approval referred to in paragraph (1) under the letter a of this article shall not be required of a husband if it is impossible to obtain the approval of his wife or wives and if she or they are incapable of becoming partner or partners to the contract, or if no information is available with respect to his wife or wives for the duration of at least 2 (two) years, or on account of other reasons requiring the judgment of a Judge on the Court of Law.

(Department of Information, 1979: 10–11)

Article 2 was one of the most controversial articles because all Muslim parties opposed the original draft, which required registration in order for a marriage to be valid, interpreting this as *civil* marriage (Soewondo, 1977: 286). As a result of compromise between secular and Muslim factions in the Parliament, Article 2 became ambiguous. Bowen points out that the relationship between the two clauses in the Article 2 is unclear: whether clause 2 modifies clause 1, with the result that unregistered marriage is invalid; or whether clause 1 allows religious authorities exclusively to decide the issue of the validity of marriage within their religion. He quotes two distinct interpretations of the Article by jurists, published in the Ministry of Religion's publication *Mimbar Hukum* in 1995. One argues that marriage registration does not affect the validity of marriage. The other differentiates between the 'validity' and the 'legality' of marriage and argues that registered marriage is recognized by law, while unregistered marriage is not. The second jurist, according to Bowen, had invoked the dual meaning of law (*hukum*): *hukum* as a matter of religious validity, and *hukum* as a matter of national law (Bowen, 2003: 182–4). This ambiguity of Article 2 is problematic in practice, especially in relation to 'secret' unregistered polygamous marriage, because a polygamous marriage cannot be registered unless there is a letter of permission from a Religious Court (Soewondo, 1977: 293).

Bowen also reports that within two years, the Supreme Court had taken two contradictory positions regarding what constituted 'valid' and 'legal' marriage (Bowen, 2003: 183–4).[26] For instance, in 1988 a court in Bandung sentenced a man who took a second wife in an unregistered marriage (without the court's permission) to five months in jail.[27] The appellate (higher) court, on the other hand, nullified the decision, arguing that only a registered marriage was valid; therefore, the man was not married to another woman but was only living with her, and he was therefore freed.[28] This case was then brought to the Supreme Court, which in 1991 ruled that the lower court had correctly interpreted the Marriage Law, ordering the man back to jail. Two years later, in 1993, the Supreme Court took a different position, in a case in a lower court in Aceh in which a man had two wives but did not register his first marriage. His first wife took him to court. The Supreme Court ruled that only a registered marriage could be considered legitimate. The Supreme Court did not regard the man as having a second marriage, because there was no official record of the first marriage taking place. Therefore, the Supreme Court ruled that the man had not committed a crime, and he was freed (Bowen, 2003: 184). These different positions taken by the Supreme Court were clearly due to the ambiguity of Article 2, which was interpreted differently by different judges in Indonesian courts.

Implications of the enactment of the 1974 Marriage Law

Many Indonesian scholars had been pessimistic about the possible outcomes of the new Law, but they saw it as successful in reducing the rate of divorce and polygamy and in enforcing the minimum age of marriage – even though they do acknowledge the contribution of other factors such as the rising standard of education and the intense campaigns surrounding family planning (Azra, 2003; Katz and Katz, 1978). The Ministry of Religion figures show a significant decrease in the divorce rate after the enactment of the 1974 Marriage Law. For instance, in West Java, in 1955, 58 percent of registered marriages ended in divorce. This rate fell to 16.53 percent in 1985, and then fell again to 14.05 percent in 1986. In Jakarta, the divorce rate between 1954 and 1975 was about 26 percent. It had fallen to 11 percent by 1985 (Azra, 2003: 88).[29] Even though there are no recent figures, Azra argues that it is possible that the difficulty in registering a polygamous marriage might have reduced the number of polygamous marriages (Azra, 2003: 89). Not all scholars agree that the Marriage Law alone brought about these changes, however. Cammack *et al*. (1996) argue that the Law did not contribute much to a reduction in the practice of early marriage. They found people in rural areas often married at an early age in a religious ceremony, and simply registered their marriage later. They argue that other factors such as education and urbanization contributed more to reducing the incidence of early marriage.

Indonesian feminist critics of the Marriage Law

A number of Indonesian feminists have been openly critical of the 1974 Marriage Law (Machali, 2005). The most vocal critics have been feminists in LBH APIK, who have also carried out their own research in relation to the Marriage Law, and reformulated a new draft, prioritizing equal gender perspectives. They argue that the Law has become a tool for justifying inequalities between men and women, by standardizing (*pembakuan*) a rigid sexual division in which women are confined to the domestic sphere, and that it fails to take into account women's interests and their unhappy experiences in polygamous marriage by allowing polygamy under any conditions (Katjasungkana, 2004; LBH APIK, 2000). The law has also been criticized as inconsistent, because in Article 3 it is stated that in principle either men or women can only have one spouse, but in the subsequent Article, it is stated that men can have more than one wife. Lastly, it has been criticized as gender biased, because it subordinates women within marriage by positioning women as 'servants' of their husbands (*Tempo*, 11–17 December 2006).

Endang Sumiarni (2004), a legal scholar lecturing at Atmajaya University in Yogyakarta, makes an additional distinctive critique, arguing that the focus on heterosexual marriage has ignored other types of marriages such as same sex marriage (Sumiarni, 2004: 1). She is also critical of the differing minimum ages of male and female marriage, the requirement that the two witnesses to a marriage must be male, the delegation of the marriage contract to a woman's *wali* (guardian) and for its permitting polygamous marriage. Critical of the way the Law implies that women are dependent on men (Sumiarni, 2004: 5), Sumiarni proposes a new marriage law based on equal gender relations, in which both husband and wife are equally responsible for domestic and public roles, and which allows them to develop their potential (*potensi*) in the public sphere. This would allow the couple to enjoy equal status and make choices based on mutual agreement, while taking into account women's reproductive function (Sumiarni, 2004: 102–3).

Criticisms of the Marriage Law are also put forward by those who claim themselves not to be feminist. For example, O'Shaughnessy (forthcoming: 230) reported her interview with a female judge who explicitly stated 'I am not a feminist'. This female judge radically criticized the Marriage Law article on male leadership as '"an extreme clause" (*pasal yang ekstrim*) that was "inequitable" (*suatu ketidaksetaraan*)'. This female judge argued that the article has often been misunderstood to say that only the husband can make every decision. Based on her marriage experience, this should not be the case and for her the ideal situation is when the decision is made together through a process of consensus (*musyawarah*). This female judge also criticizes the ideology of '*ibu rumah tangga*' (housewife), suggesting that there should also be 'a father of the household' (*bapak rumah tangga*), emphasizing the equal obligation of mother and father.

Despite the intense criticism of the Law, up until now no progress has been made in enacting a new and more just marriage law. The stronger and more visible influence of Muslim revivalism in the post-Soeharto period seems to place even more barriers in the way of this women's cause.

The New Order government regulations on marriage and divorce for civil servants

I noted in the Introduction that the New Order government had negative attitudes toward divorce and polygamy. Even though the 1974 Marriage Law restricts divorce and polygamy, the government had further tightened divorce and polygamy provisions through determining that members of the armed forces (1980), police (1981) and civil servants (1983) needed to ask their superior's permission before divorcing or practicing polygamy (Jones, 1994: 247, 280–1). It is possible that these regulations were aimed at giving more authority to the secular government in the matter of divorce and polygamy, to compensate for its failure to control them through secular courts. Among these three government regulations, the most famous one has been the Government Regulation No. 10/1983 for civil servants, PP 10. Because civil servants are regarded as models for the rest of Indonesian society and their numbers are more significant than those of the police and armed forces, I shall therefore concentrate on PP 10.

According to Suryakusuma (1996: 103), PP 10 was initiated at the request of *Dharma Wanita*. The organization reported that it often received complaints from its members about a husband's behavior, such as his seeking a divorce to marry younger women, or his practice of polygamy and a lack of financial support when he took additional wives. This situation reached its climax in the case of Dewanto, a high-ranking official (*pejabat*) in the cabinet secretariat, which was made public in the press. Dewanto's wife was the secretary to Mrs Sudharmono, the wife of the Minister of the State Secretariat (*Menteri Sekretaris Negara*) in the Soeharto era (1973–88). Every day, both Dewanto and his wife went to work, leaving their children at home with a babysitter, Rahmini. In fact, Rahmini not only took care of the children but also had an affair with Dewanto. Dewanto finally married Rahmini secretly. Later, Rahmini demanded public recognition of their marriage, when Dewanto was about to be promoted to head of the presidential palace. Afraid that her demand would endanger his promotion, Dewanto paid someone to kill her. After the publication of this incident, several wives of high-ranking officials requested the government to formulate a regulation that could protect the wives of civil servants from the men's tendency to divorce their wives or to take a second wife or mistress. There was also a rumor that the enactment of PP 10 was strongly supported by Mrs. Soeharto, the first lady and the national head of *Dharma Wanita*, who demonstrated clear disapproval of divorce and polygamy (Suryakusuma, 1996: 103–4).

In response to *Dharma Wanita*'s request, *BAKN/Badan Administrasi Kepegawaian Negara* (State Civil Service Administrative Body) formed a group to formulate the regulation in 1981. In drafting the regulation, the group referred to the 1974 Marriage Law, its implementing regulation, Government Regulation No. 30 on civil service discipline (especially chapter 2 on obligations and prohibitions), and the Ministry of Defense Decree No. 01/1/1980 on marriage, divorce and reconciliation among members of the armed forces, an amended version of a 1976 decree. PP 10 was finally enacted on Kartini Day, 21 April 1983 (Suryakusuma, 1996: 104).

The influence of PP 10 on civil servants

There are several barriers to civil servants who try to adhere to PP 10. For instance, the written application submitted to superiors ideally should be dealt with within three months. Superiors are generally very busy with their office work and permission can take more than six months. For high-ranking officials, the process may take longer. A couple may change their mind regarding their decision to divorce and try to reconcile, or they may have separated or be living under great stress owing to the long and difficult divorce procedure. In response to this situation the Supreme Court issued Circular No. 10/1984, stating that court proceedings may begin if there is no response from the civil servant's superior within six months. If the divorce is granted by the Court, there is still a possibility that civil servants will be punished by their superior, but at least their marriage problem has been resolved (Suryakusuma, 1996: 106). Suryakusuma alleges that after the enactment of PP 10/1983 an increasing number of marriages were retained for appearance only, with a growing number of men taking mistresses or using prostitutes (1996: 108).[30] But Suryakusuma does not give evidence to support her claims, and the adoption of mistresses and use of prostitutes might have been common before the enactment of PP 10/1983.

According to Suryakusuma (1996: 108–9), PP 10/1983 created a problematic situation for civil servants, because it made the process of polygamy and divorce more difficult. For instance, there is a case of a female civil servant who was beaten by her husband and kept her separation from her husband secret from her superior out of embarrassment. In this situation, when she shared her problem with other *Dharma Wanita* members they blamed her instead of expressing solidarity. Because of such incidents, Suryakusuma felt that PP 10/1983 had backfired, causing even greater problems for its members. Some wives of male civil servants were reluctant to report to their husband's superior when they knew that their husband had taken another wife secretly, had a mistress or lived with another woman without legal marriage. The wives, especially those whose husbands were the sole breadwinners, were afraid to report problems to their superior for fear of their husbands being dismissed. Instead, these women suffered and were unable to change their situation (1996: 109).

My own research confirms Suryakusuma's arguments here. For instance, one of my research participants, Eli (50), told me that she had heard from a relative of hers that her husband Yaya (51) had taken another wife secretly. Eli, who had three adult sons, was very upset. She was about to report Yaya's polygamy to his superior, but she was advised by Yaya's colleagues to reconsider reporting him for the sake of her three children. Eli took their advice and therefore did not report Yaya's second marriage to his superior, in order to protect his job and his monthly salary (interview with Eli, March 2004).[31]

This was not the only case. Four other male informants in my study, all of whom were highly educated and held senior positions in a higher education institution, also did not adhere to PP 10. These scholars did not register their second marriages, so that there would be no proof if their second marriages were reported.

This unregistered marriage can disadvantage the second wife and her children legally because they are considered 'unlawful'. Therefore they have no rights to inheritance, or to legal help if the husband abandons them. Yaya bribed marriage registration officials to obtain the marriage certificate for his unregistered second marriage, but these four men could not risk bribing the officials, for fear of undermining their positions as respected scholars.

Few civil servants seem to obey PP 10. For example, only one of my research participants, Syamsul, adhered to this regulation. He had taken another wife on the grounds that Rosa could not bear children and hence 'serve' him well. Therefore, Syamsul had 'legally acceptable' reasons for polygamy and this made it easier for him to follow the stipulated procedures. He first asked permission from his superior, attaching all the required paperwork including a doctor's certificate explaining that Rosa was infertile, written approval from Rosa, a letter from his office stating his annual income and a letter of guarantee stating that he would treat his wives and children justly, as stipulated in article 10 of PP 10. When permission was granted, he went to the Religious Court to apply for their permission to take another wife (interview with Syamsul, 5 March 2004 and the Religious Court archive 2002). It is relatively easier for civil servants to follow the Court procedures if they have obtained permission from their superior, because by fulfilling all the requirements for the permission of the superior, they have also fulfilled the Court's requirements for polygamy.[32] Once Syamsul had obtained the Court's permission, he married his second wife. Nonetheless, he seemed irritated by the time-consuming administrative procedures that he had to follow.

Even though the procedures of asking permission from civil servants' superiors seem to discourage divorce and polygamy, according to Suryakusuma (1996: 109), permission in practice can be granted easily, even arbitrarily, so long as the superior is willing. Suryakusuma suggests that military and state bureaucracy are patriarchal institutions in which the members of the 'boys' club' tend to support each other. And it is often difficult for women to obtain permission for divorce from their (generally male) superiors. In addition, female civil servants often experience considerable peer and social pressure. Many members of *Dharma Wanita*, and society in general, express disapproval of women's divorce requests. But if the female civil servant hides her marital problems and does not ask for divorce, she suffers (Suryakusuma, 1996: 112).

There are many inconsistencies in the implementation of PP 10, depending on the employee's place in the hierarchy. In the case of low-ranking employees, disobedience is grounds for dismissal; but higher-ranking civil servants who break rules may not be punished (Suryakusuma, 1996: 115–16). Suryakusuma suggests that PP 10 affects the middle and upper level of civil servants more, because the lives of high-ranking officials are more publicly visible and they are under pressure to be role models. In addition, wives of high-ranking officials may be more reluctant to lose the material benefits that their husbands' jobs bring (1996: 112–13).

The New Order era also saw reluctance by the media to cover the private lives of high-ranking officials for fear of retribution. For instance, there was no media coverage of the second marriage of Moerdiono, the Minister of the State Secretariat in the Soeharto era, even though it was a widely known event. Ironically, Moerdiono was the one who authorized the implementation of PP 10. Moerdiono met Machicha Mochtar, a young *dangdut* singer, in Bali, while campaigning for his party, Golkar. They became close and entered into a marriage in 1995, but the marriage was unregistered at Moerdiono's request. About a year after the birth of their son in 1996, Moerdiono stopped visiting Machicha. Machicha became anxious and uncertain about the status of her marriage, and pressed Moerdiono to acknowledge her son as his child. With no response from Moerdiono, she expressed her anxiety in a statement to the press in early 1999 (*Aura,* 1999; *Cek & Receck,* 1999a).

The publicity surrounding this case triggered debate on the status of unregistered marriages. Lawyer and human rights activist Nursyahbani Katjasungkana believed that Machicha's marriage is religiously valid, but illegal. Many lawyers disagreed. Two lawyers from the firm Lewis and Partners, Iwan Setiawan and Ferry Firman Nurwahyu, argued that Mordiono-Machica's marriage was invalid because the validity of marriage is not only decided by the fulfillment of the 1974 Marriage Law, article 2 (1), but also article 2 (2) that the marriage must be registered. For them, the article 2 is effective simultaneously and cumulatively. In addition, PP No. 9 1975 also states that the marriage should be undertaken in front of a marriage registration official. This means that registration is not just an administrative matter (or a matter of formality), but that the official has the authority to invalidate the marriage if there are obstacles to the marriage.[33] If the presence of the official were only a matter of formality, according to Setiawan and Nurwahyu, s/he would not have such authority (*Cek & Receck,* 1999b).

Amendments to PP 10

Suryakusuma (1996: 107) argues that there had been many problematic cases in the implementation of PP 10/1983. For instance, according to her, Sarwono Kusumaatmaja, the Minister of State for Administrative Reform, was concerned about some cases of divorce in which injustices occurred against male civil servants, including a case in which one wife wanted to divorce her civil servant husband, but the husband refused.[34] In Kusumaatmaja's view, if the Court granted the divorce, it would be unfair for the husband to be penalized by his superior for not reporting his divorce. He also opined that female civil servants should not be allowed to be the second/third/fourth wife of either civil servants or non-civil servants. In addition, the head of *BAKN* (State Civil Service Administrative Body), Waskito Reksasoedirdjo, also reported complaints from *Dharma Wanita* members that PP 10 did not protect civil servants' wives who became victims of violence (Suryakusuma, 1996: 107).

In response to these problems, PP 10 was amended in 1990 and became PP 45/1990. In summary, the amendments were as follows. First, the new regulation clearly acknowledged that civil servants could be in the position of either the litigant (*penggugat*) or the defendant (*tergugat*) (Indonesia, 1990: 5).[35] Second, the new regulation prohibited female civil servants from becoming a second/third/fourth wife at all. Therefore, all the articles of PP 10 that regulated the procedures involved in obtaining permission to become a second/third/fourth wife were deleted. Third, the new regulation stipulated that the ex-wives of male civil servants cannot receive divorce alimony if the reason for divorce was the wife's *zina* (adultery), drunkenness, drug addiction, physical or psychological violence, or desertion (Indonesia, 1990: 6). Fourth, the new regulation gives the right to alimony to the ex-wives of civil servants who initiate divorce, not only for reason of polygamy but also for reasons such as the husband's adultery, drunkenness, opium addiction, physical or psychological violence, or desertion. Fifth, heads of the state banks and companies were now required to obtain permission from the President, not the minister, before divorce or polygamy. Sixth, the new regulation applied penalties directly (without warning) to civil servants who lived with their partners without a legal marriage. Seventh, PP 10 stipulated that civil servants who do not ask the permission of their superior before initiating divorce or polygamy, and female civil servants who become the second/third/fourth wives of male civil servants or who did not ask the permission of their superior before becoming the second/third/fourth wives of non-civil servant men, would be penalized by being honorably dismissed. However, the new regulation only gave this fixed penalty to female civil servants who become the second/third/fourth wives of either civil servants or non-civil servants. Civil servants who did not report their marriage or their remarriage after divorce within a year, who did not ask permission of their superior before initiating divorce or polygamy, who lived with their partner without legal marriage, who did not report their divorce within a month or who did not report their second/third/fourth marriage within a year, would be penalized by one of the heavy penalties stipulated in PP No. 30/1980, which can be equal or less than the fixed penalty for the female civil servants who become second/third/fourth wives (Indonesia, 1990: 5–26).

PP 45/1990 seems to provide better protection than PP 10 from injustice, for either husbands or wives, in cases of divorce caused by violence, infidelity, drunkenness, drug addiction and desertion committed by either party. However, gender discrimination remains in the penalties. If the offenders are female civil servants who are married polygamously, the penalty is fixed, dismissal, the most severe penalty. But for other offenders, the penalty is flexible depending on the superior's decision. This flexibility of penalty as stipulated by the government carries the underlying assumption that men are family breadwinners while women are considered only dependants, even though this may not in fact be true. Dismissing male civil servants from their job may be assumed to cause undue suffering to their family members. The fixed penalties for female civil servants also show the government's double standards in their expectations for male and female civil servants. While it is still possible for male civil servants to practice polygamy, the government negates this possibility for female civil servants. This seems to reinforce the assumption that women bear a greater burden of moral guardianship. Female civil servants are more likely to be expected to obey the regulation or serve as role models for their society than male civil servants. In addition, the fact that the majority of high-ranking officials are male may make them more sensitive toward cases of injustice experienced by male civil servants. This can be clearly seen from

Kusumaatmaja's concern with the case of the male civil servant who was divorced by his wife. Kusumaatmaja seemed to show empathy to this man, and seemed not to expect this male civil servant to be penalized for not reporting his unwanted divorce (Suryakusuma, 1996: 107).

PP 10 in the post-Soeharto period

The workings of PP 10 during the New Order period show the power of the state in regulating civil servants' marriages and sexuality (Suryakusuma, 1996: 107–8). However, when the New Order ended in May 1998 many proponents of polygamy showed their disapproval of this regulation, even though former President Gus Dur and his wife, Sinta Nuriyah, expressed their disapproval of polygamy. For instance, Sinta Nuriyah stated: 'I do not want to be married polygamously. Therefore, I disagree with polygamy, even more if it is being related to Islamic teaching. Many people misinterpret Islamic teaching by reading the Qur'an partially. If the Qur'an is being read comprehensively, it will be clear that polygamy is explicitly not permitted in Islam' (Nuriyah, 2002: 56). Gus Dur and Nuriyah's lack of influence on polygamy among civil servants and society in general, despite their negative attitudes towards it, may be due to the short duration of Gus Dur's presidency (1999–2001). In addition, unlike Soeharto, a man from a military background with strict attitudes toward polygamy, Gus Dur was known to be a liberal person who respected diversity. Therefore, many civil servants and proponents of polygamy seemed unafraid to express disagreement with existing law and government regulations on polygamy.

In February 1999, the women's wing of one of the Islamist parties, *Muslimah Partai Bulan Bintang* (Muslim Women of the Star and the Moon Party), demanded that the government permit polygamy and abolish the current restrictions in PP 10. The government and media did not respond (Nasution, 2002: 58). But in 2000, when Khafifah Indar Parawansa, the Minister of Women's Empowerment, expressed her views on PP 10, she attracted public debate. Parawansa argued that polygamy should be a matter of personal choice, not an object of government regulation. However, even though she argued for the abolition of PP 10, she is against polygamy. She believes that the aim of marriage is to create a good and happy family, and that this is hard to achieve if a man has many wives and children (*Kompas*, 2000a). In *Femina*, she also clearly stated, 'I disagree with polygamy. Instead of debating polygamy from a religious perspective, it would be better for us as women to act more realistically: to empower ourselves' (Parawansa, 2003: 52).

Nuke Arafah, the head of LKBHIuWK (Consultative Institution and Legal Aid for Women and Family), disagreed with Parawansa's proposal to abolish PP 10. She felt that many men indeed did not have enough self-control to keep from engaging arbitrarily in polygamy. She also found that, even with clear regulations and court decisions, many ex-husbands have tried to avoid their obligations to their ex-wives. Therefore, she preferred reform of PP 10 (*Kompas*, 2000b). Many more women also disagreed with Parawansa, including the presidential spouse, Sinta Nuriyah, who felt that PP 10 protected women, and *Dharma Wanita* members interviewed by SCTV, a private TV channel in 2000 (Nasution, 2002: 57–8). During this debate on PP 10, there were also demands, such as that issued by LBH APIK, to amend the 1974 Marriage Law to abolish polygamy. These discussions largely revisited the earlier ongoing pressure from women's groups since the first enactment of the Law.

To this day, there has been no government response to the debates over PP 10. PP 10 remains in force in the post-Soeharto period, even though many civil servants ignore the regulation without fear of being penalized by their superior. These more relaxed attitudes toward polygamy were apparent during the Megawati period (2001–4). Megawati, whose father was polygamous, did not express any objections to polygamy during her presidency. Instead, she even asked that a menu from a restaurant owned by Puspo Wardoyo, a well-known polygamist (whom I shall be discussing extensively below), be served in the presidential palace when she visited Yogyakarta. She also presented an award to Wardoyo for his successful franchise business in 2003 (Suryono, 2003: 9). These two examples clearly suggest a degree at least of indirect support for Wardoyo's polygamy by Megawati.

Further evidence of the relaxed attitudes toward polygamy among post-Soeharto civil servants can be seen, for instance, in the case of one Islamic higher education institution in Bandung. A report reveals that during the Soeharto era only one among 400 of its lecturers practiced polygamy, but in 2003 at least 48 lecturers did (Nakashima, 2003). My own observation during my fieldwork confirmed this report. Ema, the first wife of one of these male civil servants, reported her husband's unregistered second marriage to his superior (the Rector) to seek protection and force him to give up his second marriage. She was very disappointed, however, because the superior took no action against her husband. Ema compared this Rector with another who, during the Soeharto period, refused permission to an employee who wanted to take another wife (interview with Ema, 14 February 2004). From these cases, I argue that the absence of role models – including among high ranking officials and the presidential office itself – has had a significant impact on subordinates' attitudes towards polygamy. Indeed, as noted in the Introduction, the Vice President's practice of polygamy during the Megawati era may be seen as encouraging the promotion of polygamy in Indonesia.

The promotion of polygamy in the post-Soeharto period

This section will explore the promotion of polygamy during the distinctive post-Soeharto era. After a long period of repression under the Soeharto government, many Indonesians, especially members of male-dominated Islamist groups, appear to have taken advantage of the freedom of expression in the post-Soeharto era. For example, the Islamist media and Puspo Wardoyo both clearly saw an opportunity to promote polygamy. Wardoyo had actively promoted polygamy since early 2000, participating in television and radio talk shows, sponsoring and giving speeches and seminars and collaborating with many journalists to promote his campaign for polygamy. He also employed Eko Suryono, a columnist at *Jawa Pos Radar Solo*, to write books supporting his campaign and promoting his restaurants. To gain general support from the majority of Indonesian Muslims, Wardoyo also collaborated with a religious scholar, Dr. Syahrin Harahap, a professor in the Institute of Islamic Studies, Sumatra Utara and some *kiayis* (religious leaders) who practiced or supported polygamy. In Bandung, Puspo Wardoyo spread his influence by cooperating with Kiayi Abdullah Gymnastiar (Aa Gym). He and his wife were willing to support Wardoyo's promotion of polygamy in radio talk shows or seminars, saying that 'polygamy is better than *zina*'. For them, if a wife did not want to support her husband's polygamy, she would be regarded as supporting her husband to commit *zina*, of which they disapprove. Muslim women were encouraged to endorse polygamy and even to look for another wife for their husbands. They were told they would be rewarded in heaven (*surga*) for allowing their husbands to take another wife.

The most controversial effort Wardoyo undertook to promote polygamy was to sponsor the 2003 Polygamy Award, which would not have been politically possible during the Soeharto period. In the next section, I discuss this Award, its background and aims, the media response and its impact on Indonesian Muslims' attitude toward polygamy. Material presented in this chapter is based on my interviews with Puspo Wardoyo and with two Polygamy Award committee members, while the media responses are based on an analysis of publications from directly before and after the Award.

Who is Puspo Wardoyo?

Puspo Wardoyo (47) was born in Solo, Central Java. After graduating from university he became a teacher in Riau, Sumatra, where in 1979 he married his first wife, Rini Purwanti (41). Dissatisfied with his small teacher's salary, he moved to Medan in 1991 and opened a small barbecue chicken business. The business became popular after an article praising his chicken was published, and sales increased from three or four to two hundred chickens a day (Nurbowo and Mulyono, 2003).

Wardoyo and Rini had been married for 17 years when he took a second wife secretly. But later, Rini found out about it. Wardoyo claimed he still loved Rini, but added: 'my desire for other women increased when I became rich'.[36] He married his second wife, Supiyanti (30), in 1996, after setting up his second restaurant, and his third wife, Anisah Nasution (28), after acquiring his third restaurant in 1997. In 1999, when he owned seven restaurants, Wardoyo married Intan Ratih Tri Laksmi (29). All of Wardoyo's additional wives were former employees of his restaurants, and held tertiary degrees, except for Supiyanti, who was a junior high school (*SMP*) graduate. After his fourth marriage, Wardoyo began campaigning for polygamy among Indonesian Muslims. He used Qur'anic verses, prophetic tradition (*hadith*) and religious slogans such as 'polygamy is part of *shari'a*', 'polygamy is better than *zina* [adultery]', and 'polygamy is *sunnah Rasul* [recommended by the Prophet]' to justify polygamy in general.

Modeling himself as the president of polygamy and claiming that his practice was Islamic, Puspo Wardoyo seemed to be trying to provide a good model for Indonesian polygamous men. He did this by seeking to treat his four wives justly, and by visiting them on regular rosters. Two of his wives lived in Medan (Sumatra), and the other two lived in Semarang and Jakarta. According to his third wife, he usually spent one week in Medan and another week in Java. When he was in Medan, he spent three days in his first wife's home and three days in his second wife's home. Similarly, when he was in Java, he spent three days in his third wife's home in Jakarta and three days in his fourth wife's home in Semarang, Central Java. Thus, each wife had three days with him every two weeks.

The background and aims of the Polygamy Award

There were two Polygamy Awards in 2003. The first was organized by the *Forum Jurnalis Muslim* (Muslim Journalist Forum/MJF hereafter), which consisted of journalists from Islamist media such as *Amanah, Fikri, Hidayah, Pelita* and *An-Nida*.[37] The background to the first Polygamy Award was as follows.

Some members of the MJF felt uneasy about publicity surrounding Inul Daratista, a *dangdut* singer and dancer who attracted widespread media interest with her sensual dancing. In May 2003, almost all the Indonesian media, including television stations, magazines, websites and newspapers (some of which were Islamist), was discussing Inul. Therefore, MJF saw a need to counter the publicity surrounding Inul, which they considered to be 'pornographic' and therefore un-Islamic, with the Polygamy Award, which they felt would promote Islamic values. Also, women activists had been energetically criticizing Wardoyo's championing of polygamy. In the view of some members of the MJF, this criticism tended to be subjective and tendentious toward Islam (interview with Darso Arief, editor of *Amanah* and the head committee of the Polygamy Award, 31 March 2004).

The MJF chose Puspo Wardoyo for the Award because of his willingness to promote polygamy – he had even founded a pro-polygamy organization in Solo. On 19 May 2003, Wardoyo, who attended the ceremony with three of his wives, expressed his gratitude to the MJF for the Award:

> I thank my journalist friends. I shall continue encouraging people to practice polygamy. Polygamy not only belongs to the *kiayi* and the rich, but it belongs to everybody. ... After practicing polygamy, my business developed. I believe that this is God's reward for practicing polygamy. Therefore, to all wives, please support your husband in practicing polygamy instead of allowing them to have extramarital relationships and commit sinful acts.
>
> (Yenni, 2003) [my translation]

Wardoyo later set up a committee to organize the Polygamy Award on a larger scale. The Award aimed to promote 'transparent polygamy' and to improve Indonesian Muslims' perception of polygamy, which until then had been generally negative (interview with Darso Arief, 30 March 2004).[38] Wardoyo provided further clarification of the reasons he wanted to present awards to 'successful' polygamous husbands:

My practice of polygamy is successful so I want to combat the women activists' attack on polygamy by looking for successful examples of polygamous marriages in order for them to become models for those who are unsuccessful. I believe that if the successful husbands are rewarded, hopefully, there will be new awareness such that we will have transparent polygamy. In a responsible polygamous marriage, it is women who gain benefits from polygamy. On the contrary, if polygamy is being challenged and regarded as taboo, women will be disadvantaged. I believe that we cannot eliminate polygamy if we are concerned about women. What we should do is to educate those who practice polygamy.[39]

(Interview with Puspo Wardoyo, 26 March 2004)

The above aims clearly show Wardoyo's opposition to many women activists' criticism of his polygamy and his opposition to 'secret polygamy'.

The Polygamy Award was advertised in both local and national newspapers on 17 April 2003. Many responses, expressions of support and willingness to participate were sent to the Polygamy Award committee. As a result, TV 7, a private Indonesian TV channel, invited Puspo Wardoyo as a guest speaker on to the *Duduk Perkara* (Focus) program, together with Debra H. Yatim, one of the leading Indonesian feminists (Suryono, 2003: 24). Those against polygamy, including numerous women's organizations, prepared a protest for the night the event was to be conducted. Several articles and letters to the editor expressing opposition to the Polygamy Award were also published in many local and national newspapers (I shall discuss these below). The Award attracted media attention and brought the issue of polygamy into the center of public controversy.

The committee recruited participants not only through television and newspaper advertisements, but also by word of mouth among people who practiced polygamy. They initially set certain criteria for those to receive the Award, such as that they must have practiced transparent polygamy and must have treated their wives kindly so that there were no conflicts among them. They must also have provided education for their children, paid alms and given money to charity, in addition to being successful entrepreneurs. These criteria were set in consultation with Wardoyo, because Wardoyo saw the need to mobilize Islamic values so that his efforts to promote polygamy could be easily accepted by Indonesian Muslims. However, owing to the limited time to prepare for the Polygamy Award and the difficulty in finding people who met the above criteria, the committee became far less rigid with the criteria. In addition, initially Wardoyo did not want to give his awards either to *kiayi* or high-ranking officials because of the negative representation of their practice of polygamy. For instance, some *kiayis* were known to take their pupils as their wives, and some high-ranking officials were known to take additional wives secretly. But because of the time constraints in preparing for the Polygamy Award, *kiayis* were among the eventual Award winners.

The Polygamy Award ceremony was conducted in Arya Duta, a five-star hotel in Jakarta, on Friday night, 25 July 2003. Hundreds of guests attended the ceremony, and Puspo Wardoyo gave 37 Awards to husbands whom he considered successful in their polygamous marriages. The Award was a placard with the name and photograph of the recipient in the middle. As the sponsor of the Polygamy Award, Wardoyo had placed his photograph everywhere: on the pin that all the Award committees wore, on the booklet and magazines distributed to all guests and on the large screen of the stage backdrop. Many of the awardees came with all their wives, some of whom were wearing the same clothing as their co-wives, possibly to show that they were the wives of the same man or to show that they got along with one another. The guests included several celebrities. Dinner was also served during the night. As well as the Award, attendees also received three books, all published with Wardoyo's sponsorship (interview with Darso Arief, 31 March 2004).

The title of the first book is *Polygamy*. Above the title there is a quote that resembles a *hadith*: 'Please get married because my good followers are those who have many wives ...' (my translation). Reading the quote at glance and literally may result in an understanding that it is a Prophet's *hadith* that recommends his male followers to have more wives. But reading it contextually and comprehensively may result in different understanding. The quote is narrated as part of the conversation between Ibn Abbas, one of the Prophet's companions, and his friend, Said bin Jubair.

Thalhah al-Yami narrates that Said bin Jubair said: 'Ibn Abbas asked me: "Are you married?" I answered, "No." Ibn Abbas said, "Please get married because the best person in this *ummat* [community] is he who has many wives' (Shahih Bukhari, cited in Abdul Kodir, 2005a: 168; [my translation]).

Abdul Kodir interprets the above quote to mean that Ibn Abbas suggested that his friend, Said bin Jubair, who was unmarried, should get married. In other narration, it was written that Said bin Jubair was still very young and answered, 'I am not interested in getting married at the moment,' and in other narration, he asked back to Ibn Abbas, 'Why should I get married?' By looking at this contextual background, according to Abdul Kodir (2005a: 168), it is inappropriate to understand that Ibn Abbas recommended his friend to practice polygamy, because Said bin Jubair was not married yet, or did not have any willingness to get married yet because of his young age, or was not yet interested in getting married. In Abdul Kodir's opinion, it is more appropriate to understand it as a suggestion to get married than as a recommendation to practice polygamy. To support his interpretation, Abdul Kodir quotes Ibn Hajar al-Asqalani's discussion on this narration: that al-Asqalani also interprets the narration as a suggestion to get married in order to leave the tradition of celibacy and that al-Asqalani does not discuss it as a suggestion to practice polygamy at all. Abdul Kodir also emphasized that the quote is not the saying of the Prophet Muhammad, only a conversation between Ibn Abbas and his friend, and therefore cannot be used as a religious justification for polygamy (Abdul Kodir, 2005a: 170).

At the bottom of the book cover, the caption reads: 'How to be successful in having many wives: The experiences of Puspo Wardoyo and his four wives.' This quote seems to promise that the book will be a practical guide for having a successful polygamous marriage. The title of the second book is *The beauty of polygamy: The experiences of the harmonious family of Puspo Wardoyo*. The title of the third book is *Profile of the Polygamy Award 2003*. There is a quote that is more like a slogan located above the title of the book which states: 'Polygamy does not belong to *kiayi* and the rich but belongs to pious and brave men.' This quote seems to try to resist the common perception that polygamy can be and is usually practiced only by the *kiayi* and the rich, suggesting that it is appropriate for any men who are pious and brave, either poor or rich, and not necessarily religious leaders. This quote also seems to challenge the existing negative perceptions of polygamous men, and to counter such perceptions by describing them as being pious and brave. Again, the writer tries to adopt the 'religious' label by using the Arabic term for pious, *taqwa*. At the very end of the first book, the text discusses 'The real polygamy', showing that polygamy exists in everyday life and is not just the object of abstract discussion. There are similarities in the way the pictures on each book are arranged, with Wardoyo located at the centre surrounded by his wives, or at the top with his wives lined up in front of him, displaying his superior position to his subordinate wives. The tone of the quotes also seems to be directed from a man to other men in general, positioning their wives as just objects to be managed. The smiles, the happy faces and the cartoon gestures seem to aim at countering the mainstream image of conflict among co-wives and miserable experiences of polygamous marriages.

Several artists who were known to support Islamist ideas played important roles in this event. For instance, Ratih Sanggarwati (a female fashion model) became the master of ceremonies, Astri Ivo (a film actress) read the Qur'an in the opening ceremony and Neno Warisman (a female singer) read a poem. Initially the Polygamy Award committee members were worried that the three artists would not be willing to support the Polygamy Award, but according to Darso Arief, they were glad to (interview with Darso Arief, 31 March 2004). Wardoyo's collaboration with several celebrities seemed to be aimed at attracting more media coverage of the event.

However, *Hikmah*, a newspaper circulated in West Java, reported that the Polygamy Award did not run smoothly owing to the presence of a number of protestors who wished to highlight the emotional damage of polygamy for women (*Hikmah*, 2003). Outside the hotel, hundreds of angry protestors were demonstrating; the group called themselves *Suara Nurani untuk Perempuan* (Voice of Conscience for Women). Some of the protestors said that polygamy had been mistakenly perceived to be part of Islam, while others carried a banner: 'Monogamy yes, polygamy, no' (Mapes, 2003; Darojah, 2003). Several public figures and artists such as Nurul Arifin opined that polygamy deprives women and children of equal rights. 'This is a kind of harassment and discrimination,' said Nurul Arifin (*Hikmah*, 2003). *Hikmah* also noted that two female protestors were able to enter the hotel room where the Polygamy Award was conducted, but were detained by the committee when they tried to approach the stage (*Hikmah*, 2003).

Wardoyo says he spent more than Rp. 1 billion (more than A$150,000) on the committee honorarium, the artists (who acted as master of ceremonies, Qur'anic reader and poem reader), hotel rent, catering, publications, transportation and accommodation for certain Award winners. Wardoyo believed that this was part of *jihad fi sabiilillah* (his sacrifice in the way of God).[40] He believed that in sponsoring the Polygamy Award he was reviving the *sunnah*, and therefore his actions constituted part of *jihad* (interview with Puspo Wardoyo, 26 March 2004).[41]

The impact of the Polygamy Award on Muslims' attitudes toward polygamy

Wardoyo considered the Polygamy Award to be successful in achieving its aims of producing a change in attitudes toward polygamy, including among those practicing it. He felt that because of it, polygamy was no longer considered taboo. He planned to hold a Polygamy Award ceremony every year in various regions of Indonesia (interview with Puspo Wardoyo, 26 March 2004). But on July 2004, when I called the head of the Polygamy Award committee to ask about the 2004 Award, he said that the event was postponed until September, after the presidential election. But to date (2009) there has not been a second Award night. Postponing the Award until after the presidential election suggests that he was politically astute, aware of the changing political climate and cautious about President Soesilo Bambang Yudhoyono's possible negative attitudes toward polygamy.

Similarly, Arief, the head of the Polygamy Award committee, saw some changes as a result of the Award. He saw several government officials and artists become more open about their polygamous marriages and admit to listening to Wardoyo's regular speeches on how to have a successful polygamous marriage. Like Wardoyo, Arief also considered the Polygamy Award to be successful because it attracted media attention. After the Award, several private TV channels such as La Tivi, Trans TV, RCTI and TV 7 broadcast it as a special event. Wardoyo had become a celebrity. He and his wives were then often invited to give talks in seminars and on television about their experience of polygamy (interview with Darso Arief, 31 March 2004).

I share the views of Arief and Wardoyo about the success of the first and the second Polygamy Awards in shifting the focus of the media from Inul to polygamy. After the Award, almost all media discussed it, and there was less coverage of Inul. The Polygamy Award also seemed quite successful in enhancing the ability of the proponents of polygamy to express their view of polygamy confidently, and to be more open about it. For instance, some members of *Partai Keadilan Sejahtera* (Welfare Justice Party) had become more open, stating their belief that polygamy is part of *shari'a* and their perception of a need to counter Indonesian Muslims' negative attitudes toward polygamy. Some of them even seemed motivated by the Award to practice polygamy, or to increase the number of their wives. Some of them, such as Jajang, Maman and Akbar, were really eager to be interviewed by me to demonstrate their pride in practicing polygamy. In my view, however, they represented a minority among Indonesian Muslims who, I am suggesting, generally hold negative attitudes toward polygamy. This general negative attitude can be seen, for instance, in the publication of responses to the Polygamy Award, which will be discussed shortly: only a few articles/letters supported the Polygamy Award, while the rest generally disagreed with or condemned it.

According to Arief, the Polygamy Award not only benefited the Islamist media including *Amanah, Fikri* and *Hidayah,* but also benefited Wardoyo's restaurant business. For example, *Amanah* sold out many editions of its magazines that carried stories about Wardoyo. After the Award, *Amanah* also published accounts of the experiences of Wardoyo's wives, one wife per issue. In addition, owing to Wardoyo's dual promotion of polygamy and his restaurants, the number of Wardoyo's restaurants increased dramatically from seven outlets in 1999 to 33 branches throughout Indonesia in 2004, with many people taking up franchise agreements (interview with Darso Arief, 2 April 2004).

According to Arief, Wardoyo's next step in promoting polygamy was to be the publication of a book of 15 stories by Arief of successful polygamous marriages. The book was due for publication in July 2004, the scheduled date of the next Polygamy Award. Arief said that the committee intended to set up criteria similar to those for the previous Award (interview with Darso Arief, 31 March 2004). But when I called Darso Arief in early July 2004, he told me that he had only completed ten chapters, because some of the polygamous husbands had changed their minds and chose not to publish information about their marriages.

I found some contradictions in Arief's attitude to polygamy. On the one hand, Arief, together with other members of the MJF, chose Wardoyo as a central figure to counter the public attention to Inul, because he saw Wardoyo as practicing one of the Islamic values, polygamy. On the other hand, when I asked Arief why there was a tendency to regard polygamy as part of *shari'a* or as an 'Islamic value', he rejected the idea that polygamy is an Islamic value:

> Polygamy is not an Islamic value. Polygamy has occurred everywhere and at all times. Islam wants to civilize the practice of polygamy. Unfortunately, there is an image that 'Muslims like polygamy'. As a result, there have been some criticisms toward polygamy that tend to slander Islam as if it is only Islam which allows polygamy.
>
> (Interview with Darso Arief, 31 March 2004)

Armando also made this point in response to the Polygamy Award (2003a). He wrote that polygamy was practiced long before the coming of Islam, by Arabians as well as non-Arabians, but before the coming of Islam there was no regulation on how to treat wives and no limit on the number of wives men could marry. He suggested that Islam, as a revolutionary religion (*agama yang revolusioner*), wanted to discourage polygamy and regulate it to avoid injustice toward women and their children by limiting the number of wives to four and obliging husbands to treat their wives justly.

Responses to the Polygamy Award

The Polygamy Award invited many responses, which were published in various media such as *Republika, Kompas, Suara Merdeka* and *Pikiran Rakyat* between

April 2003 and February 2004. (After February 2004, however, most media were focused on the national general election.) I consulted online media using a Google search of the term 'Polygamy Award'. After printing various responses to the Polygamy Award, I categorized them into those who were arguing for and those arguing against the Polygamy Award. Responses were quite polarized, but mostly negative, with only a few expressing support. Interestingly, both the proponents and the opponents of polygamy invoked ideas about benefits for women in suggesting that polygamy is either good or bad. For instance, Wardoyo believed that polygamy needed to be promoted because it benefits women, and therefore the abolition of polygamy would disadvantage women. Similarly, many Indonesian feminists, mainly women activists working for NGOs such as *LBH APIK* and *Rifka Annisa*, believe that polygamy disadvantages women and is a form of discrimination and violence against women. Therefore, for the benefit of women, polygamy needs to be abolished in Indonesia (Reyneta, 2003: 10–11).

The following letter is one example of the positive responses to the Award:

Supporting the Polygamy Award
Peace be upon you. Reading Ade Armando's writing about his opposition to the Polygamy Award, I opine that invalid *hadith* cannot be used as evidence [*hujjah*]. Please assess the validity of the *hadith* and tell who is the narrator/transmitter of this *hadith*.

In the situation when prostitution and extramarital relationships flourish, polygamy for whoever can afford it is a peaceful [*damai*] solution which is in accordance with *shari'a*. Therefore, the Polygamy Award needs to be supported and continued to be celebrated every year.

The widows of Aceh can be included in the Polygamy Association led by Puspo Wardoyo. Ade Armando can take one of them as his second wife or third wife. If he does not have enough money, he can ask for Hamzah Haz's support.

Being cynical about polygamy means being cynical about Islamic *shari'a*, the Qur'an and therefore about God. *Naudzubillah* [We seek God's protection from]. Peace be upon you.

(Ridwan, *Republika Online*, 23 July 2003)

As I shall show, the slogan 'Polygamy is part of Islamic *shari'a*' was often quoted by some of my research participants and other Indonesian literalist Muslims. For instance, one article on eramuslim.com reported outraged responses to a television advertisement in RCTI, a private television station, because RCTI advertised a television comedy entitled *Polygamy Award*, a parody of the Polygamy Award. These responses were broadcast by 95.3 RASFM radio on 4 August 2003. On this radio program, Wardoyo regarded the advertisement as degrading to polygamy. Similarly, K.H. Sulaeman Zachawerus, a military commandant, said on the radio that the advertisement was degrading to polygamy, which he believed to be part of Islamic *shari'a*, and therefore he considered the advertisement to be dangerous (*berbahaya*). He recommended that no media, including RCTI, should broadcast any program that insults Islam. Similar responses were also forwarded by Ibrahim, Komarudin, Husein and Budi, listeners to 95.3 RASFM radio. Ibrahim especially warned RCTI staff involved in the production of the advertisement that they were threatening Islamic *shari'a* and therefore they would be thrown into hell (*Era Muslim*, 2003). These outraged responses to the Polygamy Award parody clearly suggest a widespread inability among the listeners to differentiate between *shari'a* and its interpretations.

On the other hand, critics like Darojah wrote of disappointment about the Polygamy Award. One view was expressed by Tutty Alawiyah, the Rector of Universitas Islam As-Syafi'iyah Jakarta and former Minister of Women's Affairs during Habibie's presidency: 'This Award is an insult to the Islamic *Shari'a*. There are many Islamic values, its universal principles and other Muslim issues that need to be popularized other than having plural wives. I assume that MUI [*Majelis Ulama Indonesia*/Indonesian *Ulama* Councils] needs to give a *fatwa* [legal opinion] on this matter.' Darojah regarded the Polygamy Award as more like an effort to make a cult of Puspo Wardoyo, because all the committee members wore a pin bearing Wardoyo's photograph and the stage backdrop of the Polygamy Award night also included a big photograph of Wardoyo together with his four wives (Darojah, 2003).

Later, on the same day that Darojah's article was published, Kunthie sent the following letter:

> I was really disappointed when I read about the Polygamy Award in *Republika*. I thought Puspo Wardoyo was very Islamic, but in fact, he does not understand about Islam at all.
>
> You [Wardoyo] have subordinated women into the lowest level when you say that wives are cheap workers whose body can be enjoyed without being paid, *Astaghfirullah!* [I ask forgiveness from Allah]. Is this some kind of modern ignorance [*jahiliyah*]? Be careful Pak Puspo, your statement can mean that you [Wardoyo] have insulted your mother, your wives, your daughters and your sisters. Islam has raised the status of women from ignorant pre-Islamic [*jahiliyah*] tradition, but you revived that ignorant tradition [by lowering women's status].
>
> As a Muslim woman, I am not against polygamy because it is *halal* [permitted] in Islam, but you have misperceived polygamy. I suggest that you study the Qur'an first before acting as if you were a knowledgeable person ...[42]
>
> (Kunthie, 2003)

Kunthie, like the majority of Indonesian Muslims, believed that polygamy is permitted in Islam. But she felt degraded by Wardoyo's opinion of women as cheap workers whose bodies can be enjoyed without being paid for. Therefore, she regarded Wardoyo as having revived ignorant pre-Islamic (*jahiliyah*) culture.

Wita offered another criticism. In her letter to the editor Wita, like Kunthie, expressed her belief that polygamy is *mubah* (permitted), not *sunnah* Rasul (recommended by the Prophet), because the Prophet did not recommend his companions to practice polygamy and he even prohibited Ali bin Abi Thalib, his companion and son-in-law, from practicing it. According to Wita, the Prophet's polygamy had certain political and noble aims, such as building political allegiances with his wives' tribes, and could not be compared with Wardoyo's polygamy, which had a very base motive – avoiding *zina* (adultery). According to her, even though polygamy is permitted, it can destroy family happiness so that even the children could become miserable, through witnessing the misery of their mother. Wita also wrote:

> As a woman, I can accept Allah's rule on polygamy even with the base reason that it is better than *zina*. However, behind this acceptance, there is struggle to overcome very uncomfortable feelings and emotions, which I regard as a test [from God] or a calamity. Is it appropriate for Puspo Wardoyo to celebrate polygamy by giving the awards on top of a calamitous situation for women?[43]
> (Wita, *Republika Online*, 30 July 2003)

The above two views – that polygamy is permitted in Islam or is part of the religion – represent the Semi-textualists' view of polygamy. But the following letter, by a Muslim man, H. Prayitno, was closer to the Contextualists' view:

> If I make an in-depth reading of the verse regarding polygamy, it tells me that it would be better not to practice polygamy. The wording of the verse is very subtle and very deep. ... I myself would not be able to practice polygamy because I would not be able to deal with my wives justly emotionally and even biologically or financially.[44]
> (Prayitno, *Republika Online*, 30 July 2003)

Swara, the women's section of the newspaper *Kompas*, also published responses, including an article by M. Hilaly Basya, a young lecturer at Universitas Muhammadiyah, Prof. Dr. HAMKA, and a researcher at the Youth Islamic Study Club (YISC), Al-Azhar, Jakarta. Basya, a Contextualist, claimed that Wardoyo had misunderstood the Qur'anic verse 4: 3 and the Prophet's practice of polygamy. Basya believed that the Prophet was not a proponent of polygamy: the Prophet criticized the polygamy practiced by his companions who had married eight to ten wives. Basya also quoted a *hadith* written in *Jami' al-Ushul*, juz XII, 162, No. 9026, in which the Prophet became angry on finding out that Ali bin Abi Thalib, his son-in-law, would take another wife. The *hadith* reported that the Prophet immediately entered the mosque and gave this speech:

> Several families of Bani Hasyim bin al-Mughirah have asked my permission to marry their daughters to Ali bin Abi Thalib. I would let you know that I shall not give my permission, again, I shall not give my permission. I really will not give Ali bin Abi Thalib permission, unless Ali bin Abi Thalib divorces my daughter first, then I shall let him marry them. I would let you know that my daughter is part of me, anything that upsets her feelings will upset me too and anything that hurts her heart will hurt me too [my translation].[45]

Basya also believed that Qur'anic verse 4: 3 actually prohibits polygamy because the requirement of justice as stated in the verse is impossible to fulfill. For Basya, Wardoyo's polygamy was a kind of 'sexual ecstasy' (*ekstasi seksual*) because his motive for polygamy was to fulfill his 'biological' needs. In this case, he wrote, sex becomes the central focus of marriage, and turns women into mere objects who exist only to fulfill male sexual desire. Within this culture, Basya argues, human beings lose their quality as subjects and become enslaved to their lust (Basya, *Kompas*, 4 August 2003).

Pikiran Rakyat, another local newspaper in West Java, also published an article by Dewi Rahayu, an activist campaigning for the empowerment of women. She criticized the Polygamy Award for legitimating male hegemony over women, who are often regarded as the second sex. Dewi Rahayu argued that the Award is against all women's movements in the world, which have called for the abolition of polygamy because it dehumanizes and discriminates against women. From Rahayu's point of view, Islam aims to enhance women's status by liberating them from the ignorant (*jahiliyah*) pre-Islamic culture. She believes that Islam has prohibited female infanticide and slavery and has given women the right to receive *mahar* and inheritance. She believes as well that Islam has limited the number of wives that a man can have to up to four wives, with strict requirements that are impossible to fulfill. Therefore, according to her, Islam basically recommends monogamous marriage, and to endorse the practice of polygamy would be to return to 'ignorant' tradition (Rahayu, 2003).

Similar responses were published in another local newspaper, *Suara Merdeka*, in Semarang, Central Java. Misbah Zulfa Elisabeth, the director of *Sahabat Perempuan Semarang* (Friends of Semarang women), an NGO, argued that the Polygamy Award was against women's struggle for equality. Fatimah Amin Syukur, of the Women's Studies Centre of the Institute for Islamic Studies (IAIN), Semarang, was also against the Polygamy Award, claiming that the socialization of polygamy by giving awards will worsen the misunderstanding of Islam (*Suara Merdeka*, 2003).

In Magelang, Central Java, *Gabungan Organisasi Wanita*/GOW (Association of Women's Organizations) organized a public discussion titled 'The impact of polygamy on women and children'. Gusti Kanjeng Ratu Hemas, the wife of Sri Sultan Hamengku Buwono X, was the key speaker in the discussion. Hemas asserted that women in polygamous marriages might have miserable experiences, because the arrangement requires them to submit to patriarchal authority. She said that polygamy also affects children, who will experience psychological difficulties because they may feel forced to accept their father's polygamy. In addition, she said, their rights to the father's attention and care and to moral and material welfare can be neglected; conflict and violence against the powerless may also occur; and it is rare that polygamous families are free from conflict (*Suara Merdeka*, 2004).

Similarly, Ucok, who grew up in a polygamous family, wrote in *Swara* about his misery as a child of a polygamous father. He suggested that Wardoyo was being too confrontational in setting up the Polygamy Award, in a context of women's struggle for equality and discrimination against women. Ucok described how he wanted to cry when he saw his mother's face at the time his father brought home his new wife. After his father's second marriage, Ucok saw his mother's health deteriorate. She was sick for a long time, her face seemed to age too quickly and she became very thin. Her neighbors suggested that she ask for a divorce instead of continuing in a polygamous marriage. Ucok felt that his father, too, changed: he did not have enough money to support Ucok's brother's further education, and he did not even have time to be close to his children, as he had been before taking a second wife. One of Ucok's siblings said, 'Now father does not pay any attention to us because of the new wife. He prefers to be with the new wife than to be with us.' Ucok also reported his father's unjust treatment of his mother's family. For instance, his father would get angry with Ucok's mother if he suffered losses in his business, but would share his happiness with his second wife if he was happy with his business. His father also built his second wife a new house, several years before he built one for Ucok's mother, who was living in the house that had belonged to her parents. Ucok was also concerned for his father, who ideally should be able to rest and enjoy his life in his older age. The man had an incurable illness, which often required bed rest, and prevented him from earning money to support his many young children. Ucok regretted his father's practice of polygamy, but he saw it as the destiny of his family. In his opinion, 'Polygamy is like divorce, it is *halal* [permitted] but it is hated. Polygamy is permitted but I hate polygamy' (Ucok, 2003).

After the general election in September 2004, there was no media coverage of polygamy except in October 2004, when Musdah Mulia and her team launched the Counter Legal Draft of the Compilation (CLD KHI), proposing the abolition of polygamy. More recent public debates on polygamy reappeared on 30 November 2006, when *Detik* revealed the secret second marriage of a famous preacher, Kiayi Abdullah Gymnastiar (Aa Gym) (Tim Detikcom, 2006). This sparked public debate in much of the national and local media, which again points to the generally negative attitudes toward polygamy in Indonesia. It is reported that many of Aa's fans protested about his polygamy by spreading a campaign through SMS messages to boycott his preaching. As a result, his audience dropped dramatically (see, for example. *Warta Kota Bandung*, 2006a, 2006b; Dewantoro and Srihartini, 2006: 112–13; Sofyan, 2006a, 2006b).[46] Hoesterey, whose research focuses on Aa Gym in terms of *Manajemen Qolbu* (the heart management) and the broader industry of Islamic self-help psychology, reported that after Aa Gym's polygamous marriage became known to the public, the number of visitors to Aa Gym's *pesantren* was down 80 percent and the nearby souvenir shops, which usually earned A$2,000 per day, were closed owing to the absence of the visitors (Hoesterey, forthcoming). President Soesilo Bambang Yudoyono also reportedly received 9,949 SMS messages asking him to respond to Aa's polygamy. The President invited his Minister of Women's Empowerment, Meutia Hatta, and the Director General of Muslim Society Guidance (*Dirjen Binmas Islam*), Nazzaruddin Umar, to take necessary steps such as expanding the scope of PP 10, from civil servants to all members of Indonesian society (*Antara*, 2006a; Wiyana, Agustina and Bardiyah, 2006: 108). But Meutia Hatta, who might have been afraid of opposition from Muslim political leaders, and who may well belong to the Semi-textualist group, clearly agreed that 'polygamy is permitted with certain tight requirements'. For her, the current regulations, the 1974 Marriage Law and PP 10, were good enough to prevent the practice of polygamy (*Antara*, 2006b).

Conclusion

This chapter has discussed Muslim discourses on polygamy in Indonesia. As noted above, Indonesian Muslims generally believe that *shari'a* includes all legal rules in all Muslim history. This means that they regard *fiqh* as *shari'a*. The strong adherence to *fiqh* and the belief that the permission of polygamy is part of *shari'a* have led many members of Muslim women's organizations and Muslim political parties and organizations to resist any move to prohibit polygamy. But many of them personally disagree with polygamy. This disagreement with polygamy was clearly seen from responses to the Polygamy Award. Thus, it would appear from these controversies that the majority of Indonesians belong to the Semi-textualists, who do not want the door to polygamy to be wide open or closed tight. In the view of many of those who have engaged in these controversies, this slightly open door to polygamy has been misused and even abused by some polygamous men, and has caused many women and children to suffer. My informants' everyday experiences of polygamy will form the subject of the next two chapters.

4 Reactions to and negotiations around polygamous marriages

> 'I love my religion, I love my God, but I don't like polygamy.' Ramli asked, 'Why?' I answered, 'Because I am who I am. I am Risa, who wants each of us to be faithful to each other. I have been faithful to you, while you have not.'[1]

The dialogue above is between one of my informants, Risa (35) and her husband, Ramli (37). Risa rejected her husband's polygamous marriage, and preferred divorce to sharing Ramli with another woman. Her high level of education, her economic independence and her contextual approach to the Qur'anic verses dealing with polygamy all seem to have contributed to her determination to seek a divorce (her case study will be discussed in more detail later in this chapter). The quotation above shows how careful Risa was in expressing her dislike of Ramli's polygamous marriage. It is clear that she does not wish her opposition to polygamy to be judged as opposition to Islam – a fear shared by many of my informants.

This chapter will present case studies of polygamous marriages in Java, in the post-Soeharto period (see Table 4.1 for short reference list of the pseudonymic names of the people whose cases are being discussed in this chapter). As I shall show, the case studies highlight several important themes. They stress the importance of negotiating everyday marriage and household labor within the challenges posed by transparent polygamous marriages, or within the greater challenges that arise with women's discoveries of secret polygamous marriages. Many of my female informants were deeply upset and hurt when they discovered their husbands' betrayal of them. The studies also highlight the importance of kin, neighbors and workmates' responses to the discovery of polygamy in shaping women's responses.

The cases also elucidate the considerable differences among husbands in 'managing' polygamy, and the complex ways in which male informants negotiated around state regulations. The men in my study resisted secular regulations in a number of ways, including through bribery, falsifying their identity, manipulating data and even ignoring state law, to maintain unregistered additional marriages. Similarly, my research materials reveal that some supporters of Islamist ideas adhered rigidly to the belief in complementary gender roles, that men are naturally assigned to undertake public duties, while women are believed to be biologically

Table 4.1 List of informants (*dramatis personae*)

Case Study 1 (transparent polygamy)
1. Arsa (32), first wife of Jajang, Diploma in Business, a housewife, three children.
2. Jajang (34), husband of Arsa and Lia, senior high school graduate, a publishing manager.
3. Lia (28), second wife of Jajang, senior high school graduate, tailor and housewife, one child.

Case Study 2 (transparent polygamy)
1. Rosa (40), first wife of Syamsul, Bachelor's degree, a housewife, no children.
2. Syamsul (44), husband of Rosa and Indri, Doctoral degree, lecturer.
3. Indri (36), second wife of Syamsul, Bachelor's degree, former lecturer (not personally interviewed but by report a housewife), one child.

Case Study 3 (transparent polygamy)
1. Tuti (37), first wife of Rosyid, Diploma in Dance, former dancer, presently art gallery manager and part-time kindergarten teacher, three children.
2. Rosyid (39), formerly polygamous, Master's degree student, dancer and lecturer.
3. Nuri (27), former second wife of Rosyid, Bachelor's degree, housewife.

Case Study 4 (secret and unregistered polygamy)
1. Lina (39), first wife of Hadi (49), Master's degree student, secondary school teacher, six children.
2. Hadi (49), husband of Lina and Nani, Doctoral degree student, lecturer and council member.
3. Nani (35), second wife of Hadi, real estate sales, no children.

Case Study 5 (secret and unregistered polygamy)
1. Hanny (42), former wife of Asep, tertiary degree, housewife, four children.
2. Asep (46), former husband of Hanny, tertiary degree, lecturer and religious preacher.
3. Nurul (46), second wife of Asep, former divorcée, three children from previous husband, reportedly housewife.

Case Study 6 (secret and unregistered polygamy)
1. Risa (35), former wife of Ramli, Master's degree, lecturer and writer, three children.
2. Ramli (37), former husband of Risa and husband of Mamah, tertiary degree, NGO employee.
3. Mamah, second wife of Ramli, tertiary degree, no children, reportedly a housewife.

destined to undertake domestic roles (Shehadeh, 2003) (see Chapter 2), even though some of these women had higher levels of education than their husbands. In some instances men took advantage of younger women's vulnerabilities. Finally, and importantly, although none of the cases of participants recruited from LBH APIK appear in my chosen cases studies, my research shows that polygamy is associated consistently with significant degrees of emotional and physical violence.

These case studies are based on interviews with my informants, whose characteristics have been described in Chapter 1. My informants' narratives are thus a version of 'reality': their stories are a product of a particular day and interaction between informant and interviewer, and as such are inherently subjective and variable (Maila Stivens, personal communication, 18 January 2007). Each case study will consist of an account of the personal background of my research participants, their view on polygamy, their reactions to the husband's polygamous marriages, and relatives' and neighbors' reactions to the marriages. The case studies will be presented in a descriptive manner, and many of the women's views and experiences are put in direct quotes in order for readers to have direct access to their voices and experiences. The overall analysis of the case studies will be discussed at the end of the chapter.

Some Indonesian feminists seem to perceive women who are involved in polygamous marriages as 'victims' of polygamy. I argue that these women cannot merely be seen as passive, helpless victims. But as MacLeod, writing on veiling in Cairo, has pointed out, women can be both active subjects and subjects of domination at the same time (1992: 534). This point can also be argued for in the following case studies. Even though I suggest that the women are dominated by the husbands, they can also be considered as active subjects, who are struggling to make their marriages work or to improve their emotional well-being by seeking divorce rather than remaining in polygamous marriages.

I will categorize the ways in which first wives described their views about the husband's polygamous marriage and its validity within Islam in this chapter based on their approach to the Qur'anic verses: first, the women who share the Textualist approach to the Qur'anic verses on polygamy and therefore tend to accommodate the husband's polygamy; second, the women who share the Semi-textualist approach, and therefore tend to resist the husband's polygamy, which they see as not meeting the Qur'anic regulations; third, the women who share the Contextualist approach and therefore tend to reject the husband's polygamy by asking for divorce. Some women in the first, Textualist, category showed a degree of resistance to their husbands' polygamous marriages, but their resistance was not as strong as that of women in the second, Semi-textualist, and the third, Contextualist, categories – though I am aware that there are many other factors such as class, economic independence and educational level that could affect women's attitudes toward their husbands' polygamous marriage, other than their religious interpretation of polygamy.

Many of the women's attempts to resist their husbands' polygamy can be considered to have failed. Only one woman, Tuti, was able to resist her husband's polygamy, successfully bringing to an end her husband's second marriage. Tuti's case, which I shall describe below, fits very well with MacLeod's argument that

> women, even as subordinate players, always play an active part that goes beyond the dichotomy of victimization/acceptance, a dichotomy that flattens out a complex and ambiguous agency in which women accept, accommodate, ignore, resist, or protest – sometimes all at the same time.
>
> (MacLeod, 1992: 534)

Most of my participants' marriages occurred after the 1970s, and most of these marriages were based on 'personal choice': not parentally arranged, but not necessarily based on love. Most of their first marriages were celebrated with elaborate public ceremonies, with a few exceptions such as those of Arsa and Risa. It should also be noted that not all women have the social and structural support of family, because some of the women's parents and/or other close relatives had passed away, or lived far away. The cases will also show that while some women took advantage of kinship networks to escape from what they identify as an unhappy marriage, others ignored the family's concern for their unhappiness.

I will mainly focus on first wives because of the availability of data (I interviewed 16 first wives). I also interviewed nine women who were second wives but they did not speak as voluminously as the first wives. Some of the second wives seemed to feel 'guilty' for intruding on other people's marriage, while others seemed to be reluctant to reveal much of their married life. In addition, most first wives did not expect or initially did not know about the inclusion of other women in their marriage, while additional wives (the second, third or fourth wives) mostly know that their husband are already married, and therefore the latter may be emotionally more 'ready' to face the challenge of polygamous marriage. However, this does not mean that additional wives are necessarily happy. As some case studies will show, the second wives such as Lia and Nuri show their anxiety for the lack of attention from their husband and feel that they are subordinate to their first wives in terms of economic support and personal affection. Thus, as the case studies will demonstrate, either first wives or additional wives mostly feel uneasy to share a husband with other women.

Accommodating polygamy (the Textualists)

The initial case studies of polygamous marriages that I present here involve two first wives who have accommodated their husbands' polygamous marriages mainly because of their belief that Islam permits polygamy. They felt that they had to accept their husbands' polygamous marriage as a sign of their religious devotion. The first wives in these case studies were housewives who relied on their husbands economically. Both of them seemed to confront a great dilemma: whether to remain in a miserable polygamous marriage and retain their virtue as devout Muslims, or to free themselves from their unhappy situation and be seen as disavowing their religion. Clearly, divorce was not a choice in their case. For Arsa, for instance, asking for divorce might imply that she had lost her battle to win over her husband and had conceded victory to his second wife. Therefore, even though these women seemed accommodating of their situations, I shall suggest that they should not be seen as powerless victims of polygamy. Instead, they had exercised their agency to make the best of a difficult situation.

Case study 1: Arsa-Jajang-Lia

Interviewees: Arsa (first wife), Jajang (husband) and Lia (second wife)
Arsa: 'I want to smell the fragrance of heaven.'

The following case study will reveal the dilemma of a Muslim woman facing the choice of either adhering to the belief that Islam permits polygamy or facing the bitter reality of being involved in polygamous marriage. Arsa (32), who had a Diploma in Business from a private university in Jakarta, was the first wife of Jajang (34), a senior high school graduate who worked as a publishing manager. At the time of our interview, Jajang was the higher earner in the marriage, and could be categorized as a middle-income earner. As a believer in Islamist ideas of complementary gender roles, Arsa agreed to be a housewife. With the help of a maid, she was responsible for all domestic affairs such as cooking and childcare, although she was more highly educated than Jajang. As an Islamist, she believed that it was her religious obligation to wear the *hijab*.[2]

I first met Arsa and her co-wife, Lia (28, now a tailor and housewife), in a café near Arsa's rented home. I interviewed Lia first, then Arsa separately. I assumed that they did not want to be interviewed by me, a 'stranger', in their home, because they were aware of the boundaries between public and private spheres. But Arsa clearly felt obliged to invite me to her home when I told her that I needed to pray. (Islamist ideals specify that facilitating prayer for others is in itself an act of worship (*ibadah*)). She also wanted me to visit Lia's home. Even though I felt uneasy visiting Lia's home without letting her know in advance, I followed Arsa's lead, and after I had prayed we walked over to Lia's home five minutes away. Lia seemed to be embarrassed by our unexpected visit, and we only stayed for two minutes. I suspect that Arsa wanted me to compare her home and Lia's, to show that her home was located along a wider street, and was bigger and better than Lia's home, which was sited in a narrow alley.

Arsa told me that she met her husband, Jajang (34), in 1996 through a friend just after Jajang broke up with his previous girlfriend. A month after meeting, Arsa and Jajang decided to get married. It is possible that Jajang may have married Arsa in haste, perhaps as an avoidance reaction to his disappointment after the end of his relationship with the girlfriend. They did not celebrate their marriage, owing to conflict between Jajang and Arsa's parents about the wedding arrangements. Jajang wanted male and female guests to be separated, while Arsa's parents wanted the standard arrangements in which male and female guests can mingle.

Arsa's reactions to polygamy

Arsa had been married to Jajang for four years when he told her of his plan to take another wife. Arsa was shocked by the news. Arsa told me that she had felt heartbroken. She also felt that she had not yet had a chance to enjoy her marriage, because Jajang had been sick for 18 months after the marriage and the couple had been economically unsettled. They often had to seek economic help from Arsa's parents, who had even built a house for her. Jajang had just been given a well-paid job as a publishing manager when he told Arsa of his plan. She expected him to postpone his plans until their children had grown up. But Jajang could not wait that long, and described his feelings as follows:

> If I wait until they grow up, I am afraid that they would feel shocked and feel that I had been taken away. If I take another wife when they are small, the

conflict would only involve husband and wife, not children. In addition, if they get used to having two mothers, they will get used to them later.

His words suggest that Jajang was well aware of the negative psychological consequences polygamy might have for his children, and of the conflict that might arise between his wives.

Jajang said that he took another wife because of his high level of sexual desire, especially during Arsa's menstrual period and after she gave birth. According to Islamic teaching, men should restrain from sexual intercourse at these times. He had already met Lia on several occasions when he told Arsa about his plan. Lia told me how she and Jajang had met. She said that her brother worked in the same office as Jajang, and Lia had gone to this office to sell male Muslim clothing (*baju koko*). Jajang and Lia were interested in each other, and they met again and discussed the possibility of marriage. Lia told me that she was impressed by Jajang's honesty regarding his marital status, because she had found that men often claimed to be single in order to take a second wife.

Jajang told me that he believed he did not need his wife's approval to take an additional wife. However, Lia requested that he formally follow the Marriage Law requirements before taking a second wife. Therefore, Jajang told Arsa about his plan to take another wife, and whom he planned to marry. At that time, Arsa noticed that her husband paid much more attention to his appearance, even showing her the *baju koko* that he had just bought. Then, Arsa knew that he was really tempted by (*tergoda*) Lia.[3]

Even though Arsa was not happy to accept this second marriage, Jajang kept persuading her. Before she agreed, Arsa consulted her friends, who included a psychiatrist, a doctor, psychologist, and a religious expert. All were supporters of Islamist ideas regarding polygamy. She said that they told her that, psychologically, a woman has (biological) limitations (in 'serving' her husband's sexual needs) at a certain age, and they assured her that polygamy was not religiously prohibited. Thanks to their advice, even though she was hurt and shocked, Arsa decided that she would prefer that her husband practice polygamy than conduct extramarital affairs without her knowledge.

The following quote clearly demonstrates that Arsa's views on polygamy under Islam were affected by the Islamist campaigns claiming that polygamy is a 'solution' to the adulterous nature of men, a view similar to the one promoted by *ulama* in Malaysia in revitalizing the practice of polygamy (Ong, 2006).

> Women are the ornament of this world. The Qur'an states: '*Marry women of your choice, two, or three, or four.*' I also know that the Prophet Muhammad practiced polygamy. Women have a limited capacity [to serve their husband's sexual needs]. Therefore, instead of letting my husband commit adultery, it would be better to permit him to practice polygamy. In addition, if there is a woman who cannot find a good husband, while her intended husband has married another woman, this married woman would be better to not be egoistic, but to let her husband marry the woman who loves him. I do not want to deny God's law as long as it is implemented in a good way.[4]

Arsa did not want to be selfish by keeping Jajang, whom she saw as a good husband, to herself. However, as will be seen below, she seemed to regret that she had supported his marriage to Lia.

> Initially, I had a positive attitude toward polygamy. I thought that I had a 'sweet honey'. But that was only for a short time. After that, the 'honey' became poisonous. I found that Lia had disappointed me, my brother and my relatives. I found that Lia had taken many of my rights. Whenever Jajang was with me, Lia often called him even for a simple reason such as when her son was upset. I can accept polygamy religiously, but I have emotionally suffered from and am disappointed with my husband's polygamy.[5]

The term 'honey' *(madu)* is often used to refer to the co-wife. The word 'honey', according to Jennaway (2000: 147), tends to represent the male point of view about having more than one wife. For many wives, having a co-wife is bitter. Indeed, the above quotation means that for Arsa, the first wife, the 'honey' not only tasted bitter but also was poisonous because of its potential to make her sick.

Jajang's opinion of polygamy seems similar to Arsa's. It is possible that Jajang underlined the justifications for polygamy to Arsa in order to persuade her to accept the second marriage. This can be seen, for example, in his insistence that men are naturally polygamous:

> The Qur'an asks [men] to marry two, three and four in the verse: '*Fankihuu maa thooba lakum minan nisaa'i matsna. ... fawaahidatan*' [quoting the Qur'anic verse 4:3]. In my opinion, the words 'marry only one woman' here is like parents saying to their children: 'You can ride a bicycle if you are brave, if you are afraid, don't!'
>
> Polygamy is like a trial. If a wife disagrees with her husband's polygamy, her husband may have extra marital affairs. Polygamy is natural for men who want more than one source of pleasure. This is understood by God who allows polygamy, but there needs to be justice among wives. The biggest trial for women is to accept the verse on polygamy because it is hard to share their husband whom they love with another woman. That is a trial. If women are successful, like a brave man, they will pass the trial.[6]

As discussed in Chapter 3, the post-Soeharto period saw the construction of a model of femininity in which a good wife (*istri shalihah*) allowed her husband to take another wife – especially among Islamists. Therefore, if a wife disagreed with her husband's polygamy, it was often understood to be equivalent to causing or allowing her husband to engage in extramarital affairs, of which Islamists strongly disapproved. This belief was often mentioned by the proponents of polygamy, in publications or in their religious preaching. Some Islamist women seemed to be afraid of this possibility, especially the threat that they would also be responsible for the husband's sin of adultery.[7] This left a woman with two unfavorable choices: either to 'allow' her husband to take another wife or 'force' him to commit adultery.

Jajang's case also demonstrates well how one man evaded the secular legal process by falsifying the reason for his polygamy in order for his application to the Religious Court to be granted. To have his second marriage registered, Jajang, together with Arsa and Lia, sought the Court's approval, falsely testifying that his wife Arsa had a gynaecological problem (*masalah rahim*).[8] Jajang told me that it took three to four months to process the approval, and that he spent Rp. 300,000 (A$43) on administrative fees, which he considered reasonable. Jajang had the impression that the judge had made the process difficult, but he was happy that his application for polygamy was finally granted in the third hearing. Having obtained permission, Jajang and Lia were married in 2000, several months after Arsa gave birth to her third daughter. Lia's request to have her acceptance of polygamy registered is still rare, because many women seem to be unaware of the importance of marriage registration. It is possible that Lia's parents, or her sister, also a second wife, advised her to have her marriage registered for self-protection.

Relatives' and neighbors' reactions to polygamy

Arsa's case shows how her husband's second marriage disappointed her parents and her relatives, and had negative repercussions for her previously stable relationships with her family. Arsa said that her parents were very upset with Jajang when they heard about his second marriage. From then on, Arsa's parents stopped supporting Jajang financially, and only continued to provide for Arsa's children's material needs, including paying for clothes and milk. Arsa's mother hated to see Arsa so unhappy, and suggested that she ask for a divorce. This is indicative of Arsa's mother's level of concern for her daughter's well-being, which seemed greater than her father's, possibly evidence of the stronger ties between mothers and daughters than fathers and daughters noted in the literature. But Arsa did not want to ask for a divorce because she believed her husband when he told her that a woman who asked for a divorce without any reason would not smell the fragrance of heaven.

The opinions of other relatives were also important in shaping behavior. For example, Arsa told me that Jajang's mother (his father had passed away) disapproved of his polygamy because in her religion, Christianity, polygamy is not permitted. Therefore, according to Arsa, Jajang's mother regarded Lia as Jajang's mistress, not his wife. Jajang also told me that he had been isolated from his mother and sister, who both regarded him as being selfish for having more than one wife.

Arsa told me that Jajang second's marriage also changed the attitudes of Arsa's relatives and neighbors toward the couple. Arsa said that her siblings, aunts, uncles and neighbors isolated Arsa and Jajang. Some of them blamed Arsa for Jajang's second marriage, assuming that Arsa could not look after her husband well, a common tendency which might result from the construction of Indonesian Marriage Law which allows a husband to take another wife if he considers that his wife cannot do her duties to 'serve' his needs. For instance, Arsa quoted comments from her relatives and neighbors: 'You are really stupid, a fool and it is your fault.'[9] 'You are involved in polygamous marriage, so you are destroying yourself.'[10] Arsa also told me of a friend's comment to Lia: 'You are really stupid, you cannot look for a husband.'[11] Jajang also told me that he had heard some of his neighbors' comments such as, 'This man is not behaving in the usual fashion.'[12] But Jajang said that he just disregarded the comments.

The negative reactions were not only directed at a polygamous husband and his first wife, but also at his second wife. Lia told me that her father and brother did not approve of her marriage. They were afraid that Lia might become Jajang's 'plaything'. Lia's mother did not intervene, preferring her daughter to make her own choices. But after concluding that Jajang was a good person, they finally gave their blessing to the marriage. Lia also reported comments from her neighbors such as 'she has taken away another woman's husband' (*ia telah merebut suami orang*), and 'she has only married Jajang because she wanted his money'. Lia said that even though she did not hear the comments directly, but through her friends, they were upsetting. But she tried to be patient and regarded the gossip surrounding her as a trial (*ujian*).

After one and a half years, Arsa told me that her relatives no longer isolated her, even though they still could not accept that Arsa was married polygamously. Arsa's neighbors also showed their concern for Arsa and her children, and commented that it was as though the children had no father, because Jajang was always busy with his work and his second wife. Jajang also told me about one neighbor's changing attitude when this man visited him to ask for advice on how to deal with his wife's opposition toward polygamy.

Arsa's emotional well-being and her negotiation around polygamy.

Although Arsa had become weary of her husband's polygamous marriage, she tried to make the best of a difficult situation by discussing problems and attempting to work through them:

> When there was a problem in our polygamous marriage, I usually called Lia to resolve the problem. However, when the problem was too complicated to discuss on the phone, I invited Lia to spend Saturday night in my house. After several such invitations, Lia seemed to enjoy spending the night in my house. Lia often came to my house on Saturday night even without my invitation. I felt that my privacy and my time to be together with my husband had been reduced and disturbed by Lia's presence. I usually sleep with my husband on Saturday night. However, when Lia was present, I had to sleep with Lia in one room, while Jajang slept in another room with our children. For my privacy, I plan to move to another rented house, which is far from Lia's house.[13]

Arsa told me that she disliked Lia's attitude, which disturbed her marriage and made Arsa feel like she was going to 'die while standing' (*mati berdiri*). For instance, Lia became angry at Jajang when she heard that Arsa and Jajang had attended a wedding without her. Arsa told Lia that they had done so because the wedding was between two friends of Arsa's. Arsa told Lia that she would not come to a wedding of Lia's friends.

Arsa saw that Lia's attitude toward her had changed. Before the marriage, Lia did not seem jealous of Arsa. However, afterwards, Lia frequently displayed her jealousy. Her neighbors commented that it is acceptable for the first wife to be jealous of the second wife, but not vice versa. Arsa prayed to God, asking for acceptance and for the patience to withstand her unhappiness.

Throughout my interview with Arsa, her ambivalence was clear. It is possible that before the interview, Jajang asked both Lia and Arsa to convey a positive front to me. While Lia seemed able to do so, Arsa seemed to struggle. Sometimes, she sounded positive, but most of the time she could not prevent herself from describing the misery of sharing her husband with Lia. Her ambivalence, for instance, can be seen in her statements that Jajang is a good husband, but that she has not been able to enjoy her marriage since the second marriage.

Arsa's emotional well-being was clearly deeply affected by her husband's second marriage. Arsa told me explicitly that it had made her miserable, and that she was not strong enough to attend Jajang's second marriage contract (*akad nikah*), but that she and her children came to Jajang and Lia's marriage celebration. Arsa was hurt by the merriment surrounding the event, especially because Jajang did not formally celebrate his marriage with her owing to conflict over the separation of the sexes at the reception. Arsa felt that Jajang was betraying his own principles in this second marriage celebration by having a mixed-sexes party, which he rejected having at his first marriage with Arsa. She could not stand to stay any longer and went home, leaving her husband side by side with Lia. When she arrived home, she fainted and was sick for three days.

When I asked how she felt about sharing her husband with another wife, Arsa said:

> It is hurtful, very hurtful. My husband is usually beside me every night. Now, when my child is sick, he is not here. I am very upset, but when he dies I will have the same feeling of loss anyway. Therefore, when I feel jealous, I try to cope with it by involving myself with many activities, such as reading the Qur'an, playing with my children outside the house, making cookies or taking my children to my parents' home.
>
> After my husband's second marriage, I have been so stressed, I have pimples and my face is no longer smooth.[14]

Her experience was similar to that of Tuti, Rosyid's first wife, whose case will be discussed below. Nuri (27), the former second wife of Rosyid, and Lia reportedly both became increasingly demanding of their new husbands, both emotionally and economically after becoming second wives: this caused considerable distress for Tuti and Arsa, the first wives. Both second wives may well have set out intentionally to upset the first wife, so that she, feeling miserable, would ask for a divorce, and they could then be the sole wives.

Case study 2: Rosa-Syamsul-Indri

Interviewees: Rosa (first wife) and Syamsul (husband)
Rosa: 'I want a divorce but I am afraid if I did [get divorced] I would be so lonely.'

Most of the case studies discussed in this thesis are representative of the behavior of the majority of my male informants, who were able to manipulate the legal process by altering personal data, paying a bribe or failing to register a marriage. This particular case is exceptional, because it is the only case in which a husband took another wife under the reasons stipulated in the 1974 Marriage Law and PP 10. In addition, the husband also adhered to the requirements of both the Marriage Law and PP 10.

Rosa (40), a Sundanese woman, had been married to Syamsul (44), a Minang man, since 1990. Rosa and Syamsul met while studying at university in Bandung. Syamsul, who had a doctoral degree, worked as a senior lecturer in one of the state universities in Bandung, while Rosa was a housewife. They dated for two years and married when Rosa was 26 and Syamsul was 30. Before this, however, there was an important event that significantly affected Rosa's life. In 1988, just after her graduation, she was diagnosed with uterine cancer and underwent surgery that left her unable to bear children. Because of this, Syamsul told me that he was uncertain about whether or not he should marry Rosa. Therefore, he consulted two famous male *ulama* (religious scholars) in Bandung (he gave me their names). He said that they both told him to leave Rosa: 'What is marriage for if not for having children? Just search for another woman.'[15] His mother, however, advised him differently: 'How could you date her when she was healthy and abandon her when she was sick?'[16] Unlike the male *ulama*, who tend to see marriage for the purpose of procreation, as a woman, Syamsul's mother seemed to be more sympathetic to Rosa.

Feeling obliged to obey his mother, Syamsul visited Rosa and proposed marriage to her. But he was disappointed when Rosa grew to hate her new mother-in-law. Rosa explained that she often expressed her jealousy whenever Syamsul gave some money to his mother or sisters. Rosa assumed that Syamsul told them about her jealousy, making them in turn disappointed with her. I asked him whether he married Rosa out of compassion, or because he loved her. He said, 'I want to make Rosa happy, but she seems not to be grateful for my sincere desire. I married her because I loved her. I did not want to marry another woman, even though at that time, I had the chance to.'[17] Syamsul and Rosa formally celebrated their marriage. After her marriage, Rosa became a housewife. Her daily activities mainly comprised housework, including cleaning and other domestic chores. Sometimes, she joined a monthly religious gathering or visited her neighbors. As a housewife, she was economically dependent on her husband. In 2002, Syamsul, took another wife, Indri (36), who had a Bachelor's degree and formerly worked as a lecturer. He said that he needed someone to look after him and that he wanted to have children. Syamsul said that Rosa could not 'serve' and look after him well:

> Rosa was a spoiled daughter. She cannot do anything. She does not have a work schedule and her work is not carefully planned. When I went to work at

7 a.m., she got up from sleep and started to cook at 7 a.m. [He asked sarcastically] How could I eat the food that she had prepared?

I come from Padang. My parents educated their children so that they could become independent. I can do anything, from cooking to sewing. I can take care of myself.

In 2000, when I wrote my dissertation, I was sick for a year. I wondered who would look after me. Therefore, when I recovered, I discussed with my wife my plan to take another wife.[18]

The above quote illustrates Syamsul's primary expectation of Rosa: to be a 'good' wife as stipulated by the Marriage Law, and 'serve' her husband well.

Syamsul met Indri when both of them were teaching at a university in Cirebon. After marrying her, Syamsul bought another luxurious house, about seven kilometres away from his home. Since Syamsul's second marriage, Rosa has lived alone in her big house, where she and her husband had lived for twelve years. Syamsul visited her occasionally in the afternoon, while on a break from work. In my opinion, by visiting Rosa during his office hours, Syamsul seemed to be trying to lessen problems in his second marriage: Indri would presumably assume that Syamsul was in his office during that time, and not know that he was visiting the first wife. This clearly constitutes one form of male negotiation within polygamous marriage.

Rosa's views on polygamy

Rosa told me that she believed polygamy to be God's law and therefore something she must accept. But when her husband took another wife, she became depressed.

When I was studying at university, I often discussed polygamy, and I could accept polygamy because it was God's law and therefore must be accepted. As far as I know, polygamy is like an emergency exit, which can be used occasionally. In my opinion, a husband can take an additional wife even without his wife's permission, because it is our state laws [not God's law], which require the wife's permission before a husband can take an additional wife. However, a wife has the right to accept or reject her husband's polygamy. I had the feeling that I would some day be married polygamously [possibly because she was aware of her 'lack' owing to being unable to bear children]. After my marriage, I even asked my husband to take another wife. However, when I knew that my husband had a date with another woman and married her, I felt that my 'heart was hot'.[19] I was so depressed and had many psychological problems.[20]

Rosa confessed that it was her husband's polygamy that caused her to experience these psychological problems, not her parents' death or her lost uterus. In contrast, her husband never thought that his second marriage had caused Rosa's psychological problems. Syamsul told me that Rosa was mentally ill because of her shock at discovering that her father had married another woman of Rosa's age. Syamsul also told me that Rosa was very depressed when her parents passed away, and when she had a hysterectomy. But Syamsul never told me about Rosa's worsening mental state after he took another wife, and he behaved as though his second marriage had no effect on Rosa's emotional well-being.

Both Rosa and Syamsul shared the view that God's law on polygamy is superior to state law (the 1974 Marriage Law, the Compilation and the PP 10, the state laws that require the first wife's permission before taking another wife, did not need to be obeyed): 'Religious law should not be accepted in a skeptical way. We need to accept it as it is. How could religious law be subordinate to state laws such as PP 10 and the 1974 Marriage Law?' Their views indeed seem to represent the majority of Indonesian Muslims' view of the state laws, which they tend to see just as a matter of formality, subordinate to divine law. For instance, many of my participants regarded divorce outside the Court as valid. These attitudes toward the 1974 Marriage Law remind us of the history of Muslims' protests about stipulations of the 1973 draft, which Muslims felt to be contradictory to Islamic teaching.

Rosa's reaction to polygamy

A husband's intention to take another wife created an extreme dilemma for many first wives. Rosa told me about her reaction when her husband told her that he would take another wife:

> I felt unstable. I could not decide whether I wanted divorce or not, while my husband did not want to divorce me against my will. It seems to me that Syamsul's mother and siblings supported his marrying Indri because they expected Syamsul to have children, and because my relationship with them had not been harmonious.[21]

Rosa also told me that before her husband took another wife, she found that her turbulent relationship with her mother-in-law was a big problem. But she considered her husband's second marriage now to be her biggest problem. She experienced great conflict between her willingness to stay in the marriage, which seemed to cause her emotional distress, and her intention to seek a divorce, which might make her lonely.

Rosa also told me that as a woman, she wanted to make her husband happy. She felt sorry for her husband who was still young and might want to have a normal sexual life with the possibility of having children, while she was often 'too lazy' to have sexual intercourse. She supported her husband's plan to take an additional wife by signing a letter stating her consent to his second marriage. She also felt that her relationship with Indri was good before Syamsul married her. However, on the day of Syamsul's marriage with Indri, Rosa felt very hurt by her husband, because he celebrated with a big party in a rented building and invited many colleagues and neighbors. She felt that everybody seemed to be happy, and behaved as if she did not exist.

Unspoken sexual jealousy also affected a woman's ability to enjoy her sexual relationship with her husband. After her husband's second marriage, Rosa told me that she was even more reluctant to have sexual intercourse with him, because she felt that she really hated him, and was so emotionally distressed. But her husband sometimes insisted on sexual intercourse with her two to three times a month. Rosa told me, 'If I refused to have sex with him, he would verbally abuse me.'[22] She did not tell me what exactly her husband said if she rejected him.

Rosa never told me that she had a particular mental illness, but she did tell me that she suffered from psychological problems, feeling that she could hear voices, as if people were talking far away. She also felt as though she had been threatened by unknown persons. I asked her whether she shared these feelings with her husband. She said, 'No, I did not tell Syamsul because I feel that he is the one who hates me.'

Rosa also admitted her difficulties in adjusting to her husband's expectations of her:

> We have different characters. For instance, he wants me to wash clothes everyday, not to wait until they are many dirty clothes, so he can use them again whenever he needs to. He dislikes postponing any work, while I tend to be relaxed. I do not want to wash clothes everyday. I want to wait until they are many, then I will put them in the washing machine. He also expects the house to be clean, so I must mop the floor every day. Moreover, he expects me to cook, even though there would be a lot of food to throw out if I cook, because he often eats out. I often feel that he is so tough on me, even though I am very vulnerable whenever he gets angry with me. If he gets angry with me, I feel very sad, so I lock myself in my bedroom.[23]

The couple's differing attitudes to work are clear in the above quote. Syamsul, who seems to be a very hard worker, expressed his dislike of Rosa's relaxed attitudes to her work. Rosa also did not like Syamsul's 'tough' expectations of her. Therefore, she seemed to enjoy living alone after Syamsul moved to Indri's house. 'I can relax now, and I do not need to cook or mop the floor everyday. I will just buy what I want to eat and clean the house whenever I want'. The house she occupied was large (two stories), luxurious, and appeared tidy and clean. The rhythmic sound of water flowing in the small pool in the living room contributed to the relaxing and refreshing domestic environment. It may be that her new-found tranquillity, and freedom from Syamsul's authority, contributed to Rosa's unwillingness to ask for divorce.

Rosa's relatives' and neighbors' reactions to Syamsul's polygamy

Syamsul's polygamous marriage did not seem to change Rosa's relationship with her brothers. They had rarely contacted each other after they all got married, and had even less contact after their parents passed away in 1997. Therefore, Rosa could not share her feelings with her siblings. But she felt lucky that she could share her feelings with some of her old friends, who occasionally called and visited her. Rosa said that before they passed away she had had a very close relationship with her parents, who tended to be over-protective of her. She and her husband lived in the parents' house in the first two years of their marriage (1990–2) before they moved to their own house in the same city, Bandung.

Syamsul told me that when he wanted to marry Indri, she demanded that he seek permission from Rosa and her siblings. Syamsul said that he was actually very reluctant to ask their permission, but he did do it. Rosa's siblings wanted to let Rosa make her own decisions, but they gave their permission because they were aware of Rosa's physical condition.

Rosa's situation seems exactly to fit the situation stipulated in the 1974 Marriage Law in which a husband can take another wife: Rosa cannot bear children; Syamsul also felt that Rosa was unable to 'serve' him well (which is seen as the wife's duty). Therefore, Rosa's situation provides a 'licence' for Syamsul to marry another woman. In his case, polygamy can be regarded as a 'rescue', allowing him to have children, to be sexually 'served' and to be looked after properly by another woman without needing to divorce Rosa. However, her husband's polygamy improved Syamsul's situation at the expense of Rosa's mental state.

Unlike many women in developed countries, where bearing children can often be a personal choice, most Indonesian women are expected to fall pregnant soon after marriage and women who cannot bear children are seen as imperfect. Therefore, they need to prepare themselves to be 'punished' by either being married polygamously or being repudiated, even though their inability to bear children is beyond their control. This case would seem to support the critiques of the 1974 Marriage Law made by Indonesian feminists that I noted in Chapter 3: that it is biased toward men. As they suggest, within this Law women like Rosa are positioned to make men happy by serving them and bearing their children. When a woman cannot make her husband happy, he can take another wife: as if taking another wife does not have any effect on the first wife's well-being, as if women's feelings are not important to be considered in the drafting of law, and as if women are subordinate to men and therefore unimportant.

Resisting polygamy (the Semi-textualists)

The following two case studies will present instances of women showing greater resistance to their husbands' polygamous marriages, and the ways in which they represented this resistance in the context of a Semi-textualist understanding of the Qur'anic verse relating to polygamy. The women in these case studies understood that their husbands' polygamous marriages did not follow Islamic regulations. As I shall suggest, other factors such as the degree of economic independence and the availability of supportive kinship networks also seem to have significantly affected women's negotiations within polygamous marriages. The case study of Tuti shows how she initially attempted to accommodate her husband's second marriage, but finally succeeded in ending his second marriage. It will also show how Tuti tried to conform to the existing construction of a 'good wife and mother' (*istri dan ibu yang baik*), according to central cultural models of the New Order and Islamist construction of a 'pious wife' (*istri yang shaleh*). In addition, Lina's case will show how, failing to divorce her husband for the second time, Lina found her own way to resist her husband's second marriage simply by avoiding him. The construction of a 'good' mother during the New Order period seemed also to affect her negotiations around polygamy, in which she sacrificed her emotional well-being for the benefit of her children. Both cases, like the previous two case studies, will also discuss women's emotional distress upon discovering the husband's plan to marry a second wife, and even more upon discovering a secret second marriage.

Case study 3: Tuti-Rosyid-Nuri.

Interviewee: Tuti: 'I am the manager of my husband'.

Personal background

Tuti (37) had a Diploma in Dance from a higher education institution in Bandung. She married Rosyid, her classmate at the dance institution, in 1991, when she was 23 years old and Rosyid was 25. Their formal wedding celebration was not extravagant. They had three children, aged 13, 9 and 3 at the time of our interview.[24] Tuti now works as an art gallery manager and as a part-time kindergarten teacher.

Tuti told me that her husband endorsed her career and economic activities. But worrying that Tuti might have an affair with another man, Rosyid sometimes asked her to stop dancing and requested that she wear a headscarf. Tuti told me that she had many ideas about how to earn money. She rented a house near her campus and turned it into an art gallery, which she managed together with her husband.[25] She also founded a kindergarten in her parents' village, which was about four hours by bus from Bandung. While setting this up over a period of about three years, she often left Bandung for two or three weeks at a time. She had already told her husband that if he objected to her leaving the house to go to work at the kindergarten, she would stop going there. Tuti was worried that Rosyid could not restrain himself from having an affair with another woman. But Rosyid convinced her that he would be faithful. Rosyid even encouraged her to go to the kindergarten, when Tuti was very reluctant to go. Unexpectedly, one day in 2002, Rosyid told Tuti that he had a 27-year-old girlfriend, Nuri, who had studied for a Bachelor's degree. He also told Tuti that his relationship with Nuri had become too close and he asked Tuti's permission to marry Nuri.[26]

Tuti's view of polygamy

When I asked about her views on polygamy in Islam, Tuti told me that she disagreed with her husband's polygamous marriage, which she thought had different motives from those of the Prophet.

> As far as I know, the Prophet practiced polygamy in certain conditions with different motives [from those of contemporary men], not to satisfy sexual needs, but to worship God. The Qur'anic chapter on women states that it is permissible to marry one, two, three or four women if a man is 'capable' of doing

it. ... If he can lead and manage his marriage, he may be permitted to practice polygamy. Unfortunately, most men are not equal to the Prophet. I also often heard in preaching that a woman who is married polygamously would enter paradise. However, when I asked other women, even those who wore a long *hijab*, they said they did not want to be in a polygamous marriage.[27]

As stated earlier, wearing the *hijab* (head covering) is often regarded as a sign of religious piety. Some people assume that the longer the *hijab*, the more pious the woman. Tuti's anecdote seemed calculated to show me that women who are regarded as more pious than her shared her rejection of polygamy. It is clear that she did not want to be judged as the only person to reject Islam by rejecting polygamy, or being judged to be irreligious for disagreeing with polygamy.

Tuti's reactions to Rosyid's polygamy

Tuti told me that her 'heart was very hot' and she was very shocked when Rosyid told her of his intention to marry Nuri. She said that it was hard for her to believe that her husband had betrayed her, because he had always loved Tuti and been kind to her. She felt that she just wanted to run away, leaving her husband and her children. But she tried to think rationally, and asked Rosyid, 'Why do you want to marry another woman?' Rosyid said, 'I love Nuri.' Tuti asked, 'Do you still love me? If you do not love me anymore, I will ask you to divorce me and ask you to be responsible for your children.' Rosyid said, 'I still love you.' Tuti asked, 'Then what is wrong with me that makes you want to take another wife?' Rosyid said, 'There is nothing wrong with you.' The conversation between Tuti and her husband demonstrates Tuti's religious belief that polygamy can only be practiced when there is something wrong with the first wife. Therefore, she challenged her husband's intention to marry another woman.

Tuti told me that she was confused as to how to respond to her husband's request. She was reluctant to give her husband permission to marry Nuri. Tuti was afraid that it was sinful of her to forbid Rosyid to marry Nuri, however, and that she would be responsible for the sin of 'allowing' her husband to continue his illicit relationship with Nuri. Therefore, she finally gave her permission, on the condition that if his second marriage negatively affected the first marriage, Rosyid must choose to divorce either Nuri or Tuti. This points to how the Islamists' campaign for polygamy affected Tuti's decision in response to her husband's request for polygamy. Especially significant was their claim that a wife's disapproval of polygamy constitutes tacit approval of her husband's illicit sexual relationships.

To 'accommodate' Rosyid's desire to marry Nuri, Tuti was willing to attend Rosyid's hearings in a Religious Court to obtain the Court's approval for polygamy. Tuti told me that everything written in Rosyid's application to the Court was false. For instance, Rosyid testified that his reason for taking another wife was that his established wife could not 'serve' her husband sexually, owing to illness. Tuti said this was not true. In addition, Rosyid falsified his income and stated that it was in the millions, while in fact, according to Tuti, it was very low, about

Rp. 400,000 (A$57) per month, and not even enough to make their home repayment of Rp. 500,000 (A$72) per month.[28] All of this shows Rosyid's disrespect for the law, and illustrates and that the law does not necessarily provide protection for its subjects.

Before going to the Court, Rosyid introduced Nuri to Tuti in their art gallery. The meeting took place there, and not at their house, for fear that their children and neighbors would know about Rosyid's intended second marriage. Tuti was surprised that Nuri was wearing a head cover (*jilbab*). Tuti was so angry with Nuri that she said she wanted to scratch Nuri's face. But she restrained herself, instead expressing her anger by saying 'Your *jilbab* (head cover) is just an accessory. You wear a *jilbab*, but you take away another woman's husband. Oh yeah, I know a sex worker who also wears a *jilbab*.'[29]

At that time, Tuti asked Nuri what she wanted from her husband. In an attempt to prevent Nuri from marrying Rosyid, Tuti explained to Nuri that Rosyid was already married with three children, and that his income was very low. But Tuti said that Nuri did not object to Rosyid's marital and economic status. Tuti told Nuri that if she wanted to marry Rosyid, she should let Tuti arrange everything for the second marriage. Tuti told me that Nuri agreed to obey Rosyid and Tuti. In Tuti's view, before getting married, Nuri seemed to be kind and obedient. Then, the three of them went to the Court. Tuti told me of her impression of the judge in the Court: 'During the Court hearings, it seemed to me that the judge of the Religious Court was surprised to see me willing to permit my husband to take a second wife.' Indeed, it is extraordinary for a woman to express her willingness to share a husband with another woman.

Tuti even helped Rosyid to get ready for his second wedding, although she was not strong enough emotionally to attend the wedding.

> On the day of my husband's marriage, I prepared and ironed his clothes. I helped him get dressed. It was also I who provided money to pay for Nuri's *mahar* because my income was higher than that of my husband. My husband kissed my feet to ask for my forgiveness before he went out for his second marriage. I could not stand to attend the wedding. I stayed at home with my children who asked where their father was when he did not come home that night. I said to them that their father was attending a meeting. I could not sleep that night. I felt that my heart was very hot. To cool down my feelings, I spent that night praying and reading the Qur'an. My husband told me that he felt his body was very hot that night and he could not stop thinking about me and his children.[30]

By supporting her husband's second marriage, Tuti tried to conform to the new representation of a 'good' wife advocated by many Islamists during that period. As noted, the extensive promotion of polygamy discussed above had at that time encouraged women to accept their husbands' polygamy as a sign of their acceptance of their religion and their status as pious women (*wanita shalihah*). In addition, by preparing and ironing her husband's clothes, Tuti also seemed to try to conform to New Order representations of a 'good' wife, who is expected to 'serve' her husband well.

Tuti not only took control of making the second marriage happen, but also was ultimately able to end the second marriage by asking Rosyid to divorce Nuri four months later. Tuti underlined the difficulty she saw for a polygamous husband in attempting to treat his two wives justly, and how polygamous marriage could reduce a man's productivity:

> Several months after his second marriage, I noticed how tired my husband was, physically and mentally. I saw that my husband was struggling to keep both marriages working. Physically, he seemed to be worried if my sexual desire was not fulfilled. Therefore he increased the frequency of our sexual intercourse from once or twice a week into three times a week, even though I noticed how tired he was. I actually felt disgusted to have sex with him because he was the 'left overs' of another woman. But I was afraid of committing a sin by not serving my husband.
>
> When he was with me, Nuri often called him and asked him to accompany her to go to a wedding or to go shopping. ... My husband seemed anxious about both wives' requests, but he obeyed me, maybe for fear that I would ask him to divorce Nuri.
>
> Sometimes, when he was with Nuri, I did the same thing. Therefore, my husband had less time to work or to put his energy into the development of his art career. As a result, he had financial difficulties looking after his two households. Actually, my husband earned only a small amount of money, not even enough to look after one household. I then reminded my husband of the condition of his second marriage and asked him to choose either to divorce Nuri or me. My husband rejected the idea of divorcing Nuri because he seemed to be seduced by her. Nuri also did not want to get a divorce. But I insisted that he keep his promise. Finally, my husband made a decision to divorce Nuri. He might have compared his two wives' personalities during his marriage to both of us. Then both of us set up a strategy to divorce Nuri. I am the one who mostly prepared the paper work for his divorce.[31]

The above quote also shows that the issue of sexuality was significant, with unspoken sexual jealousy affecting Tuti's sexual pleasure. It also demonstrates Tuti's determination to end her husband's second marriage to prevent further economic problems for their family. Tuti told me that she and her husband had founded the art gallery and worked together on the venture from the very beginning. When it came time to reap the fruits of their efforts, however, a third person entered their married life and interfered with their ability to enjoy the rewards of their hard work. Therefore, it was for this economic reason, and because she loved her husband and her children, that Tuti was determined to save her marriage. Tuti's willingness to save her household from economic decline fits very well with Brenner's assumption that women's real concern when it comes to their spouses' infidelity is the 'draining of family resources to support extramarital affairs' (1998: 151).

However, the process of divorce took time and was also costly, because Nuri was uncooperative. She was frequently absent from the divorce hearings and demanded a high divorce settlement of 15 million rupiah, but Rosyid could only agree to 2 million rupiah. Initially, the Court agreed to Nuri's proposal for the amount of the divorce settlement because the judge assumed that Rosyid had treated her unfairly by only staying married to her for four months. Tuti then explained to the judge that Nuri's marriage to Rosyid had damaged her own marriage, with Rosyid no longer able to afford to support two wives. Tuti also explained that it was she who had financially supported Nuri's household, paid for the *mahar* and for all the administrative costs of the divorce. Tuti asked the judge what he would do if he had a daughter in Tuti's situation. After realizing the extent of Tuti's suffering, the judge ruled that Rp. 5,000,000 (A$715) would be an appropriate settlement for Nuri. Tuti initially objected, because she did not have such an amount, but because she wanted to end the case, she agreed. She was glad that she had accompanied Rosyid to court; otherwise he would have had to pay Rp. 15,000,000 (A$2,143). She opened her wallet and showed me the bank receipt from her money transfer to Nuri. She said it took her three months to finalize Rosyid's divorce case.

Tuti told me that she was happy with her current marriage because there was no other woman in it. She also told me about her pride and satisfaction in her ability to end her husband's second marriage by saying: 'I feel like I am the manager of my husband' (*Saya merasa seperti menjadi menejer suami saya*).

Neighbors' and relatives' reactions to Rosyid's polygamy

As I have emphasized, many Indonesian Muslims have negative attitudes toward polygamy, regarding it as shameful. Both Tuti and Rosyid seemed to be concerned that their relatives and neighbors might discover their polygamous marriage. But all secret polygamous marriages among my research participants were discovered sooner or later by parents, parents-in-law, relatives and neighbors of either the wives or husbands; Rosyid's marriage was the only exception: Tuti and her husband successfully kept Rosyid's polygamous marriage secret from everyone. She said that she kept Rosyid's second marriage secret from her parents because she was afraid that they would no longer respect him, and would insult him, if they found out. But it is possible that her mother suspected something: Tuti told me that on one occasion her mother visited her and told her about a dream. In this dream, her mother saw Rosyid having sexual intercourse with another woman, and, feeling disgusted, Tuti's mother kicked both of them. Tuti sat quietly listening, and could only confirm the truth of what her mother told her in her heart.

Tuti might also be ashamed if her husband's polygamous marriage became the topic of gossip among her neighbors. She said that even though she had been living in her house since 1993, she did not like to be involved in gossip in her neighborhood. She might have been worried that her neighbors would assume that she could not 'serve' her husband well, or that there might be something wrong with her, such as an inability to satisfy her husband's sexual needs. Tuti and Rosyid also did not want their children to know about his second marriage, because they were afraid that the knowledge might affect the children negatively.

Case Study 4: Lina-Hadi-Nani

Interviewee: Lina (first wife): 'Now I know the way to hurt him.'

Personal background

Lina (39) was a civil servant teaching in a secondary school, with a Bachelor's degree in Islamic Studies and taking her Master's in one of the Islamic universities in Bandung. As a local council member in Bandung and a lecturer in the university where they had both studied, her husband, Hadi, received a high income and many perks, including a good car and free petrol. Lina did not want to be interviewed in her home before she knew me personally but, after the interview, she took me to a restaurant near her place of study. She welcomed me to her large and luxurious house when I brought her interview transcript to her for checking.

Lina had married Hadi in 1985, when she was 20 and Hadi was 30. They met as fellow students: Lina and Hadi had their Bachelor's degrees when they decided to get married. They had six children (aged 18, 17, 14, 9, 7 and 5). Both Lina and Hadi continued their studies after marriage: at the time of the interview, Lina was taking her Master's and Hadi was a doctoral candidate, as well as working as a lecturer. In 1997, Hadi, who had been politically active, was elected as a council member in Bandung. Soon afterwards, Lina found out that her husband had married another woman secretly. She divorced her husband, but was prevailed on to return to him, mainly for the sake of the children.

Lina's view of polygamy

When I asked Lina about her opinion of polygamy in Islam, she quoted the Qur'anic verse 4: 3 fluently in Arabic:

> *Fain khiftum alla ta'diluu fawaahidatan* [if you fear that you cannot be just to more than one wife, then marry one woman only]. This means that Islam is in favor of monogamy. Polygamy can only be permitted in the case of a wife who cannot 'serve' her husband in many aspects. As long as the wife can do everything, polygamy is unacceptable.[32]

I have suggested that the way my participants quoted the Qur'anic verse 4: 3 was linked to their views on polygamy. Lina, who was against polygamy, only quoted this part of the verse: '*If you fear that you cannot be just to more than one wife, then marry one woman only*' – a clear Semi-textualist approach. Lina's acceptance of polygamy in certain circumstances, such as when a wife cannot 'serve' her husband, also indicated her acceptance of the 1974 Marriage Law, even though these circumstances are not stated in the Qur'an.

In this interview, Lina also wanted to express her opposition to Puspo Wardoyo's campaign that polygamy is 'good' and 'beautiful', because of the bitter reality of her life after her husband took another wife:

> I disagree with the opinion that polygamy is good. The opinion must not belong to women, or only one in ten women will say so, especially if their

husband practices unacceptable polygamy, which causes violence. The beauty of polygamy may be based on the sin committed by the couple because I assume that my husband and his lover had done something against Islamic law before they got married [Lina seemed to assume that Nani and Hadi had been sexually involved before they got married].[33]

Lina also believed that it was not only she who had suffered from polygamy, but that many women were suffering because of the husband's taking another wife.

I believe that my current sickness is caused by my husband's polygamous marriage. I believe that many other women have been suffering like me – maybe a million women have become victims of polygamous marriage. Some of them became insane; others were murdered or committed suicide because of severe depression. There are many items in the newspaper about them [murder and suicide], and it is possible that they are caused by polygamous marriage or by a husband's extramarital affairs.[34]

Lina's reactions to Hadi's polygamy

Lina found out about her husband's second wife when a man called her anonymously:

I heard a rumor that my husband had taken an additional wife, but I ignored the rumor because I felt that I had been kind to my husband. I also felt that I had become a good wife who maintained my dignity, for instance by not accepting male guests in the absence of my husband. Because I had been kind to my husband, I assumed that my husband would also treat me kindly. However, one day, a person called me and informed me that my husband had taken another wife.[35] I did not believe what the person said until the person called me for the third time. He informed me of the name and address of my husband's second wife, Nani [35].

I checked the validity of the rumor by going to Nani's house. I was really angry when I met Nani, who confessed that she married Hadi. I also asked Hadi why he had taken a second wife secretly, when there was nothing wrong with me and I had been trying to be a good wife. Hadi could not answer my questions and said, 'I did it unintentionally, it was an accident.' [This could mean that Hadi often met Nani, and their closeness might have caused them to have sexual relations. To stop committing *zina*, either Nani or Hadi initiated the marriage.][36]

As stated earlier, Lina could accept polygamy only under certain circumstances, such as when a wife could not 'serve' her husband well. She could not accept her husband's second marriage because she felt that there was nothing wrong with her: she bore six children; she felt that she could 'serve' her husband well; and she had protected her chastity and dignity by not accepting male guests in the absence of her husband. Lina found out about her husband's secret marriage when she was seven months pregnant; at that point Hadi had been married to Nani for eight months.

Lina's case shows clearly how polygamy can be associated with a significant degree of emotional and physical violence. She is a woman with substantial social resources, but these did not protect her from severe marital violence when she attempted to resist the situation that she found herself in. After she gave birth and her parturition period passed, she told me that Hadi had asked to have sexual intercourse with her. She was angry and hurt by her husband's secret second marriage and refused to 'serve' her husband's sexual needs. When she rejected Hadi's approaches, he forced her violently, hitting her face and even tying her hands together, which made her feel very powerless. She was hurt and uncomfortable having intercourse that way. She felt, quite correctly, that she had been raped by her own husband. It was not a single occurrence, either – he did it once or twice a month. Lina told me that she had actually asked Hadi to go to his second wife when he wanted to have intercourse, but Hadi kept forcing her to 'serve' his sexual needs. She assumed that for her husband, each wife might have a different sexual attraction. Lina told me that she could not stand being violently raped by her husband. Therefore, to avoid violence, she just let her husband satisfy his sexual needs. But she said to her husband, 'You can have my body but do not think that you can have my soul.' He replied, 'It does not matter.'[37]

Hadi seems to be unaware that his second marriage has taken away Lina's right to sexual enjoyment with her husband, the right of which most Muslim men and women remain unaware. He also seems to be unaware of 'raping' Lina. His unawareness of 'raping' his wife might have been influenced by classical *fiqh* and the Indonesian construction of masculinity, that a husband has the right over his wife's body and that his wife has to 'serve' his sexual needs instantly whenever he requires, ignoring the Qur'anic injunction to treat his wife kindly. If only this was happening after the enactment of *Undang-Undang Penghapusan Kekerasan dalam Rumah Tangga* (Law on the Eradication of Domestic Violence) and Lina was willing to report this sexual violence to the police, Hadi could possibly be jailed for up to 12 years or fined up to Rp. 36,000,000 (A$5,142).[38]

After discovering her husband's secret second marriage, Lina felt that overall her married life had been turned upside down:

> In the beginning, my husband's practice of polygamy was full of lies and violence in which I became the victim. I could be crazy. If I had to choose between spiritual happiness and having much money, I would prefer the former because it was easier to have much money than to attain spiritual happiness. Since I found out about my husband's polygamy, we often had arguments in which he often hit my face and kicked my feet until they were blue. Once, he pushed my body violently, which broke my left arm. Therefore, I concluded that polygamy is very painful for me as the first wife.[39]

> After he broke my arm, I reported him to the police. The report attracted many journalists' attention, especially because my husband is a public figure. Many journalists called me and requested an interview. To avoid meeting

them, and for the sake of my children, I withdrew my report to the police. I also lied to the journalists and said there was nothing wrong with my marriage. Many of my friends blamed me for lying to the journalists. However, I did it for the sake of my children, who were depressed seeing me being pushed violently, shocked by the arrival of the police and disturbed by the presence of so many journalists.[40]

After her arm was broken, Lina asked for a divorce. It is possible that her economic independence, her educational background and her family support meant that she did not hesitate to seek an escape when her husband became violent. After the divorce she lived in her parents' house. She took the three younger children with her, while the three older children lived with their father. The misery that she experienced motivated her to enhance her education. Therefore she decided to study for her Master's degree.

During her present studies, Lina told me that she had enjoyed making friends with other postgraduate students. Some of her male friends had expressed interest in her, and others tried to matchmake her with other male friends. But she expressed her discomfort about these overtures to me, saying that she did not want to be regarded as 'a cheap woman' (*perempuan murahan*), who would easily accept such proposals. She felt offended if the man who approached her was married. She said:

I needed to think many times before I could accept a marriage proposal from a widower and even more from a married man. A good woman will not want to be the second wife. It is important for women to be morally educated in order to reject being the second wife.[41]

While she was staying in her parents' house, Hadi and his three older children visited Lina each month. During these visits, Lina could see that her older children were not being looked after well, because they looked dirty and unkempt. At every visit, Hadi also gave Lina some money, which, according to Lina, was more than enough to support herself, her children and pay her tuition fees. Lina told me that she did not know why Hadi was being so generous to her. 'I did not know what he meant by giving me much money. I do not know whether he did it because he still loved me or because I am the mother of his children.'

During her divorce, Lina's oldest son had an accident. It is thought that he tried to commit suicide because of the emotional distress he suffered over his father's polygamy and his parents' divorce. For the sake of her children, she told me, Hadi had begged her to remarry him. She agreed, on the condition that he divorce Nani. Lina told me that she received a Rp. 25,000,000 (A$3571) *mahar* from her husband, which she used to pay for a pilgrimage in Mecca, a journey she and Hadi made together. During the pilgrimage, he promised her that he would improve their marriage – but he did not fulfill his promise. She told me that she regretted remarrying her husband, because he had neither divorced Nani nor treated her well. Therefore, she asked for a divorce again but Hadi told her that he would never divorce her again.

The repercussions of polygamy affected Lina not only in term of her emotional and sexual relationship with Hadi, but also in her social relationships with her neighbors. Before Hadi took another wife, Lina used to participate in the monthly religious gathering (*pengajian*) in her neighborhood. As an educated woman, she sometimes preached at these gatherings. But after she discovered the second marriage, she withdrew from any social events, because she felt ashamed and possibly fearful that her husband's second marriage had become a topic of gossip. She said that her neighbors were concerned by her withdrawal and expected her to continue to preach. Lina said that she was not mentally ready to do so because she was afraid that she could not practice what she preached; she said that she preferred to solve her marriage problems first. Even though it was her husband who had taken another wife, Lina was aware that some neighbors blamed her for not being able to 'serve' him well (*tidak bisa melayani suami dengan baik*) and for not accepting polygamy.

After she suffered both a nervous disorder and a heart attack after finding out about her husband's polygamy, some neighbors commented that Lina was like an unbeliever (*seperti orang yang tidak beriman*) because she could not accept polygamy. She replied, 'I have tried to accept it, but my body is not strong enough to deal with it.' In this difficult time, she often visited her parents, who were shocked when they first heard about Hadi's polygamy. Lina no longer had parents-in-law because both of them had passed away. She told me that she had not yet finished writing her thesis owing to her nervous disorder, which she believed to be caused by her husband's violence. In addition, she felt depressed when she saw her husband and Nani naked on their bed.

On my second visit to Lina's house, she told me that she no longer wanted to live with Hadi, but he did not want to divorce her. But every time she packed up to leave the house, one of her children would ask, 'Where are you going, Mama?' (Lina did not stop crying throughout our interview):

> If I only considered my husband's betrayal, I would not live here anymore, but I must also consider my children. Therefore, I try to be here. I often avoid my husband by locking myself in my room when my husband is home, so I can save myself from being hit or touched by him. I feel disgusted and I hate him. I only come out from my room when my husband has left the house.[42]

Because her husband neither divorced her nor treated her well, Lina chose her own way to behave around her husband.

> I like to hurt him by not talking to him, or not asking his permission whenever I go out from the house. He chose his own way so I choose mine. When I feel depressed, I just go out by myself in the car. When I feel too dizzy to drive, I just leave the car by the side of the road and then go home on public transport. I have someone pick up the car later.
>
> In the morning, I usually wake up and prepare breakfast for my children. They greet me before going to school, which makes me happy. When they have gone, I get ready myself. My husband usually gets up just after I get

> ready. When he sees me ready to go, he asks where I am going. I tell him, 'I want to go wherever I want to go. Since you have another wife, my role in this house is only as a mother of my children and I have done it for this morning.'[43]

After saying that, Lina saw her husband looked disappointed, and she felt satisfied.

> Now I know the way to hurt him, not by confronting him or by having an argument, but by avoiding and ignoring him. He seemed to be disappointed if nobody in the house asked him where he wanted to go or where he came from. It was not only me who avoided him, but also my children.[44]

The above two quotations show that Lina and her children cannot just be regarded as powerless victims of polygamy. They could not accept or accommodate Hadi's second marriage. Instead, they ignored him – 'resisted and protested' about Hadi's second marriage in their own way, to borrow McLeod's words (Macleod, 1992). Lina also told me that she wanted to be interviewed by me in order to counter the view that polygamy is positive and beautiful. She wanted other people, especially women, to learn from her misery in order to reject being a second wife and in order to provide an opposing viewpoint to this practice. Her case illustrates a number of the key themes here: the negative effects on children's well-being of polygamous marriages; the sacrifices that women, trying to be 'good' mothers (*ibu yang baik*), make in subsuming their own interests for what they perceive to be the sake of their children; the possible effects on first wives' physical and emotional well-being of such marriages; and the ways that even a highly educated, economically independent woman with a strong network of familial support could still suffer extreme marital violence.

Rejecting polygamy (the Contextualist)

In this section, I present two case studies of women who preferred divorce to remaining in a polygamous marriage. These two cases form the strongest resistance to polygamous marriages when compared to the previous four cases. Both women interviewed here are highly educated, and both tend to approach the Qur'anic verse 4: 3 in relation to polygamy contextually.

Case Study 5: Hanny

Interviewee: Hanny (42) and her two daughters: Syifa (22) and Rosiani (14).
Hanny: 'I really disagree with polygamy and I do not want to share the love of my husband with other women.'

Personal background

The following case study explores an unhappy marriage that was based on lies and betrayal, and finally ended in divorce. It will also show how seriously Hanny took the decision to divorce, and the care she took to ensure that she and her children were not disadvantaged. This underlines the extent of her agency when faced with her husband's infidelity.

Hanny cared about her appearance, dressed well and put on a head covering whenever she went out. She had just been divorced, after 23 years in an unhappy marriage. Her ex-husband, Asep (46), a lecturer and religious preacher, had claimed that he was a single man when he married her in 1980, but he was actually a married man with two children. Hanny, a housewife, found out about her husband's previous marriage when she visited his parents about six years after her marriage. Prior to that, Hanny never knew that she had become Asep's second wife.

Hanny met Asep in 1979, when he was undertaking academic social work (*Kuliah Kerja Nyata*/KKN) in Hanny's parents' village, as part of his undergraduate course requirements. Hanny – a senior high school graduate at that time – and Asep became interested in each other. Hanny's parents also admired Asep's talent for religious preaching, so they supported Hanny's relationship with him, and arranged for the two to get married. They were married in 1980, when Hanny was 19 and Asep 23. Hanny's wealthy parents celebrated their marriage, but none of Asep's family attended the celebration, not even his parents. Later, Hanny realized that Asep wanted to keep his marriage to Hanny secret from his parents, until he could divorce his first wife.

After Hanny discovered her husband's first marriage 16 years ago, she wanted a divorce. But she was unable to support herself financially yet, and her four children were still small. To prepare for a more independent life, she continued her studies by taking undergraduate courses. She also tried to save some money that she had received from her husband. In addition, she bought some land in her parents' village. Overall, her preparation took 16 years. This shows how careful Hanny was in planning her life after divorce, indicative of her agency and negotiation around her husband's betrayal of their marriage. She described her misery:

> Throughout my marriage with Asep, he often had affairs with other women such as his colleague, Yanny (39), and his student, Dina (23). Knowing my marriage was in jeopardy, I prepared myself by continuing my study in tertiary education .... In 2002, I found out that Asep had married Nurul (46), a widow, during his pilgrimage to Mecca. Since I found out about Asep's additional marriages, I refused to sleep with him, feeling disgusted and fearing I might get AIDS.
>
> I often asked for a divorce, but Asep always rejected this. He said 'Why do you want a divorce, what can you do after divorce other than selling vegetable salad?' I was furious at his undermining my ability to survive after the divorce. I said, 'Look, you will see me playing golf in Karawang [a small city located near Jakarta].'[45]

Hanny ably contrasted Asep's assumptions about her poor prospects with her playing golf, an elite sport. In saying that, Hanny used very rough Sundanese language, which shows no respect at all to the person she was speaking to, because of her anger.

Hanny's view on polygamy

When I asked Hanny about her views on polygamy, as an Islamic studies tertiary graduate she displayed detailed knowledge of the Qur'anic verses and employed a comprehensive approach in reading the verses:

> In my opinion, people tend to read the verse on polygamy partially. In fact the Qur'an says, If you fear that you shall not be able to deal justly with the orphans, marry women of your choice, two, or three, or four; but if you fear that you shall not be able to deal justly (with them), then only one. I regret that many people do not continue reading the verse until then only one. In addition, there is another verse in the chapter An-Nisa': 129 which says: You are never able to do justice between wives even if it is your ardent desire. Based on these verses, I really disagree with polygamy and I do not want to share the love of my husband with other women.[46]

Hanny's disagreement with polygamy is clear in this quote. It can also be seen from her request for a divorce, despite her husband's continued refusals. Hanny asked her children to ask their father to divorce her. In order that they understood her situation, Hanny explained to her children that she had wanted a divorce for a long time – ever since she found out about Asep's previous marriage. But she thought it would be better to wait until they grew up. Her son and daughters – Syifa (22), Amin (20), Nisa (18) and Rosiani (14) – who already knew about their father's affairs with other women, supported the divorce. They understood that their mother could no longer live with their father. It was Amin, fulfilling his mother's request, who asked Asep to divorce his mother. Hanny knew very well that Asep would listen to Amin, his only son. Syifa and Rosiani told me that they were really sad about their parents' divorce, but they did not like their father's affairs with other women. They expected that their mother would find another man who could make her happy after her divorce.

Hanny knew that she had lost the economic benefits she had received through her marriage to Asep after the divorce but, on balance, she was happier as a divorcée because his betrayals had left her exhausted. After the divorce was finalized, Hanny remained in her big, luxurious house with her oldest daughter and her granddaughter. Her other three children were studying away from home. Asep continued to support his children while Hanny began to run a small business to support herself. She realized that divorcées are socially stigmatized and therefore she avoided going out with men, especially at night. As the former wife of a civil servant, Hanny was actually entitled to one third of Asep's salary – but he gave her less than the amount to which she was entitled. Hanny did not want to argue about it, because she was concerned that asking him for money would debase her.

Case Study 6: Risa.

Interviewee: Risa, 'I could not share my husband with another woman, so I preferred divorce.'

Personal background

Risa (35) had a Master's degree in law from an Australian university. At the time of interview, she was preparing to undertake doctoral studies at an elite Australian university. She had been active in a non-government organisation (NGO) before working as a university lecturer. Risa had been married to Ramli (37), an NGO employee, for 12 years (1989–2001) and they had three children. As I shall describe, when she found out that her husband had taken another wife Risa preferred divorce.

Risa met Ramli through a friend when she was an undergraduate student. Three weeks after the meeting, they decided to get married – without courtship, or even a chance to really get to know each other. The marriage was not formally celebrated, and only Ramli's parents and relatives attended the wedding itself. Risa's parents did not know about the marriage – she had not been in contact with them since 1985, when they threw her out of their home on discovering that Risa had converted from Christianity to Islam. Seventeen-year-old Risa could survive, live independently and take a law degree at a state university in Bandung by relying on her income from writing. In addition, as a newly converted Muslim, Risa may well have felt that her Christian parents could not act as proper guardians for her marriage.[47]

Risa's attitude toward her parents' guardianship seemed to be influenced by the knowledge of Islamist teaching that she gained after her conversion. She had become a member of an Islamist religious gathering – similar to that described by Smith-Hefner (2005) at Gadjah Mada University, Yogyakarta – during her studies in Bandung. Under the rules of this religious gathering, which mostly took place in campus mosques of secular universities, courtship was discouraged.

Risa's marital happiness with Ramli lasted only a short time, because she soon found out that she could not get along with him:

> Ramli was a quiet person, so I did not have someone to share my feelings with or discuss the problems we faced. Many of our marriage problems were left unresolved because of the absence of communication. I had a higher income than Ramli and I mainly supported our family's needs. My unhappiness culminated in 2001 when I found out that Ramli had secretly married another woman, Mamah. I could not share my husband with another woman, so I preferred divorce.[48]

Risa's view on polygamy

'Polygamy is a solution in an emergency situation,' Risa told me, 'but Islam is not a polygamous religion. Islam is a monogamous religion.'[49] This view, together with her economic independence and high educational level, seemed to affect the way she reacted to her husband's polygamous marriage, which she felt was not religiously justified.

Risa's reactions to Ramli's second marriage

Risa told me that when she was taking an English course to prepare for departure to Australia to take her Master's degree, a woman called her and introduced herself as Mamah, Ramli's second wife. She asked Risa for a transparent, not secret polygamous marriage. Risa asked how long ago Mamah had been married to Ramli, and Mamah replied that she had been married to Ramli for a year. Risa told me that she was very sad knowing her husband had another wife, and felt that she lost her balance:

> When I took a breath, I felt like I lost half of my breath. When I walked, I felt like I was unstable, until one day I was nearly hit by a car in Dago. I felt that I had been treated unjustly, but I was too proud to show my jealousy. Since I found out that my husband had married another woman, I did not want to have sexual intercourse with him and preferred to live in a separate house before I finally asked for divorce. I did not want to have a roster. I even felt weird hearing that word.[50]

After finding out about her husband's second marriage, Risa visited a psychiatrist who suggested that she express her feelings to Ramli and have an argument with him. Risa obeyed the psychiatrist's suggestion, because she realized that up to that point she had never had any quarrels with her husband. Both Ramli and Risa had avoided each other instead of communicating to solve their marital problems. When she met Ramli, Risa asked him to have an argument with her, in which she expressed her feelings about polygamy, quoted at the beginning of this chapter.

After that, Risa invited both Mamah and Ramli to see her. When the three met, Risa asked Ramli to divorce her. Risa told me that Ramli actually did not want to divorce her, but Risa insisted. Risa said to Ramli, 'If I were not your wife and I see both of you sitting side by side like that, I would not feel hurt. But because I am your wife, I have a headache and my headache needs a remedy.'[51] Risa said that Ramli did not want her to suffer, and therefore he agreed to divorce her at the end of 2001.

Relatives' and neighbors' reactions to Ramli's second marriage

Risa told me that after about three months of Ramli's second marriage, Ramli's parents found out about this second marriage – nine months before Risa found out. The parents disagreed with the marriage, and asked Ramli to divorce Mamah. Ramli obeyed his parents by divorcing Mamah. Even though Risa did not know yet about Ramli's secret second marriage, she noticed something strange happened to Ramli. For instance, Ramli stayed away from home for two weeks without contacting Risa or letting her know where he was or when he would come home. Risa also felt that Ramli had been cold and indifferent to her during the marriage, and even more after he took a second wife. In hindsight, Risa realized why he had been absent and cold to her. Risa said that before his second marriage, she only had sexual intercourse with Ramli once a month, and after his second marriage, even less. Several months after Ramli divorced Mamah to obey his parents, he remarried Mamah in 2000, but

Risa only knew about his second marriage in 2001 when Mamah called her and informed her that Ramli had married her.

Risa told me that Ramli's parents disagreed with Ramli's second marriage, and were against Ramli's divorcing Risa. Risa told me that she had a very close relationship with her parents-in-law, especially Ramli's mother, a midwife, who had helped Risa during the births of all three of her children.

When Risa got a divorce, she told me that it seemed to her that none of her neighbors knew about her divorce. But Risa was not close to her neighbors in any case. Even her children, she said, seemed not to know what had happened, because they had never seen any conflict between their parents. Before the divorce took place, Risa explained to her children, 'Father has someone to look after him, therefore Father and Mother cannot live together anymore.' Her children asked, 'Then, who will look after Mother?' Ramli said, 'There will be someone who will look after Mother.'[52] This conversation shows how calm Risa remained in facing her divorce. It also shows how Ramli and Risa were used to hiding their own true feelings, and hardly communicated with each other.

Varying degrees of women's acceptance of and resistance to polygamy

The case of Arsa–Jajang–Lia highlights several important themes. First, Jajang's assumption that he did not need to ask the permission of his wife before taking another wife is indicative of his resistance to the secular government law, the 1974 Marriage Law, and is also indicative of his generalized belief that polygamy was his right. This also shows his understanding that *shari'a* includes what is written in *fiqh* books. Jajang was not the only man to display such resistance. Many other polygamous men manipulate the state legal process through such strategies as assuming different identities, paying a bribe or having an unregistered marriage, which I consider to be the strongest resistance. The case also shows us how his second wife, Lia, had recourse to legal protection. This is also illustrative of the attitude, shared by a number of my research participants, of making the best of a difficult situation. For instance, Lia may well have felt that being a second wife might be better than being a single woman with a very low income. Arsa also might well be not as confident as the other three women who preferred divorce to polygamous marriage, and not ready to face the challenge of the cultural assumption that if a marriage fails it is a woman's fault. She also might have been worried about the stigma attached to divorce. Arsa's belief, reinforced by her husband, was that by not asking for divorce and enduring the situation she would receive a spiritual reward. This view is also supported by many male religious preachers. They sometimes encourage women to accept their husbands' polygamous marriages, by saying that they will be rewarded in the hereafter and enter paradise (Jones, 1994: 279).[53] But the most important consideration for Arsa seems to be that divorcing Jajang would allow Lia, her rival, to win the battle: to be the only wife of Jajang, the possible original intention behind Lia's increasing economic and emotional demands on Jajang.

There are similarities between the cases of Arsa and Risa: they decided to get married before knowing their intended husband very well; they married without courtship (*pacaran*) because they disagreed with such courtship, believing that Islam does not favor it, because courtship may lead to *zina* (an illicit sexual relationship). The price they had to pay for not spending enough time getting to know their intended husband before marriage was that they did not know much about his character. Therefore, it is likely that they found it difficult to build a strong emotional bond. This absence of such a bond, for instance between Risa and her husband, appeared to open the door to the possibility of the presence of a third party in the marriage.

Both Arsa and Risa did not formally celebrate their marriage. As noted in Chapter 2, such absence of celebration can create uneasiness. This applied to Arsa. She felt that some of her neighbors were suspicious that she might be 'Married By Accident' or, as she jokingly called it, MBA. Arsa's neighbors might assume that she was already pregnant before her marriage, and therefore they assumed that she did not celebrate her marriage in order to hide her pregnancy. The neighbors did not know that it was the conflict between Jajang and his father-in-law over the wedding arrangements that nullified the celebration. But it was also possible that Jajang might have had another reason for requesting an 'unusual' guest arrangement in order to keep the celebration from occurring, as he might have been embarrassed to have a wedding celebration take place without his contributing any money. Jajang told me that he had no money at all on the day of his marriage:

> When I married Arsa, I only had Rp. 2,250,000 [about A$320]. I spent this money to pay for marriage administration and to buy Arsa's *mahar*. Therefore, on the day of my marriage, I did not have any money at all. During the first three years of my marriage, I was mostly economically supported by my father-in-law.

Arsa's and Risa's cases are also similar in terms of the level of education and income. Both Arsa's and Risa's level of education was higher than that of their husbands. Because Jajang had only a very low income, Arsa's parents provided for most of Arsa's household needs. Similarly, in Risa's case, her income was higher than that of Ramli, and it was she who mostly provided for the economic needs of her household. It is possible that both Jajang and Ramli felt inferior to their wives owing to their lower levels of education and income. As noted, in Indonesia, husbands usually have a higher level of education and income than their wives. They are expected to be the head of the household, and are regarded as superior to all members of their family, including their wife.

It is possible that both Jajang and Ramli felt inferior to their wives because of their inability to properly fulfill their expected responsibility in supporting their households. Their failure to provide enough money for their household members and their lower level of education compared to their wives may have violated their sense of masculinity. Their feelings of inferiority vis-à-vis their wives, together with the social factors conducive to polygamy in the post-Soeharto era, may have encouraged Jajang and Ramli to take additional wives to demonstrate their masculine superiority.[54] Similarly, Rosyid, whose income was lower than Tuti's, may have also felt inferior to her. In taking another wife, the three men had done something which Muslim women cannot do, in order to demonstrate their superiority in the Indonesian Muslim context. They had taken additional wives with similar characteristics, who were educationally and economically in lower positions than themselves. By having 'inferior' wives, their male superiority seemed to be confirmed and their sense of masculine pride was sustained. This shows the problematic nature of the 'norm' prescribed by the state through its Marriage Law which stipulates that men are breadwinner heads of the family (Article 3 and 34), regardless of the fact that not all men are superior to their wives in education and income level. These are all compelling arguments for the amendment of the Marriage Law as suggested by LBH APIK (2000).

All the established wives mentioned in the above case studies can be seen as victims of their husbands' polygamy. They were not merely victims, however. Each had actively resisted her husband's polygamy, though the degree of their resistance varied. For instance, Arsa displayed the weakest resistance; she made an effort to reconcile her beliefs about polygamy and the bitter reality of sharing a husband with another woman, to keep her marriage intact. Tuti exercised moderate resistance: she initially accommodated her husband's polygamy, but finally brought the second marriage to an end. Hanny and Risa showed the strongest resistance since both preferred divorce to involvement in polygamous marriage.

Hanny, Risa and another woman who also chose to divorce her husband, Ema, were well aware of the negative image attached to being divorcées (*janda*) in Indonesia. But they were ready to face the challenge of being stigmatized rather than share their husband with another woman. After their divorces, both Ema and Hanny were visited by men with proposals of marriage. They refused, and told me that they wanted to enjoy their freedom in not having to 'serve' men until they were truly ready to get married again.[55] Hanny said:

> I am afraid that I might not be able to get along with my new husband. I am afraid that my new husband would not like my cooking and might complain about it. Therefore, I prefer to be alone for a while and enjoy the freedom in not needing to 'serve' a husband.

Risa preferred to remarry after her divorce from Ramli. Risa told me that she was very sad about her divorce. She was in her mandatory Islamic waiting period (*'iddah*) when she went to Australia in January 2002 with two of her children to undertake her Master's studies. Many of her friends tried to comfort her, and when her waiting period was over, they looked for a prospective husband for her. Among the men from whom she received proposals, she was interested in Cecep, an Indonesian doctoral student at the university where Risa was studying. Risa finished her Master's in ten months, so she and the two children returned to Indonesia in that same year (2002). In September 2003, Cecep, a divorcé without children, proposed to her and they were married in late 2003. The marriage with Cecep was celebrated and both Risa's and Cecep's parents attended. After the marriage, Risa and Cecep lived together in Indonesia for a while, but he had to return to Sydney to continue his studies. At the time of interview (21 February 2004), Risa said that she had received another scholarship to undertake her doctoral studies in Australia. She was preparing to go there in June to study and to live with her husband. She said that she was happy with her current marriage, especially because Cecep was a communicative person.

From the case studies of the three women who preferred divorce, it is obvious that education and economic independence play important roles in giving women the resources to leave an unhappy marriage. Three of my interviewees are tertiary graduates, and have economic resources. Even though Hanny had never worked for money during her marriage with Asep, after the divorce her education level and her savings allowed her to run a business to support herself economically. As Wolf observes in relation to Javanese women, 'women's control over economic resources may strengthen their position in other decision-making processes, particularly when their marriage, [and] sexuality, ... are at stake' (Wolf, 1992: 229). In addition, Hanny's wealthy mother had always supported her, so she did not have to leave her house after her divorce because it was built on her mother's land.

All the women mentioned in the case studies above believe that Islam permits polygamy. But Tuti and Lina could only accept it under certain conditions, such as when a wife cannot 'serve' her husband well. In Rosa's words, polygamy is like 'an emergency exit', which can only be resorted to in an emergency situation. The only women who displayed unconditional 'acceptance' of polygamy were Arsa and Aida, whose cases will be presented in Chapter 5, because both of them believed that women's biological capacities to serve their husbands' sexual needs were limited by such factors as menstruation. Aida, Arsa, Rosa, Tuti and Lina all seemed to believe that, as Muslims, they had to accept polygamy as part of their acceptance of their religion, otherwise they would feel that they were not 'devout' Muslims. This feeling seems to be stronger for Arsa and Aida than for Tuti, for instance, perhaps because Arsa and Aida lived among Islamists who mostly suggest that polygamy is part of *shari'a*. Jajang, as we saw, had frequently advised Arsa to accept polygamy as a trial of her belief in Islam. Therefore, even though Arsa was unhappy and very wary of her husband's polygamous marriage, she stayed in her marriage out of her religious devotion and for the sake of her children. Tuti also told me about her regret about being unable to accept her husband's polygamy, and her fear of being labeled as a non-devout Muslim for not accepting polygamy. Tuti's initial accommodation to her husband's polygamous marriage and her later attempts to resist it illustrate the religious dilemma she experienced. On the one hand, she might feel that she was a devout woman if she supported Rosyid's polygamy. On the other, her support for polygamy caused her personal suffering and financial difficulty.

The case studies also show the importance of a woman's social network in putting more or less pressure on her to either 'accept' or reject her husband's polygamous marriage. Also, the way in which the women responded to polygamy was very much affected both by their understanding of polygamy in Islam and the attitudes of people who lived around them. For instance, unlike Arsa, who lived among militant Muslims in Jakarta, Tuti lived among moderate Muslims in Bandung, who seemed overall to have negative attitudes toward polygamy. Therefore, Tuti had less social pressure than Arsa to accept polygamy as a sign of her religious piety. In addition, Tuti could keep her husband's second marriage secret from her neighbors. Only Hanny, Risa and another informant, Ema, appeared not to be afraid of being labeled as not accepting Islam by not accepting polygamy. Even though the three of them believed that Islam permits polygamy, they seemed to interpret the Qur'anic verse 4: 3 in the terms that I have described as Contextualist.

As shown in the above case studies, all polygamous marriages received negative responses, from either first wives, their relatives or their neighbors. These negative reactions were not only directed at the husbands who took another wife, but also at the first wives, whom some neighbors assumed were unable to 'serve' their husbands well. The neighbors' assumptions were presumably shaped by the dominant Indonesian constructions of womanhood that I have described.

The cases of Aida and Arsa, who were willing to collude with their husbands' polygamy, are exceptional among my research participants. I have suggested that this was probably because they and their husbands belong to the group I have termed the Textualists, who interpret Islam as permitting polygamy and see polygamy as part of *shari'a*. As noted, both Aida and Arsa were also members of an Islamist organization, and supporters of an Islamist political party. They lived nearby, only 200 metres away from each other in an area dominated by members of the *Partai Keadilan Sejahtera/PKS* (Welfare Justice Party). The logo of the party was displayed everywhere, including on the two women's houses, because at the time of interview Indonesia was facing its general election. Indeed, Arsa tried to persuade me to join PKS by giving me a brochure on the party. Many women there dressed in a similar way to Aida and Arsa: a loose long dress with a headscarf covering more than half of the body. There were also several Islamic institutions and mosques, which became the centre of Muslim activities. Along the street between the mosques and the Islamic institutions, there were about eight bookshops selling many books written by Islamist/fundamentalist thinkers, which Arsa and Aida seemed to know well.[56]

The neighbors in all case studies seemed to react similarly to the first wives. They assumed that there must be something wrong with the wife if her husband takes another wife, as I noted in the Introduction. This assumption seemed to affect the way the first wives reacted to their husbands' polygamous marriage. For instance, both Tuti and Lina became more introverted when they found out that their husbands wanted another woman. Lina even withdrew herself from her social activities. She must have felt embarrassed or afraid that her neighbors might assume that there was something wrong with her.

The cases in this chapter show that the discovery of a husband's infidelity or secret second marriage had profound effects on the women's emotional well-being. The cases of Tuti, Lina and Rosa, for instance, show how the issue of sexuality is apparent in many of the informants' narratives – but very few wished to discuss this explicitly. Unspoken sexual jealousy can be seen from the loss of pleasure expressed by several first wives, who were very reluctant to have sexual intercourse with their husbands after discovering their second marriages. They came to see their sexual relations with their husbands as merely a 'duty' of a wife to 'serve' her husband. The emotional distress experienced by most of the first wives is evidence that their marriages cannot achieve the aim outlined in the Qur'an: to achieve peace and tranquility.[57]

Informants had many ways of dealing with their husbands' second marriages. For instance, Tuti tried to end her husband's second marriage, while Arsa wanted to take revenge on Lia by suggesting Jajang take a third wife in order to give Lia a 'taste of her own medicine'. Arsa was not the only first wife who wanted to take revenge on the second wife in this manner. Rini, Puspo Wardoyo's first wife, reportedly supported Wardoyo in taking his third wife, in order to have revenge on his second wife (Nurbowo and Mulyono, 2003). Anisah, Wardoyo's third wife, also reported Rini's eagerness to support Wardoyo's third marriage. According to Anisah, Rini even accompanied Wardoyo to visit Anisah's parents to persuade them to agree to Wardoyo's proposed marriage to their daughter. Overall, most of the first wives actively resisted their husbands' polygamous marriages. They showed their agency by trying various methods to end their husbands' polygamy. Some, like Tuti, were successful in their efforts to end the second marriage. Others, like Lina, were unsuccessful, and still have to live with the misery of sharing a husband with another woman, for the sake of the children. The cases of Lina and Hanny also fit very well with Kandiyoti's argument that it is not easy to bargain with patriarchy; even though resistance is possible, this resistance is 'always circumscribed by the limits of the culturally conceivable' (Kandiyoti, 1998: 147). The case of Lina shows that even though she was economically independent, had a high educational level and received substantial support from her family, the cultural construction of femininity, which stressed the importance of motherhood, had made her sacrifice her own personal happiness for the sake of her children. For example, Lina's report to the police of her husband's physical violence shows that she was well aware of the existing law that could protect her from a violent husband. But her consideration of family dignity, expecially the well-being of her children, made her withdraw herself from taking any legal action. Similarly, Hanny had to wait until her children grew up before divorcing her husband, even though her mother was economically supportive.

While their kinship networks were important to many of my female informants, in providing support and refuge from an unhappy marriage, not all the women I interviewed had such support. Rosa, for example, had lost both her parents. Even those women who had a supportive family did not always turn to them. For instance, Tuti preferred to hide her husband's polygamous marriage from her parents, who lived about four hours by bus from Bandung. Aida and Arsa also preferred to stay in a polygamous marriage for various reasons, even though their parents were very concerned with their emotional well-being and urged them to divorce their husbands. All of these examples are indicative of the structural autonomy of the nuclear family in Java, discussed by Geertz (1961) and Koentjaraningrat (1967), which I outlined in Chapter 2.

The case studies presented in this chapter have provided information on how women view polygamy, how they feel about, react to and negotiate around their husbands' polygamous marriages. This chapter has shown that the fulfillment of the male's interest to have children or to fulfill his desire for another woman has brought many first wives physical, mental and economic suffering. As I have shown, Arsa and Tuti shared a similar view: that the presence of their husband's second wife has taken away some of their economic rights. Lina, Rosa and Arsa had also experienced a significant degree of emotional and physical abuse. This evidence supports the arguments of many progressive Indonesian feminists, who argue that polygamy is a form of violence against women and therefore is against women's human rights (Lestari and Munti, 2003; Reyneta, 2003). As I also argue in my conclusion, the emotional distress experienced by most of the first wives is evidence that their polygamous marriages cannot achieve the aims outlined in the Qur'an ar-Ruum 21: to achieve peace and tranquility. The next chapter will explore further the issues of emotional and economic well-being within polygamous households.

5 Polygamous households

This chapter presents the first academic study of the inner working of polygamous households in Java through a series of detailed case studies. It discusses the relationships between wives in polygamous marriages in the context where Islamist campaigns had stressed acceptance of polygamy as a sign of wives' religious piety, and represented relationships between co-wives as 'good' and harmonious. Here I assess these claims by exploring the everyday relationships between wives. As I have stressed in preceding chapters, most Muslims believe that Islam requires a polygamous husband to treat all his wives equally. This equal treatment is usually measured by a husband's equal distribution of time, attention and resources among his wives. Therefore, the second section of this chapter looks at the rosters that polygamous husbands use to divide their time between wives. To explore these processes, the chapter also describes the ways in which polygamous households celebrate important days, such as the first day of *Idul Fitri*, and attend familial and official parties. I also discuss economic management in polygamous households, to see whether a polygamous husband treats his wives justly by distributing equal economic resources, and to see how polygamous marriage affects the economic well-being of first wives. As children were also involved in these households, I shall briefly examine the possible influence of their father's polygamous marriage on the emotional and economic well-being of the children. Most of the data in this section derives from the interviews with mothers, and from adult children recalling their family life.

The case studies discussed below have several important themes. They show the complexity of the relationships between wives in polygamous marriages. This depends on the way in which the husbands took another wife, and whether this took place secretly or with the first wife's consent. Financial capability to support more than one wife is stipulated in the 1974 Marriage Law as one of the requirements for polygamy. This aims at preventing injustice toward women and children who could be economically deprived if the husband/father took another wife. But as my case studies will show, many polygamous husbands disobeyed the Law. They took another wife even though they were not economically capable of supporting her. Therefore, some women had to share a household with their co-wives. My study of these Javanese households also shows the considerable differences among husbands in 'managing' their polygamous marriages, in which some of them seem to cooperate with their wives, and others just ignore their wives' feelings and acted as they wish.

Relationships between wives in polygamous marriages

The relationships between wives in polygamous marriages among my research participants can be categorized in four ways. The first category is that in which an established wife has never met her husband's second wife, and they have never contacted each other. The second category is that in which a second wife has contacted her husband's first wife by phone. The third category is a relationship in which a first wife has met her husband's second wife, but they have not had a good relationship. The fourth category is a relationship in which a first wife and a second wife have known each other and tried to have a good relationship, even though they have often felt jealous of each other.

In Bandung, two out of twelve first wives – Hanny and Ema – belonged to the first category. Both Hanny and Ema had never met or known another wife of their husbands. As discussed in Chapter 4, these women chose to ask for divorce instead of sharing their husbands with another woman. Two out of twelve women – Risa and Dahlia – belonged to the second category. Both Risa and Dahlia had been contacted by phone by their husbands' new wives. For instance, Dahlia, who had a Master's degree and worked as a part-time lecturer, was contacted by Nita, Dadi's third wife. Nita asked whether Dadi, had told Dahlia that he would divorce Dahlia.[1] Dahlia regarded Nita's call as extremely intimidating, and felt very upset by this question. She told me that she was not mentally ready to receive such a call. Seven out of the twelve first wives in Bandung – Mila, Rina, Esih (the first wife of Dadan), Linda (the first wife of Fahmi), Tuti (the first wife of Rosyid), Eli (the first wife of Yaya) and Lina (first wife of Hadi) – belonged to the third category.[2] They had met their co-wives, but the relationship between them was conflict-laden. Lina, for example, was unwilling to have anything to do with her husband's additional wife. The reason for this conflict-laden relationship may be that their husbands' additional marriages took place secretly or without the first wife's consent. Of the seven women above, only Tuti had been asked by her husband for her consent before he took another wife. Another cause of conflict might be unjust treatment on the part of the husband, or that the second wife had placed increasing economical and economic demands on the husband.

An example of a husband who took another wife secretly is Suhadi. His first wife, Mila, became uneasy when she found out that Suhadi had married Maya. Mila and Maya had known each other before Suhadi married Maya, because Maya was Suhadi's junior when she was in junior high school, and both of them had often participated in a Qur'an reading competition (*Musabaqah Tilawatil Qur'an/MTQ*). Mila told me that she was curious about Maya's motives in marrying Suhadi and invited Maya to dinner at her house. On this occasion, Maya told Mila that she would not take Suhadi's main salary, which was only for Mila. Maya said that what she wanted from Suhadi was protection, and sisterhood with Mila. Dinner did not last long, because Mila lost her temper and Maya quickly returned to her home.

Lina revealed another example of unjust treatment by a husband. During her pregnancy, Lina's husband, Hadi, mostly spent his time with Nani, his second wife. Lina displayed her sadness at this unjust treatment:

> At that time, Hadi just received a new car from his office, which he used mostly with Nani, while I had to go alone in a pedi cab [*becak*], to my obstetrical appointments, even when it was raining. Sadly, one day the pedi cab driver lost control of the pedi cab and I fell out of it. How could a polygamous husband forget his pregnant wife? My doctor told me that because of my heart attack, I could not deliver my baby normally. I had to have a caesarean section. My husband only knew of my condition a few days before I gave birth. After finding out about my condition, he reluctantly accompanied me to visit the doctor. He also took me to the hospital on the day of my delivery, but he left me with my mother at the door to the operating room. He said that he wanted to go to his office.[3]

Lina was clearly unhappy with her husband's neglectful behavior, especially because she felt he mostly spent time with his new wife. Hadi's behavior toward her contradicted the recent expectations of companionship from husbands and involvement during pregnancy and childbirth. This expectation of companionate marriage, however, seemed to be more apparent among upper-middle-class couples (such as Lina and Dadi) than lower-class (such as Yuni and the four wives of Kiayi Jamal). The lower-class female participants seemed to be more concerned with the economic support of their husband. Since the pedi cab accident, Lina was too traumatized to take public transport, and this motivated her to learn how to drive. At the time of interview, she could drive a car and she said that she was enjoying the freedom and independence driving brought. Her experience is similar to that of Dahlia, the first wife of Dadi, who also began to learn how to drive a car after finding that her husband had taken another wife.

One out of 12 wives in Bandung, Rosa, the first wife of Syamsul, belongs to the fourth category, in which a woman and her co-wife had known each other and tried to have a good relationship, even though they often felt jealous of each other. Rosa tried to have a good relationship with Indri, her husband's second wife. When Indri was pregnant, Rosa told me that she was willing to get involved in almost every stage of her pregnancy. After Indri gave birth, Rosa told me that she often visited Indri's baby; she liked children. Perhaps it was easier for them to have a cordial relationship because Syamsul's second marriage took place with Rosa's consent. But, as noted in Chapter 4, sometimes Rosa felt that Indri hated her, because Indri was occasionally sarcastic and Rosa's feelings were hurt. In response to this sarcasm, Rosa became introspective: 'She might do that because sometimes I might have verbally hurt her feelings. Now, I do not feel hurt or jealous with her anymore. Maybe because I have lost too many of my emotions, I feel that I am without feeling.'[4] Since their houses were not close to each other's (about seven kilometers apart), they did not meet very often. This infrequent contact seemed to minimize conflict between them.

In Jakarta, Bogor and Depok, three out of 19 first wives (Ijem, Yuni and Santi), belonged to the first category, in which a first wife did not know or had never met her co-wife, because either the first or the additional wife lived outside Jakarta. For instance, Ijem, Kasim's first wife, and her six children lived in Cirebon, while Kasim, his second wife, Iyah, and their children lived in Jakarta. Kasim visited Ijem occasionally, for example during Idul Fitri. None of the participants in Jakarta, Bogor and Depok belonged to the second category, in which additional wives contacted first wives. Eight of the 19 first wives – Irma, Ratna, Nunik, Tari, Tina, Nila, Ida and Nida – belonged to the third category, in which a first wife had met her co-wife and they did not have a harmonious relationship. This may be because all the additional marriages in this category took place without the first wife's consent, or were being kept secret until the established wives found out about the marriages. For instance, Lani (31), a first wife of Yoyo (36), after finding out her husband's secret second marriage, wanted to cooperate with Vivi, Yoyo's second wife. However, Lani told me that she felt Vivi did not care about Lani's feelings. Lani felt that Yoyo spent too much time with Vivi, neglecting Lani and her three children. Therefore, she asked Vivi to remind Yoyo to visit them, but Vivi refused to cooperate. Lani assumed that Vivi used black magic to keep Yoyo with her.

Eight out of 19 first wives (Edah, Nia, Hilda, Hj.Titin, Aida, Arsa, Rini and Yanti) belonged to the fourth category, in which a woman and her co-wife know each other and try to have a good relationship despite their jealousy. These women mostly lived close to each other. For instance, Hj. Titin, the first wife of Kiayi Jamal (a religious leader aged 94), lived within 200 meters of his other three wives. They cooperated with each other in organizing monthly religious gathering (*pengajian*) for their husband. They also attempted to show a united front to others, by making 'uniforms' (identical dresses), which they wore when accompanying their husband to weddings. As noted, even though the wives in this fourth category tried to have good relationships, it does not mean that there was no conflict or jealousy among them. For instance, Hj. Latifah, the second wife of Kiayi Jamal, said that she often felt jealous if her husband bought something for one of his wives and not the others. In her view, it would be better if her husband restrained himself from buying items like a washing machine or refrigerator until he could afford to buy four items at the same time, in order to avoid conflict or jealousy among his wives. Kiayi Jamal's case will be discussed later in this chapter.

Arsa, whose case I looked at in the previous chapter, also tried to maintain a good relationship with her husband's second wife, Lia, but she felt that Lia was uncooperative and demanding. Lia wanted to spend more time with Jajang, even though Jajang had rostered one day to be with Arsa and another day to be with Lia, except on Sundays. On Sundays, Arsa requested that Jajang spend time with her children, because he barely had time to be with them. Arsa said that Lia wanted to have everything that Arsa had in her house, such as a TV and refrigerator. Arsa told me that Lia often complained about having to live in a small house, and demanded to move to a bigger house like Arsa's (Arsa lived in a rented two-bedroom house which cost Rp. 5,000,000 (A$715) per year, while Lia lived in a rented one-bedroom house which cost Rp. 3,000,000 (A$430 AUD) per year). Lia herself did not express these complaints to me, because she maintained that she could accept Jajang's explanation that justice does not mean sameness: she could accept Jajang's explanation that Arsa lived in a bigger house because Arsa had more children than she did. But Lia did complain to me that Jajang spent more time at Arsa's house. Lia had told Jajang about her demands but again, Jajang explained to Lia that justice is not equal to sameness, and that he spent more time in Arsa's house because she had more children than Lia.

Similarly, Yanti (35), the first wife of Akbar, also tried to maintain a good relationship with her co-wife, Iis (31). But Yanti had felt increasingly jealous because Akbar seemed to love Iis more than Yanti. Yanti was an active member of PKS, an Islamist political party, and appeared to have been influenced by ideas about polygamous women having a strong commitment to their religion. Therefore, when her husband, Akbar (34), told her of his plan to take another wife, she 'supported' his plan (maybe for fear of being labeled as opposing Islamic teaching). Akbar, a rich entrepreneur and an Islamist political activist, told me that Yanti then chose her good friend and classmate during her tertiary education, Iis (31), a widow with a six-year-old son. Iis, who wore a waist-length *jilbab*, told me that initially she did not accept Yanti's offer because of the negative image of polygamy. However, Iis told me that in October 2002, several weeks after Yanti had informed her of her husband's plan to take another wife, Yanti gave Iis a letter stating Iis' readiness to be the second wife, ready for Iis to sign. Iis signed the letter, even though she said she was unsure as to whether she did the right thing. A week after Iis signed the letter Akbar married her in her parents' home in East Java. Iis, a religious teacher, told me that Yanti did not come to her wedding because she was five months pregnant, and could not travel from Jakarta to East Java.

A husband's even division of time and resources between wives was a key issue. After her marriage, Iis refused to live with Akbar for about four months, citing the reason that she respected Yanti, who was pregnant. Iis understood that a pregnant woman needs a great deal of attention from her husband. She also told me that she was uncomfortable with sharing her husband with another woman, but she thought if Yanti could do it, why couldn't she? In addition, she tried to view polygamy in a positive way. She told me how uncomfortable she had been as a widow: she had often received SMS messages from men asking to marry her, and had felt that marriage might alleviate this discomfort. During the initial four months, Yanti kept suggesting that Iis live with Akbar, and she also gave Iis a monthly maintenance of Rp. 2,000,000 (A$285). Iis kept the money, but did not spend it. After four months, when Yanti gave birth, Iis was willing to have sexual intercourse with Akbar and move to another rented home which costs Rp. 7,500,000 per year (A$1,070) paid for by Akbar. In this large two-story house, she lived with her son and a maidservant and Akbar often visited her. I had the impression that Akbar and Iis were happily married, and Akbar's relationship with Iis seemed to be closer than his relationship with Yanti. In fact, Akbar told me that he loved Iis more than Yanti, but said that the ratio was 'less than 60: 40'. Even though Akbar claimed to love Iis more than Yanti, he realized and appreciated that he had spent 14 years with Yanti, and had three children with her.

Iis told me that after Yanti gave birth, Akbar mostly spent his time with Iis, so her relationship with Yanti was bad. Iis, however, told me that she still communicated with Yanti. For instance, when Yanti asked Akbar for money and he said that he did not have any, Yanti would call Iis to ask how much money she received. Since Iis agreed to have sexual intercourse with Akbar, Iis told me that Akbar spent one day with Iis and another day with Yanti, because both of them lived in Jakarta but in different districts (about half an hour's drive away). Sometimes, when Akbar was too busy and tired, she would let Akbar to spend two days with Yanti. But Iis said she never allowed Akbar to spend more time with her, because she was afraid that if she granted him more time once, he would ask for more, and this could lead to injustice against Yanti.[5] This latter explanation, however, contradicts her earlier story that Akbar spent most of his time with Iis after Yanti gave birth.

Akbar told me of the changes in Yanti's attitude toward him since Iis agreed to live with him. He told me that Yanti often felt jealous, and expressed her anger by hitting him or asking for divorce or by swearing (*ngomong kotor*). She would ask his forgiveness, but then do it again and ask to be forgiven again. Akbar assumed that Yanti might know that he loved Iis more than her, and might realistically feel that he no longer belonged entirely to her. Unfortunately, Yanti refused to be interviewed, so I did not find out how she felt about sharing her husband with another woman, whom she herself chose. But from this interview with Iis and Akbar, Yanti, like Arsa, seemed to be very unhappy with her husband's second marriage.

In conclusion, most wives in polygamous marriages in this study had a conflict-laden relationship with their co-wives. The reality of their lives does not tally with Wardoyo's representation of harmonious relationships between co-wives. Only a minority of them (one out of 12 wives in Bandung and eight out of 19 wives in Jakarta, Depok and Bogor) had tried to get along with their co-wives, but even among these women, conflict and jealousy sometimes could not be avoided.

Polygamous husbands' treatments of their wives

While some husbands seemed to try to follow Islamic guidelines regarding equal and just treatment of wives by arranging a regular roster, others seemed not to care about their treatment of their wives. Some polygamous husbands had a rigid/regular roster, some of them had flexible rosters known by each wife, and others seemed not to bother about organizing a roster and visited wives on a random basis. Unlike the Balinese (Hindu) polygamous husbands studied by Jennaway (2000), who mostly could not afford to provide separate houses for their wives, most wives in Javanese polygamous marriages in this study lived in separate houses, except those of Maman and Memed. These two polygamous marriages had atypical living arrangements, which will be discussed next (see Table 5.1 for the Short Reference List of the names whose cases are discussed in this Chapter).

Table 5.1 Short reference list of informants (*dramatis personae*)

Case Study 1 (unusual living arrangement)
1. Aida (31), first wife of Maman, tertiary student and a housewife, three children.
2. Maman (31), husband of Aida and Syarifah, primary school graduate, perfume shop owner.
3. Syarifah (28), second wife of Maman, senior high school graduate, Qur'anic teacher.

Case Study 2 (unusual living arrangement)
1. Edah, first wife of Memed, primary school graduate, a domestic servant, twelve children, only six survived.
2. Memed (66), husband of Edah and Neni, year 3 primary school, casual low-paid worker.
3. Neni (49), second wife of Memed, no school, a domestic servant, two children.

Case Study 3 (regular roster)
1. Mila (42), first wife of Suhadi, year 12 (secondary school), housewife, five children.
2. Suhadi (49), husband of Mila and Maya, doctoral student, lecturer and religious preacher.
3. Maya (39), second wife of Suhadi, year 10 (secondary school), housewife, three daughters.

Case Study 4 (regular roster)
1. Kiayi Jamal (94), has four wives, secondary school graduate, a rich religious leader.
2. Hj. Titin, first wife of Kiayi Jamal, reportedly housewife.
3. Hj. Latifah (42), second wife of Kiayi Jamal, secondary school graduate (year 9), four children, housewife.
4. Hj. Mardiyah (39), third wife of Kiayi Jamal, primary school graduate, one daughter, housewife.
5. Hj. Laila (33), fourth wife of Kiayi Jamal, year 12 (secondary school graduate), two children, housewife.

Case Study 5 (irregular roster)
1. Yuni (46), first wife of Ali, no school, salad seller, three children.
2. Ali (34), husband of Yuni and Tati, year 3 primary school, *ojek* driver.
3. Tati (46), second wife of Ali, junior high school graduate, housewife, two children.

Case Study 6 (irregular roster):
1. Eli (50), first wife of Yaya, senior high school graduate (year 12), former casual administrative officer and canteen owner but became casual domestic servant since 2003, three children.
2. Yaya (51), husband of Eli and Leli, tertiary degree, civil servant (administrative officer).
3. Leli (28), second wife of Yaya, secondary school (year 9), two children, reportedly former restaurant cashier and became housewife following her marriage in 1995.

Unusual living arrangements

Case Study 1: Aida-Maman-Syarifah
Interviewees: Aida, Maman and Syarifah

Aida (31) was a tertiary student and housewife of conservative appearance, who had not worked after marriage. She was the first wife of Maman (31), a primary school graduate who ran a perfume shop out of his living room. She met Maman for the first time when she was in her final year of tertiary studies, which she did not finish. As a student activist on her campus, Aida had organized an intensive Islamic course in a nearby mosque. A few days after they met at an Islamic youth group, Aida received an envelope containing Maman's marriage proposal and biographical data. The latter explained that he was a primary school graduate with no permanent job. Given three days to decide, Aida accepted the proposal, even though her parents were against her marriage because of the difference in their educational levels and his unemployment.

Aida's parents' objection to her marriage to Maman is common among Indonesian Muslims, who expect that their daughters will marry a man of at least a similar economic and educational level. But Aida may well have been impressed by the unusual means by which Maman delivered his proposal, and seemed to disregard Maman's income and education. Aida seemed not to know that Maman, as he revealed to me, had sent the same proposal to nine women before he sent it to Aida, and only Aida accepted the proposal.

As a supporter of Islamist ideas, Aida believed that polygamy provides benefits to Muslims: 'I believe that it is not possible for God to reveal a verse which does not have any benefit or solution. I believe that if we implement the Qur'anic verse sincerely, we will be rewarded in this world and the hereafter.'[6] This belief seemed to prevent Aida from objecting to her husband's plan to take another wife. She even helped him to find a prospective second wife when Maman failed to find a suitable woman by himself.

Aida chose Syarifah (28), a member of a religious gathering led by Aida's sister. Aida accompanied Maman when he went to propose to Syarifah's parents in Purwokerto, Central Java, about twelve hours by bus from Jakarta. Initially, they only wanted to make a marriage proposal (*melamar*) but according to Aida, to save money and another visit to Purwokerto, Maman chose to marry Syarifah at that time after she accepted his proposal. Aida said that she witnessed Maman's second marriage, which took place in 2001. She appeared calm when she told me this, not sad at all – on the contrary, she seemed to be proud of what she had done for her husband. After her husband married Syarifah, Aida decided to return to study, taking another undergraduate course.

A man's reluctance to deal with marriage registration was a significant issue, as has been suggested. Unless there was a request from the women's side, men tended to avoid this marriage requirement. Maman's second marriage to Syarifah, for example, remained unregistered for about a year. After that, her parents demanded that the marriage be registered. Maman reluctantly went to the Religious Court to apply for the Court's permission to take another wife, pretending that the second marriage had not yet taken place. In Maman's view, the Court procedure was costly and difficult. First, he came to the Court to pick up the form and filled it out, then he waited for about two weeks to be called to the Court, and finally revisited the Court, where he was told that his hearing would take place in two weeks' time. But the hearing was cancelled on the day it was to take place. It took him two to three months to complete the registration procedure. In his opinion, the Court is corrupt.

He gave the example that the marriage registration fee should have been only Rp. 35,000 (A$5) but in fact he was charged Rp. 300,000 (A$43). He said that the cost of his application for polygamy was supposed to be Rp. 150,000 (A$21), but in actuality he spent Rp. 750,000 (A$107). He told me that he was really unhappy about that. As he was not wealthy, Rp. 750,000 was a great deal of money for him.

Maman's rosters

An unusual living arrangement was one in which two wives had to share a house. After Maman's second marriage, owing to financial limitations, Syarifah lived in a rented two-bedroom house together with Aida and Maman, as well as Aida's three children, for two years. Aida said that initially she felt jealous of Syarifah, but the feeling went away by itself. When she felt jealous, she told herself that Maman was with his wife and that they were not committing adultery. Maman slept with Aida for one night and then with Syarifah another night, according to his roster. As a woman who believes that polygamy is part of *shari'a*, Aida appeared to want to impress me with her harmonious relationship with Syarifah by explaining that sometimes either Aida or Syarifah gave turns to be with Maman to one another, as a gift. Aida also told me that she had never had any arguments with Syarifah. They also shared housework. Aida said that she liked to tidy up the house and take care of her children, while Syarifah was responsible for cooking and washing dishes and clothes.

After two years living under one roof with two wives, Maman set up a very modest Islamic boarding school. The school was located in a remote area of Depok, and consisted of three rooms of about 4 × 3 meters, with a separate kitchen and bathroom. Maman told me that a donor had lent him that place. He relied on donations, one of which he received from Puspo Wardoyo, and his other income to support the school. Twenty female students, aged between 14 and 18 years old, lived and studied there. They came from poor families, and were not required to pay in order to stay and study there. Syarifah, who stayed there with the students, was the only teacher. She taught the students how to read and memorize Qur'anic verses.

After his wives moved to separate homes, Maman had a flexible roster. When he was busy with his perfume business, he mostly spent his time in Jakarta, with Aida. During the weekend or when he was not busy with his business, he would spend time with Syarifah. Sometimes, Aida also visited the boarding school, to participate in teaching there.

Syarifah told me that Maman usually spent three days in Aida's home, because his business was located there, and spent one day with Syarifah. Syarifah told me that when her husband could not visit her she had no objections. In fact, she enjoyed spending time memorizing Qur'anic verses, because when her husband was around she could not do anything other than accompany and 'serve' him. But she believed that the reward from God for both actions – either memorizing Qur'anic verses or serving Maman – was the same.

When I asked Maman whether he felt that he treated his wives justly, he said:

> I have tried to be just to my wives. My wives would forgive me if I were unjust .... Even the Prophet cannot be just in term of love. He loved one of his wives more than the others. I give maintenance to my wives based on their needs, not necessarily the same amount.[7]

From the above quotation, he seems to be unsure whether or not he had treated his wives justly, because he spent more time and money with Aida – just like the situation with Jajang and his two wives. But he tried to reassure himself and justify his actions by saying that even the Prophet loved Aisyah better than his other wives.

Case Study 2: Edah-Memed-Neni
Interviewee: Memed

Personal background

Memed was part of a small group of men in my sample who did not use Islam to justify his practice of polygamy. Aged 66, he was of Batavian origin and had spent only three years in primary school. Previously, he had worked as a security guard, earning a salary of Rp. 800,000 (A$114) per month. He said that he quit the job in August 2003, because the office moved further away from his house, and his boss refused to increase his salary. Since then, he had mostly stayed at home and only worked casually when one of his neighbors needed a construction worker. Memed claimed to have two wives: Edah and Neni (49). In fact, his first wife, Edah, had passed away three months before my interview.

Memed married Edah in 1973, after two years of dating her. At the time of his wedding, he was 35, while Edah, who was a primary school graduate, was 13. It is possible that he miscalculated the date because he is uneducated. They had twelve children between 1974 and 1992, six of whom passed away. In 1984, eleven years after his first marriage, Memed married Neni, a widow who had no schooling at all, with the reluctant consent of Edah, because Neni might have had a child by Memed. He had two children with Neni, ages 22 and 17. This means that the first child was already two years old before he married Neni. All his children lived in his house except the two oldest, who lived separately with their own wives and children.

Memed's rosters

Memed had an even more unusual living arrangement than Maman. A low-income earner and uneducated, Memed had no money to pay for a separate home for Neni, his second wife. Therefore, two months after the second marriage in 1984, he brought Neni to live with him and his first wife, Edah. Because his house was small, and he had many children, Memed used to sleep with Edah and Neni in a single room, in the same bed. Memed said that one wife had the right for him each week.

He laughed as he told me that both of his wives used to prevent him from facing to another side by putting their foot on both of his feet, so he could only sleep on his back. Memed even confessed that they had sexual relations in the same room. Memed said that even though both of his wives often had arguments, they mostly cooperated with each other in doing housework. He was clearly trying to create a representation of harmonious relationships between co-wives similar to the representations promoted by Puspo Wardoyo. Memed told me that he felt that he did not treat both wives justly, because his wives brought in most of the family's income by working as domestic servants. He said that there were many advantages to having two wives: for example, it is safer and cleaner for him than having extra-marital affairs or paying for prostitutes, and it was thanks to his wives' support that he could build a better house than his previous one.

Regular rosters

Four out of 20 male polygamous participants (Suhadi, Joko, Kiayi Jamal and Jajang) had regular rosters. It seems to me that all four were well aware of the Islamic requirement of treating all wives justly, and they tried to adhere to them. While Joko and Jajang decided their own roster, Suhadi and Kiayi Jamal let their wives decide. Among my research participants, the position of senior and junior wife tended to vary. Some first wives seemed to feel superior to their junior co-wives (such as Mila, Arsa, Aida and Tuti), and therefore seemed to feel that they had the right to their co-wives' obedience. An active role for the first wife in determining and managing her husband's roster seemed to indicate a position superior to that of the secondary wives. Other first wives seemed to feel that they were 'defeated' by their junior co-wives in that they felt their husbands tended to spend more time with their younger wives (such as Lina, Esih, Eli, Dahlia, Iir, Ratih and Lani). Other relationships between co-wives seemed more egalitarian (such as those between Rosa and Indri, and among Wardoyo's and Kiayi Jamal's four wives).

Case Study 3: Mila-Suhadi-Maya
Interviewees: Mila (first wife), Suhadi (husband) and Maya (second wife)

Personal background

It was not easy for polygamous husbands to treat their wives justly, especially when justice is viewed from various positions. Mila (42) married Suhadi (49) in 1979, when she was in her final year at senior high school. She was 17, while Suhadi was 24. Suhadi was a public figure and worked as a university lecturer, Dean and religious preacher, while Mila was a housewife who was economically dependent on her husband. They had met when Suhadi was in his final year of tertiary education, in a mosque where she was studying Islam: Suhadi often preached there. Mila told me that Suhadi was actually interested in Eni, Mila's niece, and expected Mila to be his facilitator in communicating with Eni. Eni, however, was not interested in

Suhadi. Eni's mother suggested that Suhadi marry Mila instead of Eni, and he agreed. As an active religious preacher, Suhadi claimed to be a member of the *Grup Anti Pacaran* (Against Courtship Group); therefore he married Mila without any courtship. Even though the marriage was arranged, Mila said that she had come to love her husband. They lived in Mila's parents' house in the first four years of their marriage, before they finally built their own house next door. Suhadi and Mila had five children (ages 24, 22, 19, 17 and 13 at the time of our interview). Her daily activities were housework and childcare. She also regularly attended weekly religious gatherings in their neighborhood.

In 2003, after 24 years of marriage, Mila had found out that her husband had been secretly married to Maya for nine months. She told her mother and her oldest daughter, Nadira (24), an active member of *Hizbut Tahrir*, an Islamist organization, and they advised her to be patient, but she was very sad. In the first three months after this discovery, she often wept. To comfort herself, she prayed and read the Qur'an. According to Mila, her children's attitudes toward their father also changed after they found out that he had taken another wife. They were indifferent to him, and seemed to be reluctant to speak. Mila told me that one of her children said, 'I feel like I do not have a father'.

Suhadi's rosters

After Mila found out about her husband's second marriage, Suhadi let Mila arrange his roster. Mila reluctantly allowed one night, Friday night, for her husband to spend with Maya. She felt that this roster was just, because she was letting her husband spend any afternoon he wished with Maya. In fact, he did spend more time in Mila's house and gave Mila more money, because Mila had more children and he was the biological father of Mila's children. Maya, however, said that she wanted more time to be with Suhadi, not just one night. Maya used to have a husband who slept with her every night, and therefore she did not want Suhadi to only be like a guest, who visited her for a while in the afternoon and went back to Mila's house before sunset. But she tried to comfort herself by saying:

> Well, I can use my time alone to read books, to learn more. I often long for my husband, but he is with his wife. I often feel jealous, but I am aware that maybe Suhadi feels more comfortable in Mila's house because all his books are there. I often feel envious of Mila but I realize that Mila's husband's time has [also] been taken by me.[8]

From the above quotation, Maya seemed to be aware of her position as a second wife, who took away Suhadi's time with Mila. Therefore, even though she was willing to spend more time with her husband, she tried not to be demanding and used her time alone to read books.

Suhadi himself seemed unsure as to whether or not he had treated his wives justly: 'Justice means giving someone what he or she needs to accept. I cannot claim myself to be just because the Qur'an prohibits it [to claim that he had been treating his wives justly]. I tend to put aside one of my wives; but justice is not equal to sameness.' This claim is certainly the same as those of Jajang and Maman: all of them, even though they had tried to treat their wives justly, seemed to be unsure whether or not they had treated their wives justly because all of them perceived that justice is not equal with sameness.

Case Study 4: Kiayi Jamal and his four wives
Interviewees: Kiayi Jamal, Hj. Latifah, Hj. Mardhiyah and Hj. Laila

Personal background

The following case study is a typical practice of polygamy among rich religious leaders (*kiayi*). Kiayi Jamal (94), a Batavian religious leader who had four wives, all housewives, looked 20 years younger than his age. He dressed well and neatly. He sat in front of his office and was praying quietly. Many passers-by greeted him, and shook and kissed his hand as a sign of great respect. This was his daily activity when no one came seeking his spiritual help in solving problems. If they did, people usually gave some money in return for such help, which they would put in the charity box in the corner of his office, near the entrance. This office was a two-story house, consisting of his bedroom, a large guest room, kitchen and bathroom on the first floor, and a bedroom for his employees and a prayer room on the second floor. Two male employees who were responsible for cleaning the house and serving drinks to guests lived there. The office also served as a meeting place for all of Kiayi Jamal's wives and his children. His second wife, Hj. Latifah, seemed to be the manager of the house. She mostly attended to her husband's guests, and arranged his marital bed roster.

Kiayi Jamal told me that he had been married seven times, but had only ever had four wives concurrently, according to Islamic guidelines. His first wife passed away, and he had divorced two other wives. From these marriages, he had many children, whom he could recognize but could not number or name. His second wife, Hj. Latifah (42), told me that he had twenty children. All his children lived with their own mothers, whom he supported economically.

Kiayi Jamal's rosters

As noted, Kiayi Jamal's four wives' homes were close together, and he had a regular roster. He spent one night with each wife, but during the day he would stay in his office, where any wife and/or child could visit. His second wife, Hj. Latifah, would remind him whom he needed to visit that night. Hj. Latifah confessed that she did not necessarily have sexual intercourse with her husband when he was with her. She said that she was a bit lazy about intercourse, and preferred to do it only once a month. On the nights when her husband was with another wife, Hj. Latifah said that she could sleep soundly and did not feel jealous at all. Hj. Laila (33), Kiayi Jamal's fourth wife, made a similar confession, saying she too was uninterested in sexual intercourse with her husband. This may well have been because of the age gap; the wives may not actually have enjoyed intercourse with their 94-year-old husband. Only Hj. Mardiyah, the third wife, reported that she always had intercourse with her husband when he was with her.

Irregular rosters

While Suhadi, Joko and Kiayi Jamal had a regular roster, Mahmud, Ali, Yaya, Syamsul and Dadi had irregular rosters. They visited their wives as they wished. Altman and Ginat, writing about Mormon families, have dubbed this the *laissez-faire* roster system (1996: 287). Such arrangements would only conform with difficulty to the Qur'anic teaching which requires a husband to treat his wives justly. These men, except Syamsul, had taken additional wives even though they could not financially support their first wives. But, unlike the supporters of Islamist ideas, these men did not use Islam to justify their practice. These two case studies presented here will also show how men falsified their identities or paid bribes to obtain marriage certificates, as a means of manipulating the secular legal process. These cases could well be cited by Indonesian feminists as examples of what they call arbitrary polygamy: they see this as leading to injustice toward first wives who are forced to support their children themselves owing to the irresponsible actions of their husbands.

Case Study 5: Yuni- Ali-Tati
Interviewees: Ali (husband) and Yuni (first wife)

Personal background

The following case study of Ali and his wives suggests that even poor and uneducated men took risks in practicing polygamy, because they subscribed to the general belief that polygamy is permitted (*poligami itu dibolehkan*). Even though this man did not know the Islamic guidelines about just treatment of wives, he knew how to negotiate around the secular legal process, which requires marriage registration.

My interview with Ali (34) took place in his sister's house, which was near his small rented house, located in a slum area in Jakarta. Ali was born and grew up in Jakarta, but his parents originally came from Pemalang, Central Java. Ali only went to primary school for three years. He worked as an *ojek* (motorcycle vehicle) driver earning Rp. 30,000 (A$4) income per day.[9] He said that he gave Rp. 20,000 (A$3) to Yuni (46), his first wife, to pay for his children's education, and he saved Rp. 10,000 (A$1.40) for his second wife, Tati. But as Yuni claimed below, Ali had been mostly jobless and rarely gave her money.

Yuni, an illiterate woman, was a domestic servant in Ali's neighborhood the first time that Ali met her. Ali fell in love with Yuni, and married her in a free-choice marriage in 1987, when Ali was 17 and Yuni was 29. The marriage was celebrated in Solo, Yuni's hometown, even though Ali's parents disapproved of the marriage because of the age gap between him and Yuni. They had three children (ages 14, 13 and 9 at the time of our interview). When Yuni gave birth to her third child in Solo, Ali married Tati, a junior high school graduate (year 9) who worked in a *warteg* (*warung tegal*, a small fast food shop). Yuni told me that she did not know about her husband's second marriage until Ali's sister informed her of it, and was really angry when she found out about the union. She asked for a divorce, but Ali refused, saying that divorce is prohibited.

Ali claimed that his second marriage was registered, even though he took his second wife without Yuni's consent. He said that he paid a bribe of Rp. 100,000 (A$14) to obtain a letter certifying that he was single to obtain a marriage certificate for his second marriage. This again clearly shows how men have been able to manipulate the legal process to achieve the aim of marrying a second wife. After the marriage, Tati preferred to live in her village, Tegal, where Ali visited her about every two months. From this marriage, Ali and Tati had two children. Because Ali could only give Tati Rp. 150,000 (A$21) to Rp. 200,000 (A$28) every two months, Tati did not have enough money to support herself and the two children. Therefore, according to Ali, Tati cohabited with Uja, a man who had loved her since she was a girl. Ali said that Tati kept her cohabitation with Uja secret from her neighbors, telling them that he was Ali's brother. When Ali came to visit her, Ali said that Uja would voluntarily leave the house to allow Ali to sleep with his wife, because Uja knew that Tati was Ali's second wife.

Ali's rosters

Ali mostly stayed with his first wife, Yuni, in Jakarta and only visited Tati, his second wife, in Central Java, irregularly. Whenever he had enough money, usually every two months, he would go to visit Tati, staying for about a week at a time and mostly not telling Yuni in advance of the visit; instead he would lie to her, saying that he had been hired to work as a driver for a week. But Yuni always knew that whenever Ali did not come home for more than a day, he must be visiting his second wife. Yuni was very upset about that, especially because Ali, who was mostly jobless, saved any earnings for his visits to Tati.

Yuni complained that Ali rarely spent his money on her and their children. She worked hard to earn money to support her family by selling vegetable salads. She said she usually got up at 3 a.m. and then got ready to go to market to buy vegetables. She would then prepare them by 9 a.m., and sold the salads in her neighborhood from 9 a.m. until 4 p.m., usually earning Rp. 50,000 (A$7) per day.

Ali's sister told me in front of Ali that Ali was a childlike and irresponsible person. She regarded him as crazy for having two wives. His daughter, who was also there, confirmed what her aunt said about her father. Ali continued to smile when his sister and his daughter made these comments.

Case Study 6: Eli-Yaya-Leli
Interviewees: Yaya (husband) and Eli (first wife)

Personal background

The following case study shows how a man's polygamous marriage caused misery for all his family members. It will also highlight the first wife's jealousy about her husband spending his time with and money on his younger wife.

Yaya had a tertiary degree and worked as a civil servant (administrative officer) in a higher education institution. He married Eli, who had worked in the same office with him, in 1979, when he was 26 and she was 25, with full ceremonial. They had three sons (aged 24, 22 and 21 at the time of the interview). The oldest had a Diploma; the other two were attending tertiary institutions. In 1991, Yaya met Leli, a beautiful young cashier in a restaurant. He had an affair with her before marrying her secretly in 1995, when he was 42 and she was 19. As a civil servant, he was afraid of being penalized for disobeying PP 10. To obtain a marriage certificate, he paid a Rp. 400,000 (A$57) bribe to the marriage registration officer.

When Eli, who quit her administrative job after her marriage, found out about Yaya's second marriage in 1996, a year after the second marriage, she was really angry. She said to me that on that day she almost fell unconscious. She thought she had been so kind to her husband, and her husband seemed to love her and care about her. When Yaya came home, Eli shouted at him, 'I have made you happy, but you hurt me. You had a son from another woman. You are not satisfied with one woman. Your wife [Eli] is not even sick.'[10] Eli kept shouting at Yaya for five hours, until 11 pm, in order to express her anger.

Having a tertiary degree, and holding down two jobs until 2003, Yaya could be categorized as a middle-income earner. In the morning, he had worked as an administrator in a state university (civil servant), while in the afternoon he had worked as the head of the administrative staff in a private secondary school. He also borrowed a large amount of money from his office in order to support Leli's luxurious lifestyle. Eli had felt jealous of Leli's way of life at that time, as she herself lived modestly:

> I went to Leli's home to challenge her. She lived in an expensive luxurious rented house, which cost Rp. 2,500,000 (A$357) per year. There were the two (Ligna) beds, which were very expensive, a big TV and refrigerator.[11] I felt jealous at what she had in the house. I could not have such luxurious furniture unless I bought it on credit by using my own savings, because I did not want to be economically demanding on Yaya. I had never eaten out in expensive restaurants and I had never bought expensive clothes, in order to save money. However, Yaya spent most of his money on his second wife. I sometimes went to Leli's house, but she moved to another place every time I found out her address. Now, Leli and Yaya live in a very poor financial condition because Yaya was dismissed from the private school, maybe for the reason that he stole money from his office.[12]

Since losing his job in the private school in 2003, then, Yaya could be categorized as a low-income earner, and his monthly salary was mostly spent on repaying his debt. He expressed his regret to me about having two wives and neglecting his first wife and her children. He said:

I might be happier if I only had one wife. I feel guilty because I have taken another wife when I had a lot of money. Why did not I invest my money for the benefit of my only wife and her children? I have no religious knowledge so I wanted to take another wife.[13]

Thus, Yaya had clearly been ignorant of the Islamic teaching and therefore, he acted only based on his passion, not based on religious guidance, which he regretted.

Yaya's rosters

In contrast with Ali, who spent most of his time with his first wife, Yaya mainly lived with his second wife, Leli, after his first wife found out about his second marriage. Yaya gradually reduced the frequency of 'visiting' his first wife, from once a week to once a year. Eli told me that since Yaya had a secret second marriage, he no longer slept with her when he came home. Yaya used to sleep on the sofa in the living room, until he stopped coming home all together.

Since her husband stopped coming home, Eli told me that she and her children felt very lonely. But she tried to comfort herself: 'Well, I just assume that my husband has gone to war.' My children also said, 'Let us assume that father has passed away.' Eli's mother used to live in Eli's house, but when she knew that Yaya had taken another wife, she became sick, and asked to move to Eli's sister's house. Yaya had told his wife that his mother-in-law's presence in the house had brought about his second marriage, and his mother-in-law overheard him saying this. Eli's mother herself became ill, possibly because of her deep concern about Eli's unhappiness.

The celebration of important days

For Indonesian Muslims, *Idul Fitri* (*Hari Raya/Lebaran*) is the biggest day of celebration, after the fasting month of Ramadan. *Idul Adha* (*Lebaran Haji*), the day when the pilgrims in Mecca complete their ritual, is the second most important day in the Muslim calendar. On these two days, especially *Idul Fitri*, Indonesian Muslims usually get together with their family members or visit their parents and relatives. Generally, polygamous husbands in my research sample celebrated *Idul Fitri* with the first wife and her children, in their home or in the home of the first wife's parents. Then, the husbands spent the following day or evening with their other wife. This shows that husbands generally observe a hierarchy of respect for their wives. This also shows that they were cautious about negative attitudes toward polygamy among relatives and friends. There was an exception to this rule. For instance, informants with irregular rosters, such as Mahmud and Yaya, decided for themselves with whom they would celebrate the festival day. Yaya seemed to be embarrassed to return to his first wife's home to celebrate the festival with her after a long absence, and therefore he stayed and celebrated the festival with Leli, his second wife. Syamsul, who had a transparent second marriage with Indri, celebrated festivals in his mother's house together with his sisters' families and both of his wives. His first wife, Rosa, told me that, as a Minang, Syamsul looked after his relationship with his maternal kin very well, and she felt that since the birth of Indri's baby, Syamsul's relatives seemed to be closer to Indri than to her.

Dahlia, the first wife of Dadi, also told me about the different nature of the celebration of the festival before and after her husband's second marriage. She said that before the second marriage, on the first day of the festival, after prayers and breakfast, they usually visited Dahlia's parents' house. They also visited her uncles' homes. On the second day, they used to visit Dadi's parents and relatives. After his second marriage, however, Dadi seemed to be reluctant to go to Dahlia's parents' home. After refreshments, Dadi did finally go to visit Dahlia's parents, but would not visit her other relatives, such as her uncles. It is possible that Dadi was ashamed of having a second wife and therefore was reluctant to visit them.

There was also an exception among husbands who had a regular roster. For instance, Arsa told me that, one year, her husband Jajang celebrated *Idul Fitri* with her and her children in her parents' home in the morning. But Jajang went to his second wife's parents' home in the late afternoon. Knowing that, Arsa admonished him not to do so, and asked Jajang to stay in her parents' home for the first day of *Idul Fitri* in the following year. Arsa said to Jajang that as his second marriage had become shameful to her parents, Jajang should be careful not to bring more shame to her family by celebrating *Idul Fitri* in Lia's parents' home, or by bringing Lia to Arsa's parents' home.

Attending wedding ceremonies and official parties

As I noted in Chapter 2, most Indonesian marriages are celebrated with invited friends, relatives and colleagues. In response to the invitation, most guests attend wedding ceremonies with their spouses (and sometimes their children). Other than wedding ceremonies, sometimes workplaces such as universities and publishing offices also host a yearly party, to which employees are invited to come along with their spouse. When attending wedding ceremonies or official parties, most polygamous husbands preferred to go with their first wife. This can be seen in the cases of polygamous husbands such as Suhadi, Syamsul and Hadi, who preferred to go to their official parties or to attend weddings with their first wife. This may be because the first wife was regarded as the 'official' wife, whom many people already knew. They might also have wished to avoid being the object of ridicule or the focus of unwelcome attention if they came with the additional wife or wives.

While Suhadi's first wife, Mila, was happy to accompany her husband to his official parties or to weddings, Hadi's first wife, Lina, often refused to accompany her husband. Mila regarded accompanying her husband or being together with her husband in public as a privilege, inappropriate for Maya, her husband's younger wife. Lina, however, felt it was useless to support Hadi's career as a public figure by pretending that he had a harmonious family life, when in reality Hadi had physically and emotionally abused her. Similarly, Rosa, the first wife of Syamsul, said that she was reluctant to go to her husband's official parties because she was ashamed of her husband's polygamous marriage, and she often felt that she had became the centre of gossip on her husband's campus.

There are exceptions to this rule too. Maman, Akbar, Kiayi Jamal and Jajang, who were all from Jakarta and Depok and all practiced transparent polygamy, said that they often attended wedding ceremonies with all their wives. Jajang even went to his office party with his two wives. This attracted comments and jokes from his colleagues, such as, 'You have had two, you will need to add two more wives.'[14] According to Arsa, Jajang's colleagues seemed to be surprised to see the two wives getting along with each other. Arsa also told me that Lia seemed to enjoy appearing in public together with her husband and his first wife, the two women dressed alike, to parade their harmonious marriage. These public appearances were often interpreted by the people surrounding them as a sign that there was nothing wrong with Jajang's polygamous marriage. But, in fact, as my interview showed clearly, Arsa had been very unhappy, so appearances may well lie. Lia, on the other hand, may have enjoyed appearing in public together with her husband because this validation could alleviate her anxiety and need for public acceptance as a second wife.

None of the male Bandung informants were confident about attending a wedding ceremony with all their wives. As I suggested in the Introduction to this book, this may be because these participants were aware of the more strongly held negative attitudes toward polygamy in Bandung. For this reason, among others, most polygamous husbands in Bandung hid their second marriages. Even in Jakarta, where residents seemed to have a more relaxed attitude about polygamy, attending a wedding ceremony with more than one wife attracted attention and invited negative comments either from the host or from other guests.

Economic management in polygamous households

How do polygamous husbands manage their income and how does their income management affect the well-being of their wives? Pahl's (1980) and Brenner's (1998) studies, outlined in Chapter 2, are useful for understanding economic management in polygamous marriages, and how power relations are very much related to the distribution of household resources. I shall use Pahl's categorization of income management in classifying economic management within polygamous marriages. As I have argued, Brenner's discussion of the connection between controlling money and controlling one's passions also fits very well in exploring cases of polygamous husbands. Most polygamous husbands controlled their own income, which makes it easier for them to fulfill their desire for another woman. Therefore, as will be presented shortly, Dadi and Asep, who used to adopt a *whole wage system*, had to change their income management into an *allowance system*. They found the *whole wage system* to be unsuitable, because it did not allow them to freely spend their income on another woman. This changing management of household income had a negative impact on the economic well-being of their first wives and children.

Male participants can be categorized into two groups, based on their income management. The first group comprised those male participants who managed their own income. They usually gave some of the income to their wives as maintenance and kept the rest of the money for their own use and for saving: in Pahl's categories, the *allowance system*. All male participants in Jakarta, Bogor and Depok belonged to this category. They tended not to change their income management when they practiced polygamy. This may be because it was this system that helped them to fulfill their desire for another woman. Many of the first wives who usually received an allowance from their husbands, like the women in Pahl's study, did not know how much money the husband earned, saved or spent on another wife. Also, as Pahl pointed out, among the affluent husbands, this system can create inequality between husband and wife when the wife receives only a small allowance, which does not give much room to maneuver (Pahl, 1980: 331). The relationship between the husband and wife in this income category resembles that described by the mainstream interpretations of the Qur'anic verse 4: 34: the husband is the leader of his family because he is regarded as superior to his wife, and because he spends his money for his family. Therefore, the husband tends to dominate his wives. This can be seen, for instance, in the cases of Rosa, the first wife of Syamsul; Sari, the third wife of Joko; and the four wives of Kiayi Jamal (Hj. Titin, Hj. Lathifah, Hj. Mardhiyah and Hj. Laila), who were all economically dependent on their husband.

The following case shows how the allowance system sustained the wives' economic dependency on their husband. Joko, a successful restaurateur who had four wives, applied this system. Sari, his third wife, reported that she was given a monthly allowance of Rp. 10,000,000 (A$1,428), which was transferred to her bank account. She spent this money to support herself and one-and-a-half-year-old daughter, to pay for a domestic servant, a babysitter, and on car repairs and other needs including healthcare. She usually documented her spending, and would ask for more money if she found the allowance insufficient, or save the surplus when she did not spend it all. This allowance may have been too small given the very high income that Joko earned. Sari's report that the amount she received sometimes was not enough implies that she may not have had a significant amount of savings in her account, which would have left her vulnerable if she experienced marital problems. Joko might have chosen to apply this system to create sustained economic dependency in his wives. In addition, even though she lived in a luxurious big house, Sari said that the house did not belong to her. She did not even know how much money Joko spent on the house or its furniture. When she asked him, Joko told her that she did not need to know. This seems to imply that Sari only had the right to use, but not the ownership of, Joko's house and possessions. Sari said that none of her husband's wives claimed ownership. She said, 'We are not concerned with ownership. All we have is ours. None of Mas Joko's wives have such ownership. Any wife of Mas Joko can come here and feel that this house is their house too.' Sari seemed to trust that her husband would always protect her and provide her with economic security.

Joko seemed to be aware of Brenner's proposition about men in Java that 'for men sexual desire and the desire for money, two manifestations of *nafsu,* are often seen as two sides of the same coin; it is assumed that a man must have money in order to find satisfaction for his lust' (Brenner, 1998: 152). Joko took full control of his own money in order to sustain his control over women (his wives), in order to satisfy his sexual needs.

Another example of participants in Jakarta who used the allowance system was Jajang, married to Arsa and Lia. As discussed previously, Jajang was mostly economically dependent on Arsa's parents in the first four years of his marriage, owing to his very low income. Soon after he began to earn a higher income, he married another woman and implemented the allowance system. Arsa, his first wife, told me that she disliked the situation after Jajang married Lia because Arsa felt that she and Jajang had been struggling together toward a more stable financial position. When his income went up, however, another woman entered their marriage, and enjoyed the results of their struggle. Arsa said that no matter how justly Jajang tried to treat her, she felt that many of her entitlements had been taken away. This situation is illustrative of Geertz's suggestion (1961: 131) that when women are older and have children, their primary concern regarding infidelity (or polygamy) is with 'the loss of money that might otherwise be spent in the family's interests'. Similar concerns were also clearly expressed by Tuti, but not Rosa and Lina. Before her husband took another wife, Rosa was very concerned with her husband's money. She often openly expressed her disapproval when Syamsul gave money to his mother. But Rosa did not seem concerned with her husband's spending on his second wife. This may have been because of her emotional distress over her husband's polygamy. Similarly, Lina did not display any concern with money matters, because she had her own income, and she told me that she put emotional happiness above economic luxuries. Thus, her main problem with her husband's second marriage seems to have been his betrayal of their commitment.

The second category comprises those male participants who usually gave all their income to their wives to manage. They might retain a small portion of the income for discretionary use, such as to buy petrol or cigarettes. In Pahl's category, this income management is called the *whole wage system*. The wife usually spends the money on daily household needs and the children's education, and saves the rest. The relationship between husband and wife in this income category tends to be more equal than that in the first category. In this second category, the husband and his wife tend to discuss expensive purchases, such as those of land or houses, together beforehand, signifying a more equal relationship. This approach to financial decision-making is very different from that seen in the first category, where a husband may buy something very expensive, such as a car or a house, without first consulting his wife. Nine men from 19 households of Bandung participants employed the *whole wage system*, while the rest used the *allowance system*.

Some husbands in this second category of income management tended to change their usual income management after they took additional wives: from the *whole wage system* to the *allowance system*. They no longer gave all of their income to their first wife. This might be done in order to be able to distribute money to their additional wives without needing to ask their first wife's permission. Only a minority of these men did not change their income management. This change of income management affected the economic well-being of some first wives and their children, who often received less after their husbands took additional wives. This can be seen, for instance, in the cases of Dadi and Asep, who changed their income management from the *whole wage system* into the *allowance system* when Asep married another woman.

Dahlia, Dadi's first wife, and Hanny, the former first wife of Asep, explained these economic management changes to me. Before his second marriage, Dadi usually gave all of his income – at least Rp. 10,000,000 (A$1428) per month – to Dahlia to manage. But after his second marriage, Dadi no longer did this. Dahlia had the impression that giving all his income to her might reduce Dadi's freedom to spend his money on additional wives. When Dahlia managed the income, she spent this money on the servant's salary, the children's tuition and pocket money, and the household bills. However, since taking another wife, Dadi gradually reduced the amount he gave to Dahlia, until the amount was only Rp. 1,500,000 (A$214) or Rp. 2,000,000 (A$286) per month. According to Dahlia, this was far from enough to fulfill her usual household needs. But Dahlia did not want to complain because she was afraid of disturbing Dadi's feelings and affecting his service to his community. Therefore, she preferred to sacrifice her own personal savings that she earned as a part-time lecturer, which soon ran out, to cover the gap. Because she did not have enough money, she asked her children to ask their father directly for pocket money and tuition fees. She also gave all the bills to her husband so he would pay them.

Dahlia also told me that Dadi's second marriage had negatively affected his career. As a professor, Dadi intended to stand in the election for Dean and also Rector. But Dadi did not seem confident about his chances of success. He told her that when he was in America with Dahlia, he had called a friend who told him that it was rumored that Dadi had three wives. He did stand for election to Dean but he was defeated, and thus did not proceed to stand for the position of Rector.

Dahlia also told me about changes in her husband's relationship with the West Javanese Governor that followed the rumors about his polygamy. She said that before the second marriage he had had a good relationship with the Governor, and had been entrusted with the management of a large mosque in West Java. He was also given some capital to develop an Islamic boarding school cooperative (*koprasi pesantren*). If he needed money, the Governor could easily help him, said Dahlia, and the Governor often called Dadi's home. But after the Governor heard about Dadi's second marriage, he no longer contacted Dadi who's proposal for some money was met with no response.

Dahlia's case is similar to Hanny's. Hanny explained the economic changes she experienced from the time of her marriage until the time she asked Asep for a divorce. In the beginning of their marriage, Hanny and Asep were economically supported by Hanny's mother, because Asep was still in the final year of his tertiary study. After graduation, Asep earned an increasing income from his job as a lecturer and as a well-known religious preacher. He initially gave all his income to Hanny to manage, but he gradually reduced his maintenance for Hanny when he took additional wives. He might have needed much more money to support his two other children from his previous marriage, his other wives and his step-children.

Before Asep took his additional wives, Hanny usually received Rp. 10,000,000 to Rp. 15,000,000 (A$1,428–2,143) per month. Afterwards, Hanny only received Rp. 3,300,000 (A$471) out of Rp. 4,500,000 (A$643), Asep's monthly salary as a lecturer, and Rp. 300,000 (A$43) from Asep's preaching honoraria. Hanny told me that Asep, as a famous preacher, usually received between Rp. 1,000,000 (A$143) and Rp. 2,500,000 (A$357) each time he preached, and he usually received up to eight invitations per month. Thus, his preaching honoraria could be at least Rp. 8,000,000 (A$1143) per month. Because Asep no longer gave her all his income, Hanny could only cover her daily household necessities, and did not have enough for her children's tuition and other needs. When her children asked for money, she asked them to ask their father directly, as did Dahlia. Her children would complain, because Asep often replied that he had no money.

The above two cases clearly show that a husband's practice of polygamy negatively affected the economic well-being of first wives and their children. But what happened to Mila, the first wife of Suhadi, and Esih, the first wife of Dadan, was not as drastic as what happened to Dahlia and Hanny. Suhadi, Mila's husband, and Dadan, Esih's husband, still gave all their official salary from their main job to their first wife, but kept their supplementary income from other projects for themselves and their additional wives. But supplementary income could be higher than main income, as in the cases of Asep and Dadi, Suhadi and Dadan. All of them would have been able to save more to pay for their children's education, or buy more properties, had they not taken additional wives.

Eli suffered even more economic difficulty than Dahlia and Hanny. Her husband's second marriage turned Eli's life upside down. She had previously lived a comfortable life with him, but her financial situation was now very difficult. Eli told me that 1991 was Yaya's most prosperous year, because he had two sources of good income. In addition, Eli herself earned much money, from opening a canteen within the university where Yaya worked. They had their own house and car. But Yaya's affair with Leli changed everything, said Eli, making him act irrationally. To keep his love affair a secret from his wife, in 1991, Yaya asked Eli to close her canteen business. Eli suspected that Yaya had been afraid that she would find out about his affair with Leli if she continued to run her canteen on her husband's campus. In addition, since Eli always provided lunch for her husband in her canteen, he had no reason to go to the restaurant where Leli had worked as a cashier.

> Before he took a second wife, we never borrowed money. However, after his second marriage, he borrowed a lot of money to support his second wife's luxurious life. Therefore, now his income is significantly cut to pay his debt. Yaya's income is actually Rp. 1,400,000 [A$200] but I only receive Rp. 600,000 (A$86) per month, while Rp. 800,000 [A$114] was debited directly to pay Yaya's debt. I use this money to pay for electricity and water bills and transport for the children. My two sons spend Rp. 20,000 [A$3] daily for public transport.
>
> Since April 2004, I have only received Rp. 250,000 [A$36], which is a very small amount. My youngest son has had to take a leave of absence from his university because I do not have any money, even to eat. I usually can buy 1 kilo

of rice every two days, which I eat with salt. I only eat once in two days because the important thing for me is that my children can eat. Sometimes I help my neighbors with housework and in return, they give me food. Some of my relatives, whom I often helped when I had money, sometimes also give me rice. On the day of *Idul Fitri*, I did not buy anything, but my husband also told me that he did not buy anything for his second wife and her children.[15]

Rosyid's polygamy also caused him to have a huge debt. At the time of our interview (February 2004), Tuti told me that Rosyid still had a Rp. 7,000,000 (A$1,000) debt to pay. Rosyid's and Yaya's cases, whose polygamy caused economic difficulties, are not rare. Many of the additional wives were willing to be married to gain economic benefits from their polygamous husbands, as in the saying quote earlier about bees that take honey from flowers and fly away when the honey is gone. Husbands had a reputation of doing anything to fulfill a younger wife's demands, even if it meant borrowing or stealing a large amount of money. Some polygamous husbands became bankrupt and or had no income at all. For instance, Yaya lost one of his jobs as a private school administrator because he was stealing money from this school in order to support the luxurious lifestyle of his second wife. Mahmud, a wood seller, and Kasim, a Chinese food seller, had also been bankrupt since the Indonesian monetary crisis in 1997. Mahmud, who had previously had four wives, divorced all his wives except Hilda, his second wife. At the time of our interview, Mahmud had put his only house on the market, in order to survive. Kasim also had to change his job, and went from selling Chinese food, where he earned at least Rp. 150,000 (A$21) per day, to working as an *ojek* driver, with a daily income of only about Rp. 30,000 (A$4).

As discussed in Chapter 3, the enactment of the Marriage Law aimed to prevent arbitrary polygamy, with strict requirements on husbands who intend to take another wife, including the stipulation that the husband must be able to provide maintenance to more than one wife. But since many polygamous husbands disobeyed the Law, as these cases show, it clearly does not necessarily protect women from such arbitrary polygamy.

The influence of polygamy on children's emotional and economic well-being

Polygamous marriages not only affected the emotional and economic well-being of first wives, but also the children in these polygamous households. This section will look more closely at how children felt about their father's polygamous marriages. As will be clear, not all children in polygamous marriages knew that their father was polygamous. This was because the father kept his additional marriage secret, or because some children were too young to understand the situation. As noted, I interviewed a small number of children from such households who were now of adult age, but much of the information in this section was obtained from their parents. I found that most children suffered economically within polygamous families, apart from the few very wealthy cases. But even though children of wealthy fathers were not economically affected by their father's polygamous marriage, many of them suffered emotionally.

For example, Lina told me that her children did not know about their father's polygamy until the day that Lina brought Nani, her co-wife, to her house to ask her husband Hadi to pronounce the triple *talak* (divorce formula) to Nani. Hadi refused to do so. Lina's oldest son, Budi (18), was wondering why there was a woman who was bold enough to sit side by side with his father in front of Lina in the living room and asked Lina who the woman was. Lina said that she was another wife of their father. Shocked by the news, Budi went to the backyard to look for a sword. Lina said that he was really angry and wanted to kill Nani, but he was able to restrain himself from doing it. He released his anger by hitting the back door with the sword. Lina also reported that Budi had run away from school, because he was ashamed when some of his friends found out about his father going out with another woman who was not Budi's mother.

I reported above Hadi's violence toward Lina after the second marriage. Lina reported that on one occasion Hadi saw his two children quarrelling. Hadi hit one of his children and kicked the other. He even pulled out his daughter's hair while dragging her. Lina told me that her children became even more upset after Lina was divorced from Hadi: I described the son's suicide attempt above. Lina told me that she would feel too guilty to leave the three older children with their father after her divorce. Economically, however, Lina's children seemed unaffected by Hadi's second marriage. Lina told me that Hadi always gave her enough money for her children. Lina had the impression that her children needed their father's money but they did not like him:

> My children told me that they only need their father's money. They also often stayed in their room when their father was home. When they knew that their father had gone out of the house, they came out from their rooms and asked me: 'Did Papa [father] give you money? I want to buy something.'[16]

These reactions by the children are clearly unusual, but perhaps they were disappointed that their father, a respected local council member and a lecturer in a higher education institution, had treated them and their mother violently. They were probably also afraid, and felt that hiding in their rooms was the best way to avoid their father's violence.

Unlike Lina's children, Hanny's children were both emotionally upset and economically deprived after their father's other relationships. Syifa (22), the first daughter of Hanny and Asep, told me about discovering her father's affair with a girl of her own age:

> I was ashamed of my father's love affair. I initially heard a rumor that my father has wives everywhere. I did not believe it, so I just ignored the rumor. I assumed that the rumor was spread by the people who were jealous of my family. However, one day, I found a letter in my father's office. The letter was from Dina's parents stating that they rejected my father's marriage proposal to Dina,

who was the same age as me. For me, his having an affair with a girl of my age was like his having an affair with his own child. However, he did not think that way.[17]

After realizing that her father had two other wives, Syifa realized that his income needed to be shared among more people. She was sad that whenever she asked her father for money, her father often said that he had none. Therefore, she decided to stop her tertiary studies to look for a job to pay for her own education, and to allow her father to pay for her younger brother's and her sisters' education.

Similarly, Rosiani (14), Hanny and Asep's youngest daughter, told me that she was really angry with her father and his new wife. She said that she disliked her father having any woman other than her mother and she could understand her mother's choice to divorce. She expected that her mother could now find a man who would make her happy.

Dahlia's children were also emotionally and economically affected by their father's polygamous marriage. Dahlia, the first wife of Dadi, described the emotional and economic changes experienced by her children after Dadi's second marriage. Dahlia told her oldest child, Dadan (25), about her husband's secret marriage at the same time that she herself found out about it. Dadan was silent, but seemed to suffer from a sense of loss and disappointment. Soon, Dahlia's other children found out about her father's polygamy. Her second child commented, 'Father will never stop doing it before something bad happens to him.' Her youngest son, Kiki (12), seemed to no longer trust his father. Dahlia told me that one day, Kiki called his father and asked him where he was. After the call, Kiki told Dahlia that his father had told him that he was on the way to somewhere, but Kiki told Dahlia, 'It seems to me that *Bapak* [Father] lies to me. I think he is not on his way to anywhere.'

Dahlia had the impression that Dadi had tried to introduce his children to Titin, his second wife. Dahlia said that one day, Dadi took his first son, Dadan (25), to visit Titin. Dadi asked Dadan to shake Titin's hand, but he refused. Titin was crying, because she felt rejected by Dadan. Dahlia also told me that Dadan prohibited Dahlia from accepting Titin. When Titin was pregnant, Dadi told Dadan that he would have another sibling, but asked Dadan not to tell Dahlia. Dahlia assumed that her husband had kept it secret from her in order not to hurt her.

As described above, since marrying another woman, Dadi no longer gave Dahlia all his income. Dahlia needed to ask her children to ask their father for money for their education. But Dahlia told me that in the first year of Dadi's polygamous marriage, even though he had more income, Dadi was often angry with his children when they asked him for money. Dahlia heard Dadi's saying to his children, 'If you need money for tuition, give me plenty of advance warning.' Dahlia was sad because she knew that it was difficult for his children to communicate with a father who was rarely at home.

Dahlia said that it was Kiki, her youngest child, who seemed most affected emotionally and economically by his father's polygamy. Before Dadi's second marriage, Kiki was indulged and received a great deal of attention from his father. For instance, Dadi and Kiki usually went to the supermarket to do the weekly shopping and to buy Kiki's favorite food and snacks. When Kiki did not want to eat at home, Dadi would take him to KFC. Dahlia said that Dadi stopped these outings with Kiki after taking another wife, and mostly spent his time with his second wife rather than his children.

While Hanny and Asep's daughters were emotionally affected by their father's taking additional wives, Iin (12), the youngest daughter of Suhadi, who had two wives, seemed unbothered by her father's polygamy. Iin told me that her father had often been away from home. She missed him when he was away. She said that when her father was not at home, he might be at meetings or might be 'there'. I asked what she meant by 'there'. She said, 'With his young wife' (*ke yang muda*). She told me that she had seen her parents arguing, which made her sad, but she could do nothing about it. She also said that her father had brought her to visit his young wife, Maya. Iin said that she spent her time there watching television and listening to Maya's story about her *kosidah* song performances.[18]

Similarly, in contrast to the children in other polygamous marriages, Nadira (24), Suhadi's first daughter, did not show any objection to her father's polygamy. She seemed to be well-prepared when I met her for the interview. She also showed me a book entitled *Sistem Pergaulan dalam Islam* (Relationship System in Islam), which she had read in order to be more informed about polygamy in Islam before I interviewed her. As an activist in one of the Islamist organizations, *Hizbut Tahrir*, she wanted to defend polygamy.

> I believed that polygamy is permitted in Islam, and I am happy that my mother understands Islam by not rejecting polygamy. What I wonder about is whether my father practices polygamy based on God's order or not. I do not like my neighbors' attitudes toward polygamy, which they showed by comforting my mother and showing their pity to my mother. This attitude toward polygamy is un-Islamic. Polygamy is permitted in Islam, and I reject the requirement for justice in polygamy because it is impossible for a man to be perfectly just to his wives, especially in terms of love and sexual relationship. I also believe that a husband does not need his wife's permission to take another wife, because *shari'a* did not ask to do so.[19]

Nadira's strong adherence to Islamist ideas on polygamy emerged from her Textualist, literal approach in understanding the Qur'anic verse 4: 3. Given her strong support for polygamy, which she regarded as permissible in Islam and therefore demanding tolerance and acceptance, I wondered whether she would agree to her (hypothetical) husband taking another wife. She indirectly said no: 'I only express my belief; in practice, it is different. There is a difference between belief and practice.' As noted in the Introduction to this book, I have found many Islamist ideas problematic when it comes to practice, especially in terms of the relationship between husband and wife.

One of Kiayi Jamal's sons, Rahman (25), showed an unusual response to polygamous marriage, seeming able to 'accept' and enjoy his status as the son of a rich *kiayi* who had four wives. Rahman, the only one of Kiayi Jamal's children to have a tertiary degree, felt that he was economically comfortable. He knew that his father had a considerable amount of money, so there was no question of economic problems being posed by polygamy. Other than giving spiritual help to his patients, his father earned money from renting party facilities, and from managing school foundations. In his view, his father supported his children's development by supporting any activities that could give benefit to his children. For instance, he was supportive when Rahman wanted to continue his study to a tertiary level, while his other sisters and brothers stopped studying when they finished senior high school.

Rahman said that his father was temperamental, stubborn and did not give his children enough attention. He said that his father was not a busy person but he had too many children – 20 children – so he could not give them enough attention. Indeed, as noted, Kiayi Jamal could not even remember how many children he had and what their names were when I asked him. Rahman said that he was happy with his father's polygamous marriage. He regarded his mother as a friend, while he saw his father's other wives as being like his own mother. However, Rahman told me that his mother had in fact asked for a divorce a long time ago, when she found out that Kiayi Jamal had secretly taken another wife during her third pregnancy.

In contrast to Suhadi's daughters, Iin and Nadira, whose father's polygamous marriage seemed not to have any negative effect on their emotional and economic well-being, Tio (21), the youngest son of Yaya and Eli, found that his father's polygamy had caused misery for his mother, himself and his two brothers. Tio told me that he had to take a leave of absence from his university studies, owing to problems with having no financial support. He told me:

> I found out about my father's second marriage when I was in my second year of junior high school. Initially, I felt hurt, but I tried to forget it. What could I do? We have been suffering because my father spent more money on his second wife, even though we needed more money for our education. Now, I do not want to think about it. I just want to think that I do not have a father anymore. I do not want to be like my father, who has more than one wife.
>
> Years ago, my mother was often angry whenever my father called her. She was also often angry whenever she watched a TV drama about a husband who takes an additional wife. She often discussed it and gave us advice in order not to follow in our father's footsteps. I felt bored by such advice. We tried not to talk about our father. There is no benefit in talking about him, because he does not care about us anymore. The important thing for us now is how to survive.[20]

The above quotation shows that he no longer cared about a father who had not cared for him, his two brothers and mothers for a long time. As discussed in Chapter 4, his father took a very young wife secretly in 1995, and after this came to light in 1996, his father abandoned his mother and her children to live with his younger wife, causing them to suffer economically and emotionally.

A bargain with patriarchy and settling for polygamy

Household arrangements among my informants mostly fit with the descriptions given by Geertz (1961) and Koentjaraningrat (1985: 133). They suggest that in Java, soon after marriage, a couple are expected to establish their own separate nuclear family, although many couples temporarily live in either the wife's or the husband's parents' household, with some preference for the wife's. Even though married couples tend to live in separate houses, according to Vreede-de Stuers (1960: 30), they are closely bound to both sides of the family and tend to help each other if they experience difficulties. Parents from either or both sides usually help the newly established household, but later it is the couple that mainly support their parents in old age. Some aged parents live in their children's households, but generally prefer to live with their daughters rather than daughters-in-law (Koentjaraningrat, 1985: 142). This tallies well with the arrangements among my informants, like those of Lina, Tuti, Rosa, Aida, Mila, Hanny and Arsa.

Some case studies, in either Chapter 4 or Chapter 5, demonstrated men's reluctance to obey the Law in relation to marriage registration, only doing so if their younger wife demanded it. Therefore, unless the woman is aware of the importance of marriage registration, the Law affords her no protection. In addition, unless polygamous men choose to obey the Marriage Law's restrictions on polygamy, arbitrary polygamy cannot be avoided. It is also clear that polygamy can bring shame not only for those who practice it, but also for their first wife, their children and their parents.

There are similarities between Joko's practice of polygamy and Kiayi Jamal's. Both of them were rich men who had four wives. We can suggest that all their wives sacrificed their negative feelings of sharing a husband with three other women in order to retain the social status and economic security that their husbands offered. Using Kandiyoti's concept of the patriarchal bargain (1988: 283), we can argue that these women have exchanged their discomfort at sharing a husband for the social status and economic security that they received from their husband.

In contrast, since Memed was poor, it was clear that both of his wives, Edah and Neni, did not have any especial economic motives. It is not known what motivated these women to stay in the polygamous marriage because I did not interview them. It is possible, however, to assume that it might have been better for Neni and her children to have a husband/father who had another wife, rather than no father at all, and she may have also wanted to avoid the social stigma that accompanied having 'illegitimate' children. For Edah, it might have been better for her to 'accept' her husband's second marriage rather than seek a divorce, which was also socially stigmatized. Thus, these women had made a choice in of a difficult situation. Again, according to Kandiyoti's concept of the patriarchal bargain (1988: 283), these women had sacrificed their feelings about sharing a husband in exchange for the social status of having a husband. Memed was not the only poor man who took another wife. Ali did too.

Why did Leli, a young attractive girl, want to marry Yaya, who was far older than her? According to Eli, Yaya's first wife, Leli came from a very poor family. Eli told me that Leli's mother, who was divorced, had appeared to ask Leli to marry Yaya, because Yaya had a car and hence the mother assumed that Yaya was rich. Eli said that Leli did not love Yaya, and Leli knew that Yaya was already married with many children. Eli assumed that Leli, Yaya's second wife, was already pregnant when Yaya married her, because Leli had had a boyfriend before she met Yaya, and that Leli's first child was not Yaya's: in 1997, two years after Leli's marriage to Yaya, her son was two years old. From this information, it is possible to argue that Leli 'exchanged' – borrowing Kandiyoti's word – her beauty and youth for apparent economic security and social status for her child. Thus, Leli cannot be seen as merely a victim; she fulfilled her side of the bargain by marrying an older man.

The fact that Nita, a highly educated woman, was willing to become the third wife of Dadi, seems to negate some of my assumptions. I assumed that the more educated the woman, the more capacity she would have to be economically independent. In addition, I assumed that the more economically independent women were, the more choices they would have in relation to marriage. Nita was not the only educated woman who was willing to be an additional wife. All of Puspo Wardoyo's wives, except for his second wife, had university degrees, but were still willing to be involved in polygamous marriages. I speculate that they might have chosen to take advantage of the economic luxuries their husbands could provide, rather than earning their own living. However, my assumption seems to apply only in four cases: those of Hanny, Ema, Risa and Lina, who preferred divorce to polygamous marriage.

The cases of Yaya and Ali are similar. Both of them had irregular rosters with their wives and did not use religion as the motive or justification for their practice of polygamy. They appeared not to know or to care about religion and did not try to fulfil the religious requirement of treating wives justly. Other informants behaved in a similar fashion: Mahmud for example, told me that he only started to learn Qur'anic verses about polygamy after reading media coverage of Wardoyo's polygamy. Ali and Yaya confessed that they did not know much about Islamic teaching. Three of them took additional wives because they were tempted to do so. As a result, their own needs and interests dominated their treatment of their wives, and they were often seen as treating their wives and children unjustly. Their cases of polygamous marriage would appear to negate the Qur'anic guidelines stated in verse 4: 129:

> You are never able to be fair and just as between women, even if it is your ardent desire; but turn not away (from a woman) altogether, so as to leave her (as it were) hanging (in the air). If you come to a friendly understanding, and practice self-restraint, God is Oft-forgiving, Most Merciful.
>
> (Ali, 1989: 227)

In contrast, Suhadi, Kiayi Jamal, Jajang and Maman, who used religion to justify their practice of polygamy, seemed to try to follow religious instruction to treat their wives justly by having a regular roster. Suhadi's case seemed to be the only one that truly fitted the context of Qur'anic verses 4: 2–3: polygamy as a 'solution' to protect orphans from unjust treatment, with the requirement that a man must treat his wives justly. His second marriage, however, had created discomfort for his first wife, Mila, and undermined her happiness. Dadi's case seemed to be exceptional. Even though he was rich and highly educated, he did not seem to be willing to treat his wife justly, and for more than six months at a time would avoid visiting his first wife and children. Syamsul also had an irregular roster with his first wife, Rosa. He visited Rosa only occasionally, in the afternoon, because he was too busy with his career as a high-ranking academic. But unlike Dadi, Syamsul displayed a sense of responsibility for Rosa. For instance, he gave her a monthly maintenance allowance. He also sent her his car and his driver when he could not accompany her to doctor's appointments. On the day of my first interview with her, in the late afternoon, Syamsul's driver came to pick up Rosa to go to her doctor. On my third visit to Rosa in the mid afternoon, her husband was there. Syamsul also seemed to care about Rosa's feelings: he let her decide whether to stay in the marriage or to seek a divorce. He did not want to divorce her against her will.

Thus, some polygamous husbands knew of the Qur'anic guidelines regarding just treatment. Some husbands appeared to try to follow these guidelines by adopting a regular roster with their wives, but other husbands just ignored them. Yet, the wives whose husbands tried did not necessarily feel that they were being treated justly.

In addition, most of the first wives, except Lina, Rosa and the wives of Kiayi Jamal, suffered economically after the husband's second marriage, and this also had negative repercussions for their children. Syifa (23), Hanny's daughter, and Tio (21), Eli's son, had to drop out from their studies because of the absence of economic support from their fathers. Most of the adult children in polygamous marriages in my study were both economically and psychologically disadvantaged, and ashamed of having a father who married another woman. Via (22), Ratih's daughter, never allowed friends to visit her house, for fear that they might ask about Vic's father, who had not returned home since marrying other women. Dadan (25), Dadi's son, had similar concerns about his friends. His situation was complicated by the fact that he and his friends studied at the university where his father taught. Dadi's polygamy was widely known (he was known as a *tukang kawin*, 'maker of marriages'). This could potentially damage Dadan's reputation and make it difficult for him to find a wife (cf. Grace's study in Lombok, 2004). Many of these adult children felt traumatized by their experiences, and therefore they were determined not to practice polygamy themselves (e.g. Tio and Ucok, whose case was presented in Chapter 3).

6 Conclusion

> Polygamy is a religious rule, we could not change that ...
> (Ibu Hayinah in Wieringa, 1995: 81)

Ibu Hayinah is a woman's activist in Aisyiyah, the women's wing of Muhammadiyah, and her view of polygamy, related in the quotation above, is one held by the majority of Indonesian Muslims. From Kartini's era until the present, this belief that polygamy is a religious rule has persisted, as if the claim that 'polygamy is permitted in Islam' is the only truth; as if this belief has to be taken for granted; as if this belief is divine and therefore cannot be challenged or changed; and as if challenging polygamy is equivalent to challenging Islam. In contrast, this book argues that polygamy is not a religious rule or an Islamic value. Polygamy is a pre-Islamic practice which has been regulated by Islam in order to prevent injustice to powerless orphans. Thus, what is Islamic in the Qur'anic verses 4: 2–3 is not 'the practice of polygamy itself' but 'the importance of being just to the powerless'. As this research suggests, polygamy can lead to unjust treatment of women and their children. This book takes the view that to prevent such injustice (and given that preventing injustice is an Islamic value accepted by all schools of Islamic thought), the Indonesian Marriage Law should be modified to abolish the practice of polygamy.

Qur'an is divine, while its interpretation is human

As an activist who was involved in the Marriage Council of the Ministry of Religious Affairs, Ibu Hayinah often had to deal with cases of polygamy. She found many men used this religious belief as a license to practice polygamy. This made her concerned with the practice as she found many polygamous men had abused the practice by not following Islamic guidelines (of treating wives justly). But due to her literal understanding that 'Islam permits polygamy', she was not so bold as to challenge what she believed to be a religious rule (Wieringa, 1995). Similarly, many other Muslim women's activists (discussed in Chapter 3) and the research participants often faced a similar dilemma. On the one hand, they personally disagreed with polygamy. On the other hand, they were afraid of rejecting polygamy for fear of being accused of rejecting Islam because of the belief that polygamy is a religious rule. This book has shown that the belief that 'Islam permits polygamy' is only one among other interpretations of the Qur'anic verses 4: 3. The Qur'an itself is divine, but its interpretations are human products, therefore they cannot be regarded as an absolute truth, but they can be challenged.

I have argued in Chapter 3 that Muslim discourses on polygamy revolve around three different interpretations of the Qur'anic verse 4: 3: the Textualists, who believe that Islam permits polygamy; the Semi-textualists, who believe that polygamy is permitted under certain circumstances; and the Contextualists, who believe that polygamy is prohibited. The majority of Indonesian Muslims belong to the Semi-textualist group, and as such, their interpretation of polygamy gained significant support and was therefore adopted in the 1974 Marriage Law. Many members of this group regard their interpretation of polygamy as the religion itself and fail to differentiate between the Qur'an, which is understood to be divinely inspired, and its interpretation, which is human and therefore fallible. The failure to differentiate between the Qur'an and its interpretation also occurred among my research participants who mostly felt that Islam permits polygamy and therefore they should accept it as a sign of their acceptance of their religion.

Ultimately my research emphasizes the difference between the Qur'an and its interpretations. It has argued that the claims made by some Islamists such as that 'polygamy is part of *shari'a*' or 'Islam permits polygamy, therefore its prohibition is against Islamic teaching' represent only one interpretation. Therefore, in opposition to the assumption that rejecting polygamy is equivalent to rejecting Islam or not accepting Islam comprehensively, this book argued that rejecting polygamy is not equivalent to rejecting Islam, but involves a view of polygamy which is different from the mainstream interpretation. As human interpretation, the claim that 'Islam permits polygamy' is fallible. Moreover, such an interpretation should not invalidate other interpretations, such as the view that 'Islam prohibits polygamy'.

The conception that 'Islam prohibits polygamy' is not new. Countries with a Muslim majority population, such as Turkey and Tunisia, have adopted this interpretation into their family law since the 1920s and 1956 respectively. What is new is the Islamists' campaign advocating polygamy on the basis of such claims that 'polygamy is better than *zina*' (adultery) and 'polygamy is *sunnah Rasul*' (recommended by the Prophet). These campaigns to promote polygamy have the potential to impact on many Indonesian Muslim women, not only the women whose cases are discussed in this book. Such encouragement of polygamy can threaten all monogamous marriages because the increasing religious legitimacy granted to polygamy plays a very real role in everyday life for all women in Indonesia. Women live with the constant and increasing worry that someday their husband will ask their permission to take another wife or, even worse, simply inform them after the fact that he has taken another wife for 'religious' reasons.

The campaigns advocating a polygamous lifestyle also present a challenge for women's organizations such as the women's wing of Muhammadiyah and NU who promote *keluarga sakinah* (peaceful families) and *keluarga maslahah* (virtuous and prosperous families) respectively – free from polygamous practices. Some male scholars, such as Mustofa (2007), Gusmian (2007) and Abdul Kodir (2005), have criticized the aforementioned Islamists' claims. Abdul Kodir (2005), for instance, argues that none of the classical Qur'anic exegetes holds such pro-polygamy opinions. Even Takariawan (2007), a leading figure in PKS party, which is commonly labeled as an Islamist party, criticizes such claims and makes public his opposition to the rising incidence of polygamy among his party members.

The need for a contextual approach in reading the Qur'an

This book has shown that throughout the history of the Indonesian women's movement since the early twentieth century, polygamy has been a crucial issue alongside issues such as child and forced marriage, unilateral divorce and female education, leading to marriage law reform. The book has discussed the ways in which polygamy has been widely admitted to have caused social problems, such as deserted wives and neglected children, in the first half of the twentieth century. Even though most Muslim women's organizations knew about this problem, they have been unwilling to support the abolition of polygamy proposed by secular women's organizations such as *Istri Sedar* and *Perwari* owing to their reluctance to confront their male organizations and their belief that they cannot prohibit something that is permitted by their religion. Again, this shows that they have failed to differentiate between religion and its interpretation, which can be fluid and contextual: therefore any law should be changed if it contradicts the intended purpose of *shari'a*.

The women's organizations' struggles to reform the marriage law faced many obstacles. President Soekarno's practice of polygamy has been seen as betraying women's support for national struggles of independence. In addition, even though the Soeharto government supported the marriage law reform, the government had to seek a compromise with Islamist groups by giving authority to religious courts, not civil courts, in dealing with cases of polygamy and divorce. The minimal involvement of women in these decisions prior to the enactment of the 1974 Marriage Law led to the marginalization of women's issues within the heated debates between secular and Muslim parties in the Parliament. As a result, many contemporary Indonesian feminists regard the Marriage Law as discriminating against women. They also see this Law as a government tool to homogenize a gender ideology that serves to 'domesticate' women. Furthermore, the Law also has been criticized for its ambiguity in relation to marriage registration. This ambiguity has caused continuing debates between secular and religious groups about whether or not registration is a requirement for valid marriage. It seems to me that similar debates will be likely to occur in the future if the Marriage Law is not amended. Therefore, to avoid such lack of clarity, I would support Indonesian feminists' efforts to amend the 1974 Marriage Law: to protect the rights of women and children, it would be better to have unregistered marriage declared invalid. But cooperation with *ulama*, especially the conservative ones, is important to enlighten them first on the benefits of marriage registration and to convince them that marriage registration is not against *shari'a*.[1]

I have discussed extensively how the New Order government demonstrated negative attitudes to divorce and polygamy by placing further restrictions on police, armed forces and civil servants in matters of marriage. They had to obtain the permission of their superior before divorcing or taking additional wives. In practice, however, these regulations were problematic. Very few adhered to them and many others manipulated the requirements for polygamy or failed to register polygamous marriages, all of which disadvantaged women and their children.

The post-Soeharto period was marked by widespread re-Islamization which introduced a new context for debates around polygamy. In contrast to the Soeharto period, many proponents of polygamy have become more vocal in expressing their opposition to the restrictions on polygamy and have even promoted polygamy as part of Islamic values. But this promotion has been mostly countered by moderate and progressive Muslim feminists. Thus, throughout Indonesian history, polygamy has become an object of the conflicting interest between various groups, in which secular western-educated Muslims argue for the abolition of polygamy; conservative Islamist Muslims argue for allowing polygamy; and the mainstream moderate Muslims argue for its restriction.

Using Fazlur Rahman's approach of a *double movement* in understanding Qur'anic verses 4: 2–3 in relation to polygamy discussed in Chapter 3, one can infer that the verses are not about the permitting of polygamy, but rather that they stress the importance of justice – justice for the powerless orphaned girls and justice for women. To maintain the relevance of the Qur'anic spirit, I would suggest that this intended message of the Qur'an ideally be applied in the current context of Indonesia. This book has shown that when polygamy was permitted in an unregulated way (prior to the enactment of the 1974 Marriage Law), it was practiced arbitrarily, causing the social problems of neglected wives and children. Similarly, at the present time, when polygamy is restricted, many Muslim men in Indonesia manipulate and flout the restrictions on polygamy, because of their literal understanding that polygamy is permitted in Islam. Therefore, as this book has shown, polygamy has created many cases of injustice to women and children. Such injustice is clearly against Islamic teaching. Therefore, in line with Rahman's argument that the rules can be changed in order to change the present situation to conform to the spirit of the Qur'anic verse, I would support the abolition of polygamy in order to prevent this injustice.

This argument is supported by Abduh's concept of *maslahat* (welfare or public interest). Abduh argues that *law is just a tool*; its main and ultimate *aim is to create social welfare* for all human beings (cited in Nasution, 1996: 20, my emphasis). This suggests a flexible and contextual interpretation of the Qur'anic verses, rather than a rigid, literal interpretation which stresses only symbolism, and not the essence. Accordingly, it would be a mistake to retain the law if human welfare is ignored or neglected. Similarly, as Wadud and Barazangi argue, because of the changing and the diverse context of Muslim lives, to maintain the relevance of Islamic teaching in a contemporary situation, Qur'anic verses must be continually reinterpreted (Barazangi, 2004; Wadud, 1999). The relevance of these two arguments in relation to polygamy is that it would be a mistake to retain a law which 'permits' or 'restricts' polygamy if the practice of polygamy had caused injustice to women and children. To prevent such injustice, the law has to be changed from 'permission' in the classical *fiqh* texts and 'restriction' in the 1974 Marriage Law to 'prohibition' of polygamy. Such reform is important because in the long run, the prohibition of polygamy, like the prohibition of slavery (which is similar to polygamy, in that both of them are not explicitly prohibited in the Qur'an), will hopefully create more stigma for those who practice it and therefore can further discourage its practice.

The above arguments suggest the importance of the contextual approach in reading the Qur'anic messages. However, I am aware that it is not easy to employ this approach. To employ this approach, a person has to have relevant knowledge of Islamic studies such as Arabic language, *fiqh* (Islamic jurisprudence), *tafsir* (Qur'anic exegesis), *usul al-fiqh* (principles of Islamic jurisprudence), *asbab al-nuzul al-Qur'an* (the context where the Qur'an was revealed) and knowledge of the current context in which he or she lives. *Pesantren* and IAIN/UIN (the Institutes or Universities for Islamic Studies) would be the important institutions to prepare a person to have a contextual approach to the Qur'an, especially since the early 1970s. Azyumardi Azra, the former rector of UIN Jakarta and one of the leading liberal thinkers in Indonesia, reported that since the early 1970s, the leading scholars of IAIN such as Nurcholish Madjid, Harun Nasution and Mukti Ali, three of whom were western-educated scholars, reoriented the direction of Islamic studies in Indonesia from a normative approach to a historical, sociological and empirical approach. This reorientation, according to Azra, is useful because the normative approach tends to see Islam as an 'idealistic religion', which often leads Muslims to be 'trapped into "spiritual satisfaction"', neglecting the socio-historical realities (Azra, 2002: 100). Indeed, even though a normative approach to Islamic studies has advantages, such as to guide Muslims how to be Islamic adherents, this approach tends to see Islam as idealistic religion and can lead Muslims to ignore Muslim realities. This can be seen, for instance, in the case of Ibu Hayinah and other members of Muslim women's organizations prior to the 1990s, who knew that the permission or the restriction of polygamy had been abused by many Muslim men but did not use this knowledge of realities to challenge the existing majority's interpretation that 'Islam permits polygamy'.[2]

As one of the IAIN graduates and a western-educated Muslim, I claim this research as one of the examples of this reorientation in Islamic studies. It is an empirical research on the everyday practice of polygamous marriages, not merely an idealistic view of polygamy. This research can provide useful information for *ulama* in their *ijtihad* on polygamy, in order that their *ijtihad* is not merely based on a male normative perspective, but also takes into account the perspectives of women and children who have been involved in polygamous marriages. This will hopefully ensure increased connections between ideals and realities so that legal changes can occur to accommodate changing times and circumstances (*taghayyurul ahkaami bi taghayyuril azminati wal amkinati wal ahwali*) in order to enhance social welfare for all human beings.

In addition, since the early 1970s, IAIN employ various perspectives in Islamic studies that encourage students to be more open and tolerant to various religious interpretations (Azra, 2002). However, Azra points out that even though many western-educated scholars have been influential in this process of change within IAIN, the influence of many Middle Eastern graduates, who mostly stress the textual normative approach in Islamic studies, is still apparent. Thus, as he suggests, 'the IAIN has become the meeting place for these two orientations within Islamic studies' (Azra, 2002: 101). The 'battle' of influence between western-educated Muslims, who are mostly in favor of a liberal and contextual approach to Islam, and Middle Eastern graduates, who are mostly in favor of a literal or textual normative approach not only occur within IAIN/UIN but also in their higher level, the Ministry of Religious Affairs (MORA).[3] This can be seen, for instance, in the case of Abdurrahman Mas'ud, one of the western-educated scholars who attempted to be more open to the liberal and progressive thinking of Islam. He was recently dismissed from his position as the Director of Islamic Higher Education for allegedly being too liberal. Just before he was dismissed from his high position in MORA, Mas'ud organized two conferences in which he invited Nasr Abu Zaid, an Egyptian Muslim scholar who was expelled from his country for his liberal and contextual approach to the Qur'an, as one of the guest speakers.[4] Even though Abu Zaid could travel from the Netherlands to Indonesia, he was allegedly being prevented by the leading authority in MORA, who was a Middle Eastern graduate, from attending these two conferences.

The above case shows the apparent fear of the influence of a liberal and contextual approach to Islam, which some Middle Eastern graduates who work in IAIN/UIN and MORA thought to be 'too western'. To prevent the spread of this 'western' influence, some 'subtle' efforts have been undertaken within both IAIN/UIN and MORA. For example, one of my colleagues, who had done her MA under the supervision of Nasr Abu Zaid and had been teaching Semiotics and a Hermeneutical approach to Qur'anic interpretation, was shocked when she was told that she could no longer teach this course. She was told that this subject could not be offered to Qur'anic studies students because it was no longer needed. In addition, several western doctoral graduates could not teach in the postgraduate program, even though they were previously sent to the West to fill in the position of the postgraduate lecturers in IAIN/UIN. Finally, on 28 April 2008, MORA issued a circular to stop sending students or lecturers within MORA to western countries such as America, Europe and Australia to study Islamic Studies or Religious Studies for the reason that there are a sufficient number of the scholars already in this area.

This circular can be one of the ways to lessen the growing influence of western-educated scholars within MORA and Islamic higher education institutions. It also shows the success of some Islamists or conservative Muslims who may not be in favor of a liberal and contextual approach to Islam in influencing those who are in power within the Department of Religious Affairs. All of these cases show that the success or failure of the proposal to abolish polygamy in the projected amendment of the marriage law will likely depend on who is in power in the MORA (and the Ministry of Women's Empowerment). If Siti Musdah Mulia, one of the leading Indonesian progressive Muslim feminists, is selected to be in one of the two positions, the proposal will likely to be successful. She seems likely to be selected to be the Minister of Women's Empowerment (depending on who is the next elected president), but since religion is still a male-dominated area, she will be unlikely to be selected to be the Minister of Religious Affairs. Even though the issue of polygamy can be dealt with by the Ministry of Women's Empowerment, it is still regarded as a religious issue which will likely be highly controlled by the MORA. It is my hope that a man or woman with pro-gender justice views and who favors a contextual approach to Islam will lead MORA.

There are also other strong reasons to amend the 1974 Marriage Law in relation to the abolition of polygamy. First, as part of the international community, Indonesia ratified the Convention on the Elimination of All Forms of Discrimination against Women (CEDAW) in 1984. This means that Indonesia has agreed to make any necessary changes, including amending its laws in accordance with the Convention. In addition, it means that Indonesia has agreed with the international monitoring on the implementation of the Convention and has agreed to provide reports on any achievements that Indonesia has made in implementing the Convention (Alimi *et al.*, 1999: 41). As previously discussed, Indonesian Marriage Law adopts monogamous marriage, but it allows (only) a man to have more than one spouse if he has an intent to do so and if he can fulfill the state requirements for it. This means that the 1974 Marriage Law has treated men and women differently on the basis of their sex. This contradicts the CEDAW Article 1 which defines discrimination against women as follow:

> For the purposes of the present Convention, the term 'discrimination against women' shall mean any distinction, exclusion or restriction made on the basis of sex which has the effect or purpose of impairing or nullifying the recognition, enjoyment or exercise by women, irrespective of their marital status, on a basis of equality of men and women, of human rights and fundamental freedoms in the political, economic, social, cultural, civil or any other field.
> (Department of Economic and Social Affairs, 2004)

Since Indonesia has ratified CEDAW, Indonesia has to amend its Marriage Law by adopting monogamous marriage, with no exception being given to either sexes.

Second, several cases in this study such as the cases of Dahlia, Eli and Lina show that some polygamous marriages tend to violate the 2004 Law on the Eradication of Domestic Violence. As the cases have shown, Dahlia and Eli have both experienced economic neglect by their husbands since their husbands took an additional wife, while Lina has experienced sexual violence because of her reluctance to have sexual relations with her husband since she knew of her husband's additional marriage. Most of the women in the case studies also experienced psychological violence. For example, Arsa and Risa had to visit psychologists to discuss the psychological problems generated by their husbands' choosing to live polygamously. This shows that the law allowing the practice of polygamy, which violates other state laws, needs to be amended.

Third, the cases in this research such as those of Lina, Dahlia and Tuti clearly show how a husband's taking another wife has taken away the first wife's sexual enjoyment. Women's right to sexual enjoyment is one of the women's reproductive rights in Islam – a feature that is still largely unknown among the majority of Muslims. In Indonesia, these rights have been advocated especially by *Perhimpunan Pengembangan Pesantren dan Masyarakat/P3M* (Indonesian Society for Pesantren and Community Development), which was founded in 1983.[5] Even though this NGO was not legally affiliated with NU, its activists and leaders such as Masdar F Mas'udi and Lies Marcos came from the NU circle. This NGO organized gender training and advocated women's reproductive rights in some NU *pesantren* beginning in 1994 in response to the existing unequal gender relations which mostly emphasize a man's rights with regard to his spouse and a woman's responsibilities/obligations toward her spouse (Marcos-Natsir, 2000).[6] For example, many Muslims men and women tend to see sexual relations as man's rights and woman's obligation. As a result, many husbands require their wives to 'serve' their sexual needs regardless of the unreadiness or unwillingness of their wife to do so. Mas'udi's book (1997) tries to radically change some of the common Muslim beliefs about women in Islam. Unlike most of the books on women, which tend to stress the women's obligations, Mas'udi's book emphasises women's rights. The book argues that women have the right to choose their spouse (arguing against arranged marriage), that women have the right to sexual enjoyment (arguing against the belief that women are obliged to 'serve' the husband's sexual needs), that women have the right to have or not have children (arguing against the social pressure on women to have children after their marriage), that women have the right to decide when and whether to be pregnant (including their right to abort an unwanted pregnancy), that women have the right to decide how to take care of their children (arguing against those who see child care as women's obligation), that women have the right for reproductive leave such as being free from daily prayer during menstruation, and that women have the right to divorce a spouse (arguing against the belief that only a husband has the right to divorce his wife). This means that to protect women's rights, the 1974 Marriage Law, which allows polygamy, needs to be amended.

I am aware that the prohibition of polygamy in the projected amendment of the marriage law would be likely to invite resistance from many Textualists and Semi-textualists who believe that Islam permits polygamy. In addition, as this research has shown, many polygamous husbands disobey the law and therefore the law does not necessarily provide protection for women and children. This can probably be anticipated, for instance, by publications that stress the difference between the Qur'an and its interpretation. Special training for religious leaders and *ulama* could also be provided to stress the fallibility of *fiqh* works and the importance of the concept of welfare in applying certain laws. This social education certainly will not be an easy task, especially in the present situation, when the Islamist influence seems to be growing stronger. The campaigns by Sisters in Islam (SIS) in Malaysia to counter the monopoly of male *ulama* in interpreting the Qur'an could provide a useful model for Indonesian Muslim feminists in countering dominant discourses about polygamy (Ong, 2006). In Indonesia, groups similar to SIS, such as the women's studies centers in IAIN/UIN (State Institutes/Universities for Islamic

Studies) throughout Indonesia, the Institute for Religious and Gender Research (LKAJ) under the Department of Religious Affairs led by Musdah Mulia, and NGOs that are concerned with women and the use of religion to justify injustice toward women such as Rahima, Puan Amal Hayati, Nasyiatul Aisyiyah of Muhammadiyah, Muslimat and Fatayat of NU and LBH APIK in Jakarta, have also been attempting to challenge the dominant male interpretation of the Qur'an. Their endeavors are important in continually providing alternative views that are friendlier to women; therefore they deserve to be supported.

Most of the discussion in Chapter 4 and Chapter 5 is based mainly on the perspectives and lived experiences of first wives, even though polygamous marriages affected not only first wives but also additional wives and their children. As these chapters showed, even though some additional wives of rich men could derive economic advantage from their husbands, many other additional wives suffered from a lack of economic and emotional support from the husband. This can be seen, for instance, in the cases of Nuri and Lia, who had become increasingly demanding economically and emotionally, not to mention those women who had been married secretly. The latter could not claim their rights if their marriages were problematic because they had no legal proof of the marriage. Thus, further research could focus more on the perspectives and lived experiences of additional wives. In addition, even though my findings about the impact of polygamy on the well-being of children were only based on my interviews with 11 children from polygamous families and have been mostly mediated by their parents, my research has brought the previously ignored children's perspective into the center of the discourse on polygamy. Further research which focuses more on the impact of polygamy on the emotional and economic well-being of children would be very important to support the campaigns for the abolition of polygamy in order to protect children from unjust treatment. Finally, I hope this research will begin to fill in some of the gaps in our knowledge of women's experiences in polygamous marriages, as noted earlier by Blackburn 2004a).

Notes

1 Introduction

1 'Saya tidak setuju dengan poligami yang dilakukan sekarang ini yang kebanyakan hanya berdasar nafsu belaka. Misalnya, seperti yang dilakukan suami saya yang belum mapan secara ekonomi. ... Beberapa bulan setelah pernikahannya yang kedua, dia punya banyak utang dan uang SPP anak-anak tidak terbayar. Dengan utang yang besar seperti itu, saya pikir saya harus menghentikan pernikahannya yang kedua sebelum keadaan ekonominya tambah memburuk.'
2 For ethical reasons, all participants' names are pseudonyms.
3 Rahman (2005: 76) pointed out the absence of data on women's experiences in polygamous marriages by saying: '*Tidak pernah ada data yang memperlihatkan bagaimana pengalaman perempuan pada berbagai perkawinan poligami.*'
4 See for example Blackwood's study of Minangkabau women rice farmers (2008), in which she highlights women's agency. Blackwood sees that these women farmers have actively redefined the term 'housewife' by including their work on the farm as part of their domestic work, not following the New Order state ideology of housewife. Blackwood also regards these women, not simply as victims of poor economic condition, but as being active in creating new work practices and labor networks.
5 PP 10 is an Indonesian government regulation that requires civil servants to ask the permission of their superior before divorcing or practicing polygamy, which will be discussed in Chapter 3.
6 'Secular' is a contested term. It is often understood as meaning 'non-religious'. For the purpose of this thesis, I shall use Vanaik's (1992) and Engineer's (2003) definition that secularity is state neutrality with regard to religion. This, according to Vanaik, 'can mean either a fundamental separation of the state from religious activity and affiliation, or state impartiality on all issues relating to the religious interests of different communities' (1992). This definition implies that secularity does not necessarily imply being non-religious. Someone can be religious, but may disagree with the state's partiality toward certain religion.
7 Literalist Muslims, or in Saeed's category the Textualists and the Semi-Textualists, adopt a literalistic approach to the text. They mainly rely on the linguistic criteria in understanding the meaning of the Qur'anic verses, not taking into account the socio-historical context of the Qur'an and the contemporary context (Saeed, 2006b: 3).
8 Though I am aware of the existing distancing from western feminism forwarded by some Muslim women, for instance, in Malaysia, by preferring to use the term 'womanist' to 'feminist'. The reasons for this distancing, according to Stivens (2003b: 129), are, for example, suspicion that feminism would carry an 'alien' neo-colonial agenda, and a disagreement with the assumed stress on sexuality in 'western' feminisms. Similarly, I am aware of the view that Islam and feminism are mutually exclusive, and that for some Muslims, especially Iranian radical Islamists, the term 'Islamic feminism' is totally unacceptable (Tohidi, 2006: 631).

9 This definition is based on my understanding of Badran's (1991: 202, 1995: 19–20) and Karam's (1998: 5) definitions of feminism.
10 *Dharma Wanita* (Women's Duties) was founded by the Soeharto government, commonly called the New Order government, in August 1974. Membership to this organization was compulsory and the position of members in this organization depended on their husband's position (Sunindyo, 1996: 124). *Dharma Wanita* has branches in every government institution throughout Indonesia, from the highest to the lowest-level institution.
11 These *Panca Dharma Wanita* stress women's responsibilities without stating their rights. For more information about these organizations, see, for instance, Sullivan (1983, 1994), Suryakusuma (1996, 2004), Bianpoen (2000), Buchori and Soenarto (2000).
12 Jakarta Charter is a gentlemen's agreement signed just before Indonesian independence. It is written in the *Preambul* of the 1945 Constitution that the 'Indonesian state … is based on: the belief in God, with the obligation to implement *shari'a* for its adherents [*Negara Indonesia… berdasarkan kepada Ke-Tuhanan, dengan kewajiban menjalankan syariat Islam bagi pemeluk-pemeluknya*]'(Anshari, 1986: 32, my translation). The last seven words are commonly called the 'seven-words' (*tujuh kata*). The 'seven-words' were removed from the *Preambul* soon after Indonesian independence, in a meeting on 18 August 1945, which was mostly attended by secular nationalists (secular nationalists are Indonesian political leaders who fight for independence and preferred Indonesia to be a secular state in which the state is neutral to any religion). According to Anshari, the majority of Islamist nationalists felt betrayed and disappointed with this unilateral removal of the 'seven-words' (1986: 59–63). Therefore, many Islamists seem to try to re-include them in the Constitution whenever possible.
13 Similar tensions between Muslim feminists and Islamists or conservative Muslims in defining the ideal gender relations can also be seen in other Muslim majority countries such as Malaysia (see Ong, 2006) and Iran (Tohidi, 2006).
14 For example, Abu Bakar Bashir, the *Jama'ah Islamiah* spiritual leader, expresses his opinion on polygamy: 'Polygamy is *shari'a*. Whoever rejects it becomes an infidel' (Forbes, 2006).
15 For example, women's activists of *Hizbut Tahrir Indonesia* Yogyakarta had a long march supporting polygamy by carrying posters such as 'Mengharamkan Poligami = Menentang Hukum Allah' (Forbidding polygamy is against God's law), 'Larangan Poligami Dukungan Seks Bebas' (Forbidding polygamy is supporting free sex), 'Kesetaraan Gender = Penjajahan Bangsa Melalui Perempuan' (Gender equality is colonizing the nation through women) and 'Poligami Halal vs Free Sex Haram' (Polygamy is permitted vs free sex is forbidden) (PMII UGM, 2006).
16 Similar phenomena can be observed in Iran, where a state-run television had a series of programs promoting polygamy, which was protested by some 250 Iranians, mostly women, in Tehran on 28 April 2004 (Rene, 2004); and in Malaysia, where Muslim clerics (*ulama*) were campaigning for polygamy. As in Indonesia, they argue that polygamy is a 'solution' to the adulterous nature of men, the high rate of unwed women and prostitution. This campaign, however, has been challenged by progressive Muslim feminists of Sisters in Islam (see Ong, 2006).
17 It is important to note that I had completed my fieldwork when this Law was enacted. Therefore, I was not in the position to inform my female participants on the availability of this Law and how this Law could be useful for those who experience economic neglect or violence – physical, psychological or sexual.
18 Mormon fundamentalism is one of several Christian religious movements in the USA. It was established in 1830 (Altman and Ginat, 1996: 21). The fact that polygamy has been practiced by Mormons and has been part of African culture refutes the claim often made by many literalist Muslims that polygamy is part of *shari'a* and is solely an Islamic practice.
19 They mostly come from Muslim countries but they were primarily educated and employed in the West.

20 Both of these women writers criticize the practice of polygamy, which has negative impact on the socio-psychological well-being of women. Mulia, one of the most outspoken Indonesian Muslim feminists, especially argues for the amendment of the 1974 Marriage Law to abolish polygamy.
21 The fact that most books here mainly belong to the first group is not intentional. I went to a bookshop near my campus in Bandung and asked the bookshop staff to provide me with any books on polygamy. I then bought all the books he provided me.
22 Traditional villages were relatively isolated and small, and mostly relied on their food production; the villagers were mostly nominal Muslims who practiced animistic rituals. In contrast, Islamized and modern villages were more oriented toward a market economy and considered animistic rituals as pagan (Krulfeld, 1986).
23 Unlike the *pesantren*s described by Doorn-Harder (2006), which are mostly affiliated with Nahdlatul Ulama (NU), my *pesantren* has no affiliation with either NU or Muhammadiyah, the two moderate Muslim organizations. It employs the curriculum from Gontor, one of the modern *pesantren*s in East Java. We did study classical *fiqh* but have no exposure to the books which are generally taught in NU *pesantren* such as the well-known male-biased *fiqh* book of *Uqudulujjain*, which teaches women's obedience and subservience to their husband. There is no different curriculum for male and female students even though we had sexually segregated classes.
24 'Standpoint feminism' tries to reconstruct knowledge from the perspectives of women's lives. Smith, a standpoint feminist, argues that sociology has been predicated on a universe grounded in men's experiences and relationships; and it has been regarded as men's 'territory' (1990: 13–14). Therefore, based on the standpoint feminist theory, I see the need to reinterpret Qur'anic verses from women's perspectives and to reformulate the marriage law based on women's experiences.
25 It is possible that the strong negative attitudes toward polygamy found in Bandung exist because Istri Sedar, a women's organization founded in Bandung in 1930, strongly opposed polygamy (Vreede-de Stuers, 1960: 91).
26 I am aware that this economic categorization is too simplistic because, as Sen (1998) suggests, Indonesian income level is highly stratified. This categorization is applicable only among my research participants.
27 As noted in the Glossary, this approximation is based on A$1=Rp.7000.
28 For the purpose of this book, I classify the class of female participants according to their income and level of education. Thus, even though all the four wives of Kiayi Jamal (Hj. Titin, Hj. Latifah, Hj. Mardiyah and Hj. Laila), for instance, have a rich husband, because they have low educational level and their daily income, which they receive from their husband, is only Rp. 50,000 (A$7), they are categorized as low-class participants.
29 This research is different from the usual anthropological research undertaken by western anthropologists on non-western societies (e.g. Berninghausen and Kerstan, 1992; Brenner, 1998; Firth, 1966; Geertz, 1961; Sullivan, 1994), who usually lived for at least one and half years in one village. Given the absence of separate polygamous communities and the rare incidence of polygamous marriage in Java, I had no choice but to travel from my accommodation to places where my research participants lived.
30 The term 'halfie' was first introduced by Lila Abu-Lughod (1991). It refers to 'people whose national or cultural identity is mixed by virtue of migration, overseas education, or parentage' (Abu-Lughod, 1991: 137). My positionality as a 'halfie' is gained through my overseas education.

2 Polygamy in context: family and kinship

1 Kuwait placed no restrictions on men who wanted to practice polygamy. In this country, polygamy is exclusively governed by classical *fiqh* (An-Na'im, 2002: 124).

2 According to Lev (1972: 141), from 1947 to 1972, the Indonesian divorce rate was 50 percent to 58 percent of registered marriages, with only 5 percent to 10 percent of reconciliations among the divorces.
3 Kinship in the USA is usually defined as relationship between persons based on descent or marriage. The relationships between persons that are based on descent are called consanguineal ('blood') – relatives such as mother, sister and father; while those based on marriage called affinal – relatives such as mother-in-law, sister-in-law. However, in other societies kinship could be formed on the basis of social, economic or political structure (Stone, 2006). There has been a debate among western anthropologists, in which a later generation of anthropologists challenged earlier claims that kinship is natural and universal (e.g. Carsten, 2004; Collier and Yanagisako, 1987; Faubion, 1996; Hobart, 1991; Schneider, 1984; Strathern, 1992, 2005).
4 Reenen (1996: 211) reported changes over the past few generations, in which a husband has become a more permanent resident in his wife's house, and therefore may become much more attached to his wife and children.
5 *Matrihouse* is an extended kin group living in one house (Blackwood, 2005: 12).
6 For an elaboration of matrilineal kinship system in Minangkabau and women's power within it, see also, for instance, Thomas (1977: 107–115) and Blackwood (1995, 2001).
7 The tradition of *sentana* ('heir') in Bali is the exception to this general rule of inheritance within the patrilineal kinship system. This occurs when there is no male descent. A woman will inherit from her father, and when she gets married her husband will come to her house as a 'wife' (*meawak luh*, to be as a woman) – a *nyentana* marriage. The woman will be in charge of all financial matters, and manage production, acting as if she were a man (*meawak muani*). If she has a daughter, she will ensure that her daughter has a *nyentana* marriage. If she does not have any children, she will adopt a daughter, who could have a *nyentana* marriage in order to could keep the property within her father's patriline. She would not adopt a son, fearing that her property would fall to her adopted son's natal patriline. When her husband dies, he is believed to join the ancestor group of his wife (Branson and Miller, 1988: 5). Even though women in *nyentana* marriages seem to be in an advantageous position, they are, according to Branson and Miller (1988: 13) 'agents of the patrilineage and its glorification of male ancestors', within which women are politically and religiously devalued.
8 Indonesia is one of the countries located in Southeast Asia.
9 The term *ibuism* (the ideology of motherhood, as *ibu* means mother) was first introduced by Djajadiningrat-Nieuwenhuis in the early 1980s, and was further popularized by Suryakusuma as 'state *Ibuism*' in a Masters thesis that she completed in 1988 in the Netherlands (2004).
10 In contrast, Wolters (1991: 177) argues that extended kin networks do play an important role in the social organization of village life in Watulawang (Banjarnegara regency, Central Java) and more generally in Java.
11 On matrifocality, see also, for instance, Reenen (1996) and Blackwood (2000, 2005). Female-centred kinship is also found in Rembau, Negeri Sembilan, Malaysia, which has a matrilineal kinship system (Stivens, 1988: 86, 1996).
12 This contradictory representation of masculinity and femininity is also found among Malay society in Rembau, Negeri Sembilan, Malaysia. Peletz found that the *official* (hegemonic) representation that men are reasonable and responsible is contradictory to the *practical* representation that women are more reasonable and responsible (Peletz, 1995). He also highlighted class differences of the women's acceptance of the official gender representation, in which upper-middle-class women tended to accept this official representation more than the lower-class women.
13 For more comprehensive and latest elaboration of the changing patterns of marriages in the world, see Therborn (2004). Like Jones (1994, 1997), Hirschman and Teerawichitchainan (2003), Therborn argues against universal changes in family patterns in the world, asserted earlier by Goode (1970).

14 This is in contrast with Thai tradition which marks the girl's entry to adulthood, not by her marriage but by the birth of her first child. The birth of her child changes a woman's status into that of a mother; therefore she is considered mature or adult (Yoddumnern-Attig, 2002).
15 Similarly, Jaspan and Hill (1987: 2), who conducted field research in Sewon, a small village in Bantul, Yogyakarta, in 1956–8 reported that the average age of first marriage for girls was 16 to 20, while their second marriage usually took place when they were in their twenties. Boys could be married at age 18 to 20, but most often they married in their twenties. If their first marriage failed, they usually married again in their late twenties.
16 Clifford Geertz was the first to use this category to explain variations in individuals' commitment to Islam. An *Abangan* is a Muslim who is still very much influenced by Hinduism, while a *santri* is a pious Muslim (Geertz, 1956: 98, 121). An *Abangan* is also often called a nominal Muslim, while a *santri* is often called a devout Muslim.
17 Djamour reported that the presence of young and attractive *jandas* was feared by married women. Since many *jandas* preferred secured legal union, a married man who was willing to marry a *janda* might divorce his wife. Thus, the breakdown of one marriage might lead to the breakdown of another marriage. Some *jandas* who did not have kin to depend on, could not find a husband and were unwilling to engage in poorly paid jobs might have casual affairs with men, and finally became prostitutes (Djamour, 1965: 129).
18 That was why his recent publication emphasizes that the issue is no longer 'When to Marry' but 'Whether to Marry' (Jones, 2004).
19 One of the explanations for this phenomenon is that, according to Jones (2004: 20), women do *want* marriage, but they face many obstacles. For instance, in the context of traditional attitudes, men still prefer to marry women who have a lower educational level, and women have been unwilling to 'marry down'. As a result, well-educated women and poorly educated men are 'stranded' in the marriage market.
20 Romantic love is a modern concept which appeared in the late eighteenth century: 'It is a process of attraction to someone who can make one's life, as it is said, "complete"' (Giddens, 1992: 40).
21 This was the same period in which similar novels were also published in Malaysia (see Hooker (2000) for her analysis of the novels' effect in bringing changes within Malaysian society).
22 MBA is of course the abbreviation for Master of Business Administration, a reputable degree which may assist graduates in gaining a favourable job. On the contrary, the parodic term (Marriage By Accident) gives the women and their parents great shame.
23 See Brenner (1996) for more elaboration of the Javanese women's motives to veil themselves.
24 See Chapter 3 for further elaboration on the promotion of polygamy in Indonesia.
25 O'Shaughnessy's study (forthcoming) reveals how the New Order Indonesian government has contributed to the stigmatizing of divorce by constructing it as a shameful act that contradicts the idealization of marriage.
26 Pure relationship is one of the examples of the transformation of intimacy, in which the relationship does not necessarily consist of a heterosexual couple – it could also be a homosexual couple. This form of relationship is a challenge to the unequal gender relations that often occurred within heterosexual 'permanent' marriage (Giddens, 1992). In a situation similar to that in the West, where homosexuals have been struggling to challenge the 'normal' heterosexual marriage, in Indonesia this group has become more visible, and has challenged the 'idealized' form of heterosexual relationship (e.g. Boellstorff, 2005; *Femina*, 2006).
27 For influential feminist literature see, for instance, Gittins (1985), Barrett and MacIntosh (1991), Thorne and Yalom (1992), Segal (1995) and Jagger and Wright (1999). For earlier influential non-feminist scholarly critique of the family see, for instance, Mark Poster (1978) and Jacques Donzelot (1980).
28 Judith Stacey (1986) regards the emergence of conservative 'pro-family' feminists as a

160 *Notes*

backlash stemming from feminist critique of the family. She argues that 'the new feminist conservatism discards the most significant contributions of feminist theory and, more alarmingly, provides in their place a feminism that turns quite readily into its opposite' (Stacey, 1986: 235).

29 See, for example, the writings of Rayna Rapp (1992), Kath Weston (1992), and Patricia Hill Collins (1992).

30 Visweswaran (1997: 595), however, notes an earlier date of the birth of third-wave feminism (1980s). This was marked by the emergence of critique from queer theorists and women of colour, targeting second-wave feminism for generalizing from the perspectives of white, heterosexual, middle-class women, and for its failure in dealing with the practical and theoretical questions of class, sexual identity, homophobia, race and racism within the movement.

31 As in the case of NGOs in Malaysia described by Stivens (2003: 135), these NGOs are mainly composed of 'middle-class educated women with close links to global feminist circuits, agendas, and funding'.

32 But Indonesian feminist critique of marriage and the family has existed since the colonial era. As will be discussed in Chapter 3, Kartini (1879–1904), who was also a western-educated Javanese feminist and was, according to Blackburn, deeply influenced by western feminism (Blackburn, 1997: 1), believed that marriage existed only to fulfill men's needs (Kartini, 1992).

33 See Brenner (1999) for more information on the problematic construction of femininity in the media during the New Order Period, in which women were expected to be good mothers and wives and know their *kodrat*. Therefore, whatever the role women have outside their house, they are expected to be 'instinctive and emotional, gentle, caring, and nurturing' (Brenner, 1999: 29).

34 Born to upper-class diplomat parents, Suryakusuma's socioeconomic and educational background gave her many international connections which conferred a degree of privilege on her and allowed her to express her criticism of the New Order state ideology more freely, even though she has also admitted her fear of the military government in a recent publication (Suryakusuma, 2004). Other than indigenous Indonesian feminists, a number of western feminists with a research interest in Indonesian women have also expressed criticism of the New Order government ideology, which they see as tending to domesticate women (see, for instance, Wolf, 1992; Sullivan 1983, 1994; Brenner, 2005).

35 This Dutch colonial promotion of motherhood and domesticity for women is also reported by Blackwood (2001: 136).

3 Muslim discourses on polygamy in Indonesia

1 'Secara pribadi saya tidak suka dan membenci poligami karena memiliki banyak dampak negatif. Terkadang saya mempertanyakan kok aturan Islam yang ini terasa berat untuk perempuan kalau pelakunya seperti suami saya. …Mencegah poligami merupakan tantangan yang berat bagi perempuan, sebab orang selalu menggunakan Al-Qur'an dalam melegitimasi praktek poligami mereka.'

2 Muslims believe that the Qur'an was revealed to the Prophet Muhammad through the Angel Gabriel (*Jibril*). Qur'anic verses were memorized by early Muslims and were written during the Prophet's era. Therefore, Muslims believe that the validity of the Qur'an is *qath'i* (without doubt). Muslims regard *Sunnah*, the normative behavior of the Prophet Muhammad, some of which is recorded in *hadith*, as written Prophetic tradition and the second source of *shari'a*. Unlike the Qur'an, Muslims need to be cautious in accepting the *hadith* because even though it is regarded as a divine or 'un-recited' revelation (Saeed, 2006b: 38), *hadith* was forbidden to be written down during the Prophet's period, for fear of being mixed with Qur'anic verses. Therefore, its validity is *dzanni* (with doubt). In accepting the *hadith* as a source of *shari'a*, Muslims need to be critical of its chain of narration and verify whether or not its content is contradictory with

Qur'anic verses. The different quality of the narration affects the quality of the *hadith*. See Mernissi (1991) for one of the critical studies of the *hadith*.

3 'Ashmawy (1998: 97) notes that this tendency also occurred towards the word *Torah* in Judaism. *Torah* means 'way of guidance'. However, later, it is used to refer to the legal rules in Torah. Over time, it comes to mean the new rules and interpretations written by rabbis.

4 An-Na'im (2002: 1) seems to be an exception to this statement. Even though he is a proponent of contextual reading of the Qur'an, he tends to define *shari'a* as a human product of interpretation: 'The term *Shari'a* refers to the general normative system of Islam as historically understood and developed by Muslim jurists, especially during the first three centuries of Islam.' Consequently, he argues for the abandonment of *shari'a* as a necessary step to achieve a more egalitarian society (An-Na'im, 2002: 19).

5 Nik Badli Shah (2004: 117) discusses similar phenomena in Malaysia, where campaigns for monogamy were regarded to be against Islam.

6 Barlas' book provides an excellent discussion of this. This book has successfully uncovered the root of Muslims' unconscious elevation of *Sunnah* (the Muhamadan tradition), *tafsir* (the Qur'anic exegesis) and *fiqh* above the Qur'an. According to her, this began in the ninth century. Syafi'i (d. 819) and Tabari (the great exegete of the tenth century) unconsciously claimed their opinion not as 'my opinion' but as 'the will of God'. The canonization of *Sunnah* (the consensus to make the *Sunnah* the second source of Islam) and the formation of the four schools of law have made the Qur'an more untouchable and removed the right of contemporary Muslims to conduct their own *ijtihad*, and to understand the Qur'an directly. Barlas also reveals the political interest behind the closure of *ijtihad*. The government of the Muslim medieval era took advantage of the 'intellectual stability' of the time by having its people only refer to the existing four schools of *fiqh*: Syafi'i, Hanafi, Maliki and Hanbali. This tradition of *taqlid*, referring to the existing products of *ijtihad*, has been maintained up to the present time. Consequently, according to her, many contemporary Muslims tend to refer to the human products of *fiqh* and *tafsir* rather than the Qur'an.

7 According to Saeed (2006b: 3), this group tend to approach the Qur'an literally, without taking into account the socio-historical context, but they package the meaning derived from the text in a somewhat 'modern' idiom, often within an apologetic discourse.

8 *Mahar* is a gift, usually gold or money, paid to the bride herself by the bridegroom. In Indonesia, it is commonly called *mas kawin*. According to Hooker (1970: 164), '*mas kawin* [in Indonesia] originally meant money paid by the bridegroom to the bride's parents but, by confusion with *mahar*, is now [1960s] paid (or more usually promised and left as an outstanding debt) to the bride herself'. *Mahar* is often mistakenly translated as dowry, valuables given to the husband from the wife's family at the time of the marriage ceremony, or bride price, payment made by the bridegroom to the bride's family. *Mahar* is also often mistakenly interpreted as a means for the bridegroom to 'buy' a bride. Therefore many men assume that their wife belongs to them when they have paid *mahar*.

9 Among others, Tabari and Rida based their account on the following *hadith*: *Shahih Bukhari, Volume 7, Book 62, Number 2:* Narrated 'Ursa:

> that he asked 'Aisha about the Statement of Allah: 'If you fear that you shall not be able to deal justly with the orphan girls, then marry (other) women of your choice, two or three or four; but if you fear that you shall not be able to deal justly (with them), then only one, or (the captives) that your right hands possess. That will be nearer to prevent you from doing injustice' (4.3). 'Aisha said, 'O my nephew! This Verse has been revealed in connection with an orphan girl under the guardianship of her guardian who is attracted by her wealth and beauty and intends to marry her with a *Mahar* less than what other women of her standard deserve. So they (such guardians) have been forbidden to marry them unless they do justice to them and give them their full *Mahar*, and they are ordered to marry other women instead of them.'
>
> (Bukhari, 2006)

10 In his tafsir, which was compiled by his student Rida, Abduh argues that marrying more than one woman is definitely prohibited for fear of being unjust (*anna ta'addudu 'l-zaujaat muharromun qoth'an 'inda 'l-khauf min 'adami 'l-'adli*) (Rida, 1973: 350).
11 As in Indonesia, the interpretations of polygamy in other Muslim majority countries are not homogeneous. These various interpretations of polygamy, except those of the first group, are reflected in the Muslim Family Laws throughout Muslim countries. For example, Syria, Egypt, Pakistan, Algeria, Morocco, Iraq, Iran, Pakistan and Malaysia restrict polygamy. Like Indonesia, they mainly require the permission of the court before a man may take additional wives (Abdurrahman, 1992; Esposito, 1982; Mahmood, 1972; Pearl, 1990). Only a small number clearly prohibit polygamy (Turkey, Tunisia, Albania and Muslim states of the Soviet Union) (Jones, 1994; Mahmood, 1972; Nasir, 1990). None of the Muslim majority countries permits polygamy without any restriction, apart from Kuwait (An-Na'im, 2002: 124).
12 Kartini is identified not only as an Indonesian feminist but also as a nationalist. Her nationalist view can be seen from her protest against Dutch colonialization (Cote, 2005).
13 Some of the most important organizations were *Wanita Oetomo, Aisyiyah, Poetri Indonesia, Wanita Katolik, Wanita Mulyo* and the women's department of the SI (*Serikat Islam*), the *Jong Islamieten Bond* (League of Young Muslims) and *Taman Siswa*. Three educated women – Nyi Hajar Dewantara, Nona Sujatin and Ibu Sukonto – organized this conference with the aim of unifying the women's movement throughout the archipelago (Wieringa, 1995: 77).
14 I cannot detail every women's congress and the issues addressed there in this limited space, but for more information about the congress, see also KOWANI (1978).
15 For a similar view expressed by Aisyiyah leaders that polygamy is a religious rule, see Wieringa (1995: 81).
16 Other male proponents of the emancipation of women and the protection of their rights during the colonial era were, for instance, Achmad Djajadiningrat, Dr. Soetomo and Dr. Tjipto Mangoen Koesoemo.
17 Since the Ethical Policy of 1901, there had been an increasing number of indigenous men studying in the Netherlands, which had led to the possibility of their marrying Dutch women, such as Syahrir (Wieringa, 1995).
18 These are the most important women's organizations, such as *Kongres Perempuan Indonesia* (Indonesian Women's Congress), *Taman Siswa* (Student Association), *Istri Indonesia* (Indonesian Women), *Istri Sedar* (Aware Women), *Pasundan Istri* (PASI) (Sundanese Women) and *the Sumatran Sarikat Kaum Ibu Sumatera (SKIS)* (The Sumatran Women Association) (Locher-Scholten, 2000: 199).
19 The standardized *taklik talak* consists of the husband's promise to give his wife the right to divorce if the husband breaks one of the four following stipulations:

1 If he leaves his wife for six consecutive months
2 If he does not give her proper maintenance for three consecutive months
3 If he physically hurts her
4 If he neglects her for six consecutive months (Azra, 2003: 80–1; Mahmood, 1972: 193–4).

20 Before the enactment of the 1974 Marriage Law, Indonesians acted within four different marriage laws:

1 Muslims acted within the Muslim marriage law (*fiqh*)
2 Christians acted within the Ordinance of 1933
3 Europeans and Chinese acted within the Civil Code (Burgerlijk Wetboek), which regulated marriage among the people subject to the Western law
4 Non-Christian and non-Muslims acted within *adat* law (Azra, 2003: 79 and Hanifa, 1983).

21 This unilateral step taken by government was the critical event that caused Muslim

objection and resistance to the marriage law. Up until now, many Muslims still regard the enacted Marriage Law as a government top-down approach for secularizing Islam. Resistance to the Marriage Law can be seen, for instance, in some male Muslims' unwillingness to register their marriages and to adhere to the government restriction on polygamy. This resistance has disadvantaged women and the children born from these unregistered marriages because they cannot protect their rights, such as for maintenance or inheritance, since they do not have a proof of marriage.

22 The New Order government seems to copy the step taken by the colonial government in reducing the authority of Religious Court. As a result, this marriage law draft was strongly opposed by Muslim parties and organisations, as in the previous Muslim resistance to the 1937 Ordinance.
23 This Faction consisted of the four Muslim parties: *Partai Serikat Islam Indonesia, Nahdlatul Ulama, Muslimin Indonesia* and *Perti* (Soewondo, 1977: 285).
24 As noted earlier, the original draft of the marriage law proposed by the government required the intervention of the Civil Court for cases of divorce and polygamy. But as a compromise with the Muslim parties, Muslim cases of divorce and polygamy must be dealt with by the Religious Court, not the Civil Court.
25 A Court of Law here means a Religious Court.
26 The Supreme Court, as the highest-level court in Indonesia, deals with cases unsatisfactorily resolved by the lower courts, either Religious or Civil Courts.
27 This court believed that his second marriage was 'valid', but because he did not follow the state's procedure before taking another wife, he was regarded as having committed a crime.
28 The appellate court took the secular position that registration is the requirement for valid marriage.
29 Bowen (2003: 201) suggests being cautious of the rates of registered divorce because they may not necessarily show the actual number of divorces, some of which are unregistered.
30 This means people persisted with marriages for the sake of appearances. The wife usually stays in the marriage for the sake of her children, and the husband usually stays in marriage for the sake of his career.
31 For further information on Yaya's case, see Chapter 5.
32 On the Court's requirements for polygamy as stipulated in the 1974 Marriage Law, see articles 4 and 5. All these requirements are also necessary to obtain permission from a civil servant's superior, because PP 10 was drafted in reference to the 1974 Marriage Law.
33 There are several obstacles that can prevent the validity of marriage, e.g. that the bride and the groom are related by blood, the bride is still in the 'waiting period' after her divorce from another man, and/or if the bride is under 16 years old, the minimum age at which women can marry (Department of Information, 1979).
34 In classical *fiqh,* a wife has the right to repudiate her husband by giving back her *mahar* or by paying a certain amount of money agreed by both parties. This dissolution of marriage initiated by women is called *khulu',* while the dissolution of marriage initiated by men is called *talak*. Women's and men's respective rights regarding divorce are also stipulated in the 1974 Marriage Law, articles 23–25, and as an attempt to prevent unilateral and easy divorce, either party should submit an application for divorce to a Religious Court if they are Muslim or to a Civil Court if they are non-Muslim (Department of Information, 1979).
35 The wife is the litigant if she initiates divorce and consequently the husband is called the defendant. The husband is the litigant if he initiates divorce and consequently the wife is called the defendant.
36 This confirms Brenner's discussion about the common representation of men as lacking control over their desire, and the danger of men having control over money as they tend to spend it on [other]women (1995; 1998: 150).

37 These media tend to promote the implementation of *shari'a*, with the literal approach to the Qur'an.
38 'Transparent polygamy' is a practice of polygamy in which the husband lets his established wife/wives know of his new marriage and advises when he will visit each wife, rather than having secret marriages.
39 'Poligami saya termasuk poligami sukses sehingga saya ingin melawan gerakan perempuan yang menyerang poligami dengan mencari figure-figur sukses poligami untuk dijadikan sebagai teladan/contoh bagi yang tidak sukses Saya yakin jika para suami yang berpoligami diberi hadiah, diharapkan ada kesadaran baru untuk mempaktekan poligami yang transparan. Dalam poligami yang bertanggung jawab, perempuanlah yang akan diuntungkan. Sebaliknya, jika poligami terus dihujat dan dianggap tabu, maka akan merugikan perempuan. Bagaimana pun poligami tidak bisa diberantas, jika kita peduli pada wanita. Yang harus dilakukan adalah mendidik para pelaku poligami.'
40 *Jihad* is commonly interpreted as 'fighting against the enemy with the sword', but in fact it has a broader meaning. One of the Prophet's traditional *hadiths* states that the biggest *jihad* is to fight against our own anger. Some Muslims interpret *jihad* as 'making a sacrifice in the name of God'. Wardoyo has his own interpretation of *jihad*. For him, reviving or promoting the practice of polygamy, which was practiced by the Prophet Muhammad, is *jihad*.
41 Wardoyo believes that polygamy is *sunnah Rasul. Sunnah* can mean 'a practice which is recommended in Islam'. Muslims will be rewarded for doing something considered *sunnah*, and will not be punished for it. *Sunnah Rasul* here means the practice undertaken by *Rasul*/the Prophet Muhammad. The Prophet practiced polygamy, therefore it is interpreted that the Prophet recommends polygamy. Wardoyo believes that a man will be lucky if he practices polygamy, and will regret if he does not practice it, because he believes that polygamy is part of Islamic *shari'a* and is necessary for both men and women (Suryono, 2003: 24).
42 'Membaca tulisan mengenai poligami award di Republika, saya merasa sangat kecewa, ternyata bapak Puspo Wardoyo yang saya kira sangat Islami ternyata hanyalah seorang yang lupa daratan dan tidak memahami agama Islam sama sekali.

'Anda telah merendahkan martabat wanita ke titik terendah dengan mengatakan bahwa wanita adalah tenaga kerja murah tak perlu dibayar dan tubuhnya dapat dinikmati, Astaghfirullah! Apakah ini yang dinamakan Jahiliyah modern? Ingat pak Puspo berarti anda telah menghina ibu anda dan istri-istri anda, anak perempuan anda, kakak-adik perempuan anda. Islam mengangkat martabat perempuan dari tangan Jahiliyah tetapi anda berusaha menghidupkan kembali.

'Saya pribadi (seorang muslimah) sangat tidak menentang poligami, karena poligami hukumnya halal dan boleh dalam Islam, tetapi Anda telah salah persepsi mengenai poligami. Tolong pak Puspo anda belajar Al-Qur'an dahulu sebelum bertindak sok pintar ...'
43 'Sebagai wanita kami sangat dapat menerima ketentuan Allah tentang poligami meskipun dengan alas an yang sangat rendah yaitu daripada zina. Tetapi di balik penerimaan tersebut ada suatu perjuangan untuk mengalahkan emosi dan perasaan yang bergejolak. Sehingga dapat dikatakan hal ini adalah cobaan dan musibah. Apakah pantas di atas cobaan dan musibah ini saudara Puspo Wardoyo merayakannya dengan memberikan Award?'
44 'Saya pribadi kalau mengkaji lebih dalam mengenai ayat yang menyangkut masalah poligami tersebut adalah sebaiknya jangan berpoligami, karena kalimat-kalimat itu sangat dan teramat halus serta teramat dalam .... Jadi untuk saya pribadi tidak sanggup berpoligami karena dimulai dari segi hati ataupun perasaan saya terhadap istri pertama ataupun kedua saya belum bisa adil apalagi sampai pada kebutuhan biologis ataupun harta.'
45 'Beberapa keluarga Bani Hasyim bin al-Mughirah meminta izin kepadaku untuk mengawinkan putri mereka dengan Ali bin Abi Thalib. Ketahuilah, aku tidak akan

mengizinkan, sekali lagi tidak akan mengizinkan. Sungguh tidak aku izinkan, kecuali Ali bin Abi Thalib menceraikan putriku, kupersilahkan mengawini putri mereka. Ketahuilah, putriku itu bagian dariku; apa yang mengganggu perasaannya adalah mengggangguku juga, apa yang menyakiti hatinya adalah menyakiti hatiku juga.'

46 Apparently, Aa was extremely angry and disappointed with *Detik*'s revelation. He planned to keep his second marriage secret, and wait for the 'right moment' to tell his wife and children, expecting them to smile and happily receive the news of his second marriage directly from him. He found this publication unethical because he was not informed of it. Therefore, he regarded it as a betrayal designed to destroy his career. He demanded that the publication of his second marriage be stopped, because of its negative effects for his first wife and children. He said that after this publication, his first wife was crying and his children were sad because their friends had ridiculed them (Mardiana, 2006).

4 Reactions to and negotiation around polygamous marriages

1 'Saya cinta agama saya, saya cinta Tuhan saya namun saya tidak suka poligami,' Ramli bertanya, 'Mengapa?' saya menjawab, 'Karena saya adalah saya. Saya Risa yang ingin saling setia antar pasangan. Saya setia sama kamu, tapi kamu tidak setia.'
2 Many 'conservative' Muslim women believe that wearing a headcovering (*hijab* or *jilbab*) is a woman's obligation, and it is regarded as a sign of religious devotion. But some liberal Muslim feminists regard it as a sign of identity (Rinaldo, 2006). Therefore, the ways Muslim women cover their hair vary from using a very short headscarf to the longer one. Some commentators feel veiling may also be a matter of fashion for some women.
3 In an earlier draft I wrote that 'Jajang was falling in love with [*jatuh cinta pada*] Lia', but Arsa corrected my written version with 'tempted by [*tergoda oleh*]' when she proofread the result of my interview with her.
4 'Perempuan itu adalah perhiasan dunia. Al-Qur'an menyebutkan: 'Nikahilah wanita yang kamu cintai dua, tiga atau empat.' Saya juga mengetahui bahwa Nabi Muhammad berpoligami. Kemampuan perempuan itu terbatas. Ketimbang membiarkan suami berzina, lebih baik mengizinkan suami berpoligami. Selain itu, jika ada seorang perempuan tidak dapat memperoleh suami yang baik, sementara calon suami yang baik itu sudah menjadi milik orang lain, maka istri dari suami tersebut hendaknya tidak egois, melainkan hendaknya merelakan suaminya untuk menikah dengan wanita yang menginginkannya. Saya juga tidak ingin mengingkari hukum Allah, asal tata caranya baik.'
5 'Pada mulanya saya memiliki sikap positif terhadap poligami. Saya kira saya memiliki "madu yang manis". Sayangnya, itu hanya sebentar. Setelah itu "madu" nya jadi beracun. Lia telah mengecewakan saya, kakak saya dan saudara-saudara saya. Lia sudah banyak mengambil hak saya. Saat Jajang bersama saya, Lia sering menelpon Jajang meski hanya dengan alas an yang sepele seperti saat anaknya rewel. Secara agama, saya bisa menerima poligami, tapi secara emosi saya menderita dan kecewa dengan poligami suami saya.'
6 'Qur'an menyuruh untuk menikahi dua, tiga, atau empat dalam ayatnya "*Fankihuu maa thooba lakum minan nisaa'i matsna ...fawaahidatan*" Menurut saya, kata *fawaahidatan* disini merupakan analogi, seperti orang tua yang berkata kepada anaknya: "Jika kamu bisa naik sepeda maka kamu harus berani, namun jika kamu takut, ya diam saja."

'Poligami merupakan ujian. Jika istri menolak suaminya poligami, bisa saja suaminya selingkuh. Poligami adalah fitrah laki-laki, yang ingin memiliki lebih dari satu kenikmatan. Ini dimengerti oleh Allh, sehingga dibolehkan, namun harus adil. Ujian yang terbesar bagi perempuan adalah menerima ayat tentang poligami karena berat bagi perempuan untuk membagi orang yang dicintainya. Itu merupakan ujuan. Jika perempuan berhasil, maka seperti pria yang berani, ia lulus ujian.'

7 The threat that a woman should be responsible for the sin committed by her husband's extramarital affair if she did not allow him to take another wife contradicts the Qur'anic verse Az-Zumar: 7, which states that no one should be responsible for other people's sin: '*No bearer of burdens can bear the burden of another*' (Ali, 1989: 1182) On this verse, Ali noted that it means no one else can carry your sin.
8 Jajang was not the only person who had to lie regarding his reason for polygamy. All male polygamous participants, except Syamsul, who submitted their application for polygamy to the Court, manipulated the reasons for polygamy or falsified their personal data in order for their application for to be granted. They mostly, however, used the reason that their wife 'was unable to fulfill her duties as a wife', the easiest (because they do not need to provide doctor certificate) and the most acceptable reason for polygamy (because it is stipulated in the 1974 Marriage Law).
9 'Lu bego lu, tolol, salah lu sendiri' (Batavian dialect).
10 'Lu poligami lu, ancur lu.'
11 'Lu bego lu, kagak bisa cari suami.'
12 'Macem-macem nich laki-laki yang satu ini.'
13 'Ketika ada masalah dalam pernikahan kami, saya biasanya menelpon Lia untuk menyelesaikan masalah tersebut. Akan tetapi, jika masalahnya terlalu rumit untuk didiskusikan lewat telpon, saya mengundang Lia ke rumah saya pada Sabtu malam. Akan tetapi, setelah beberapa kali diundang, sepertinya Lia merasa senang bermalam minggu di rumah saya. Setelah itu, Lia sering datang ke rumah saya di malam Minggu walaupun saya tidak mengundangnya. Saya merasa privacy saya terganggu dan waktu untuk bersama suami saya terkurangi dan terganggu dengan kehadiran Lia. Biasanya saya tidur bersama suami di malam Minggu. Namun jika Lia datang ke rumah saya, saya terpaksa harus tidur sekamar dengan Lia, sementara suami saya tidur bersama anak-anak di kamar yang satu lagi. Untuk menjaga privacy, saya berencana pindah ke rumah kontrakan lain yang jauh dari rumah kontrakannya Lia.'
14 'Sakit, sangat sakit. Biasanya suamiku selalu di sampingku setiap malam. Sekarang, saat anak sakit, dia tidak di sini. Saya sangat kesal, tapi kalau dia meninggal nanti, saya pasti akan merasakan kehilangan yang sama. Oleh karena itu, saat saya merasa cemburu, saya mencoba mengatasinya dengan menyibukan diri dengan berbagai aktivitas, misalnya membaca Al-Qur'an, bermain di luar bersama anak-anak, membuat kue atau membawa mereka ke rumah orang tuaku.'

Setelah suami saya menikah lagi, saya sangat stress, saya berjerawat dan muka saya tidak lagi mulus.
15 'Untuk apa menikah kalau bukan untuk memiliki anak? Cari saja perempuan lain.'
16 'Kenapa kamu menyukai Rosa saat dia sehat saja, tapi ketika sakit ditinggal?'
17 'Saya ingin membahagiakan Rosa. Namun Rosa tidak merasa tertolong dengan ketulusan saya. Saya menikahinya karena saya mencintainya. Toh disodori perempuan lain selain Rosa saat itu, saya merasa tidak srek.'
18 'Rosa anak manja. Ia tidak bisa melakukan apa-apa. Kerjanya tidak terprogram dan tidak memiliki pola kerja. Masa suami pergi bekerja jam 7 pagi, ia baru bangun dan mulai masak jam 7. Bagaimana saya bias memakan yang disiapkannya?

'Saya berasal dari Padang. Orang tua saya mendidik anak-anaknya agar bias mandiri. Saya bisa melakukan apa saja, dari masak sampai menjahit bias. Saya bisa mengurus kehidupan sendiri.

'Pada tahun 2000, saat hendak menulis disertasi, saya sakit keras selama setahun. Saya memikirkan siapa yang hendak mengurus saya. Maka setelah sembuh, saya berbicara pada istri saya untuk melaksanakan niat saya menikah lagi.'
19 Hot (*panas*) is a mixed feeling of jealousy, anger, sadness and disappointment.
20 'Saat saya masih kuliah, saya sering mendiskusikan tentang poligami dan saya bisa menerimanya sebagai hukum Tuhan yang harus diterima. Sepengetahuan saya, poligami itu seperti pintu darurat yang terkadang bisa digunakan. Menurut saya, seorang suami bisa menikah lagi walaupun tanpa izin istri karena hukum Negara kitalah yang

mengharuskan izin istri sebelum menikah lagi. Akan tetapi, seorang istri berhak menerima atau menolak poligami suaminya. Saya sendiri sudah merasa bahwa suatu saat saya akan dipoligami. Setelah menikah, bahkan saya meminta suami saya untuk beristri lagi. Tapi saat saya tahu suami saya pacaran dengan wanit alain dan menikahinya, saya merasa hati saya panas. Saya merasa sangat depresi dan banyak mengalami masalah psikologis.'

21 'Saya merasa labil. Saya tidak dapat memutuskan apakah saya ingin bercerai atau tidak. Sementara suami saya tidak mau menceraikan saya tanpa kemauan saya. Sepertinya, ibu dan kakak-kakaknya Syamsul menyetujui pernikahan Syamsul dengan Indri selain karena mereka mengharapkan Syamsul memiliki keturunan juga karena hubungan mereka dengan saya kurang harmonis.'

22 'Jika saya menolak berhubungan sex dengannya, dia suka melemparkan verbal abuse pada saya.'

23 'Kita memiliki karakter yang berbeda. Misalnya, dalam hal cucian, suami saya menginginkan agar cucian dicuci setiap hari, tidak ditumpuk sampai banyak supaya jika diperlukan bisa segera digunakan. Suami saya tidak suka menunda-nunda pekerjaan, sementara saya cenderung santai. Saya enggan mencuci setiap hari. Saya ingin cucian itu dikumpul sampai banyak dulu, baru kemudian dicuci. Toh ada mesin cuci. Selain itu, dalam masalah bersih-bersih, suami saya ingin agar rumah selalu bersih sehingga saya harus mengepel setiap hari. Meskipun jika masak sering banyak terbuang, suami saya tetap mengharapkan saya memasak. Saya sering merasa dikerasi suami. Padahal saya merasa rentan jika dimarahi (Teu kaop dicawad, langsung pundung). Jika dimarahi suami, biasanya saya sedih dan mengurung diri di kamar.'

24 The dates of Tuti's marriage and the birth of her child strongly suggest that she was pregnant at the time of the marriage. Only a few female participants revealed that they were already pregnant when they got married; most would try to hide what they considered a shameful fact. But I could mostly tell, from calculating the date of their marriage and the first child's date of birth.

25 I interviewed Tuti in the art gallery, because she did not want the interview to take place in her house, owing to her fear that someone, such as her children or her servant, might find out about her husband's previous second marriage.

26 This might mean that Rosyid had a sexual relationship with Nuri. Realising that having sex without marriage is unlawful in Islamic law, he preferred to marry Nuri because he had fallen in love with her.

27 'Sepengetahuan saya, Nabi berpoligami dalam keadaan dan dengan tujuan yang berbeda, bukan karena nafsu seperti sekarang, melainkan untuk ibadah. Dalam Al-Qur'an surat An-Nisa disebutkan bahwa boleh menikah dengan satu, dua, tiga atau empat jika "mampu" ... Jika ia bisa memimpin dan mengatur, boleh saja. Namun sayangnya kebanyakan laki-laki sekarang ini tidak bisa disamakan dengan Nabi.
Saya sering mendengar dalam ceramah bahwa seorang perempuan yang mau dimadu akan masuk surga. Tapi saat saya tanya perempuan lain, sekali pun yang jilbabnya lebar, mereka bilang gak mau dimadu.'

28 It is possible that Rosyid's income was higher than Tuti reported, if Rosyid teaches in two institutions. But as a casual teacher, it is possible that his income is lower than one million rupiah. He sometimes performed as a dancer, but not very often.

29 'Jilbabmu itu hanya asesoris [perhiasan] semata. Kamu pakai *jilbab* tapi merebut suami orang. Oh ya saya kenal pekerja seks yang juga pakai *jilbab*.'

30 'Pada hari pernikahan suamiku, sayalah yang menyiapkan dan menyetrika bajunya. Saya juga yang mendandaninya. Saya sediakan uang untuk membayar mas kawin untuk Nuri karena penghasilan saya lebih besar dari suami saya. Suami saya mencium kaki saya dan meminta maaf sebelum pergi untuk menikah lagi. Saya tidak tahan untuk hadir menyaksikan pernikahannya. Saya tinggal di rumah bersama anak-anak yang bertanya kemana ayah mereka saat mereka tahu bahwa dia tidak pulang ke rumah malam itu. Saya katakana pada mereka bahwa ayahnya ada rapat. Saya tidak bisa tidur malam itu. Saya

merasa hati ini begitu panas. Untuk menenangkan perasaan, saya shalat dan mengaji semalaman. Suami saya memberitahu bahwa pada malam itu badannya terasa panas dan pikirannya senantiasa teringat pada saya dan anak-anak.'

31 'Beberapa bulan setelah dia menikah lagi, saya perhatikan begitu lelahnya suami saya, baik secara phisik ataupun mental. Saya lihat suami saya berusaha agar kedua pernikahannya berjalan dengan baik. Secara phisik, nampaknya dia khawatir kalau hasrat seks saya tidak terpenuhi. Maka dia meningkatkan frekuensi persetubuhan dari sekali atau dua kali per minggu menjadi tiga kali per minggu, walaupun saya perhatikan begitu lelahnya dia. Saya sebenarnya merasa jijik melakukan hubungan seks dengannya karena dia bekas orang lain. Namun saya takut kalau saya berdosa jika tidak melayani suami saya.

'Saat dia bersama saya, Nuri sering menelponnya untuk minta ditemani pergi ke undangan atau belanja. ... Suami saya sepertinya bingung dengan permintaan kedua istrinya tapi dia menurutinya, mungkin karena takut saya menyuruh menceraikan Nuri.

'Terkadang, saat dia bersama Nuri, saya juga melakukan hal yang sama. Jadinya suami saya hanya punya waktu sedikit untuk bekerja atau mencurahkan energinya untuk mengembangkan karier seninya. Akibatnya, dia merasa kesulitan untuk memenuhi kebutuhan dua rumah tangga. Sebenarnya, penghasilan suami saya Cuma sedikit, untuk membiayai satu rumah tangga pun tidak cukup. Kemudia saya mengingatkan suami saya pada perjanjian sebelum dia menikah lagi dan meminta dia untuk memilih apakah akan menceraikan Nuri atau saya. Suami saya menolak ide menceraikan Nuri karena nampaknya dia tergoda oleh guna-guna Nuri. Nuri juga tidak mau diceraikan suami saya. Namun saya mendesak supaya dia memenuhi janjinya. Akhirnya suami saya memutuskan menceraikan Nuri. Dia mungkin sudah membandingkan pribadi kedua istrinya selama masa pernikahannya. Kemudian kami berdua membuat strategi untuk menceraikan Nuri. Sayalah yang menyiapkan hamper semua persyaratan administrasi untuk perceraian.'

32 '"*Fain khiftum alla ta'diluu fawaahidatan.*" Artinya, Islam lebih menyukai monogamy. Poligami hanya boleh dilakukan jika si istri tidak dapat melayani suaminya dalam segala segi. Selama istri bisa memberikan segalanya, poligami tidak wajar terjadi.'

33 'Saya tidak setuju dengan pendapat bahwa poligami itu manis. Kalau ada yang mengatakan bahwa poligami itu manis, pasti itu bukan suara perempuan. Saya yakin jika ada 10 sample, pasti hanya satu yang bisa mengatakan bahwa poligami itu manis, apalagi kalau poligami dilakukan secara tidak wajar sehingga menimbulkan kekerasan. Letak keindahan poligami mungkin indah dalam dosa. Sebab saya yakin saat pendekatan, suami dan pasangan selingkuhnya sudah melanggar rambu-rambu Islam.'

34 'Saya merasa bahwa penyakit yang diderita saat ini adalah akibat dari poligami suami saya. Saya pun yakin masih banyak perempuan lain yang menderita seperti saya, mungkin jutaan perempuan telah menjadi korban poligami. Ada yang sampai gila, terbunuh ataupun bunuh diri karena depresi berat. Di Koran banyak berita tentang hal tersebut, bisa saja itu adalah akibat poligami ataupun perselingkuhan suami.'

35 Lina did not know the person who called her, but the person must have known Lina and Hadi well, and perhaps disapproved of Hadi's betrayal of Lina.

36 'Saya mendengar selentingan bahwa suamiku menikah lagi namun saya tidak menggubrisnya karena saya merasa bahwa saya sudah bersikap baik kepada suami saya. Saya juga merasa bahwa saya telah menjadi istri yang baik yang memelihara kehormatan, misalnya, dengan tidak menerima tamu saat suami tidak ada. Karena saya sudah berbuat baik pada suami saya, maka saya kira suami juga akan memperlakukan saya dengan baik. Akan tetapi, suatu hari ada orang menelpon saya dan memberitahukan bahwa suami saya telah beristri lagi. Saya tidak percaya dengan apa yang dikatakannya sampai orang tersebut menelpon untuk ketiga kalinya dan memberitahukan secara detail nama dan alamat istri kedua suami saya, Nani (35).

'Saya mengecek kebenaran berita tersebut dengan pergi ke rumah Nani. Saya sangat marah saat bertemu Nani yang mengaku bahwa dia telah menikah dengan Hadi. Saya juga bertanya kepada Hadi mengapa dia beristri lagi secara diam-diam padahal tidak ada yang salah dalam diri saya dan saya telah berusaha menjadi istri yang baik. Hadi tidak bisa menjawab pertanyaan saya dan berkata, 'Tidak sengaja, semacam kecelakaan.'

37 '"Kamu bisa mendapatkan tubuhku, tapi jangan harap kamu bisa mendapatkan batinku." Hadi menjawab, "Biarin".'

38 Article 5 of the Law states that anybody is prohibited from doing violence to any members of the household, either physical, psychological, sexual or by economic neglect. Article 8 describes sexual violence as forcing someone who lives in the household to have a sexual relationship; or forcing someone in the household to have a sexual relationship with others for commercial or other certain purposes. Article 46 specifies the punishment for the perpetrators of sexual violence, that they could be jailed for up to 12 years or fined for up to Rp. 36,000,000 (Republik Indonesia, 2006). As noted in Chapter 1, my fieldword ended on April 2004, while the Law was enacted in September 2004. Even though the Law has been enacted since 2004, it will certainly require much time to socialize it and to change people's attitude toward domestic violence, which has often been regarded as a private matter for a long period of time.

39 'Poligami yang terjadi pada saya pada awalnya banyak kebohongan dan kekerasan sehingga istri benar-benar dikorbankan. Dari sisi batin, bisa membuat gila. Jika saya harus memilih antara ketenangan batin dan kemegahan materi, saya memilih ketenangan batin karena kemegahan materi lebih mudah didapat. Sejak saya tahu suami menikah lagi, saya sering bertengkar. Saat sedang bertengkar, sering menampar dan menendang sehingga pipi dan kaki saya membiru. Bahkan pernah suami mendorong saya sehingga mengakibatkan tangan kiri saya patah.'

40 'Setelah tangan saya patah, saya melaporkannya ke polisi sehingga tercium oleh wartawan karena suami saya sudah menjadi public figure. Banyak wartawan yang menelpon dan mengejar saya untuk wawancara. Untuk menghindari mereka dan demi anak-anak, saya menarik kembali laporan saya kepada polisi. Saya juga berbohong kepada para wartawan bahwa rumah tangga saya dalam keadaan baik-baik saja. Banyak teman-teman saya yang mengatakan saya bodoh dengan berbohong kepada wartawan. Namun saya melakukannya demi kesembuhan anak-anak saya yang mengalami depresi karena melihat saya didorong dengan kasar, kaget dengan kedatangan polisi serta terganggu oleh wawancara para wartawan.'

41 'Saya masih perlu berfikir berkali-kali sebelum menerima lamaran dari seorang duda, apalagi dari pria beristri. Seorang perempuan yang baik tidak akan mau menjadi istri kedua. Perempuan harus terdidik secara moral supaya mereka bisa menolak menjadi istri kedua.'

42 'Kalau saya hanya mempertimbangkan suami yang menyeleweng, pasti saya sudah tidak tinggal di sini, namun saya juga mempertimbangkan anak-anak. Maka saya mencoba bertahan di sini. Saya sering menghindarkan diri dari suami dengan mengunci diri di kamar saat suami berada di rumah untuk menghindari agar tidak dipukul atau disentuh oleh suami. Saya merasa jijik dan dendam padanya. Saya baru keluar kamar saat suami saya sudah meninggalkan rumah.'

43 'Saya senang menyakitinya dengan tidak bicara dengannya atau tidak meminta izin saat saya pergi dari rumah. Dia sudah memilih jalannya sendiri, maka saya pun memilih jalan saya sendiri. Saat saya merasa depresi, saya pergi saja sendiri bawa mobil. Kalau kepala saya terlalu pusing untuk menyetir, saya tinggalkan mobil di pinggir jalan dan saya pulang pake kendaraan umum. Biar saja mobil itu diambil nanti.

'Di pagi hari, saya biasanya bangun dan menyiapkan sarapan untuk anak-anak. Mereka memberi salam sebelum berangkat sekolah yang membuatku bahagia. Saat anak-anak sudah pergi, saya segera bersiap-siap. Suami saya biasanya bangun setelah saya siap untuk pergi. Saat melihat saya hendak pergi, dia akan bertanya kemana saya pergi. Saya bilang: "Saya mau pergi kemana saja saya mau. Sejak kamu punya istri lagi, peranan saya di rumah ini hanyalah sebagai ibu dari anak-anak saya dan saya sudah melaksanakan peranan tersebut untuk pagi ini."'

44 'Sekarang saya tahu cara menyakitinya, bukan dengan memarahinya atau bertengkar dengannya, namun dengan menghindari dan mengacuhkannya. Dia tampak kecewa jika tidak ada seorang pun di rumah yang bertanya padanya kemana dia akan pergi atau dari mana dia datang. Bukan hanya saya yang menghindarinya, anak-anak juga.'

45 'Selama pernikahan saya dengan Asep, dia sering berselingkuh dengan wanita lain seperti teman sekerjanya, Yanny (39), dan mahasiswanya, Dina (23). Tahu bahwa pernikahan saya dalam bahaya, saya menyiapkan diri dengan melanjutkan kuliah. ... Di tahun 2002, saya mengetahui kalau Asep telah menikahi Nurul (46), seorang janda, saat mereka pergi haji ke Mekah. Sejak saya mengetahui Asep menikah lagi, saya menolak tidur bersama dengannya karena jijik dan takut terkena AIDS.

'Saya sering meminta cerai namun Asep selalu menolaknya. Dia katakan 'Mengapa kamu ingin bercerai sementara yang kamu bisa lakukan setelah bercerai paling-paling jualan lotek?' Saya sangat marah dengan penghinaannya atas kemampuan saya bertahan hidup setelah bercerai. Saya katakan, "Deuleu ku sia, aing rek maen golf di Karawang" ("Lihat, kamu akan melihat saya bermain golf di Karawang.")'

46 'Menurut pendapat saya, orang cenderung membaca ayat tentang poligami sepotong-sepotong. Sebenarnya Al-Qurán mengatakan, *Jika kamu takut tidak bisa berbuat adil terhadap anak-anak yatim, nikahilah perempuan yang kamu sukai dua, tiga atau empat; namun jika kamu takut tidak bisa memperlakukan mereka dengan adil, maka satu saja.* Sayangnya banyak orang yang tidak melanjutkan membaca ayat tersebut sampai maka satu saja. Selain itu, ada lagi satu ayat, dalam surat yang sama An-Nisa':129 yang mengatakan bahwa Kamu tidak akan pernah bisa berbuat adil di antara istri-istrimu walaupun kamu sangat menginginkannya. Berdasarkan ayat ini, saya sangat tidak setuju dengan poligami dan saya tidak ingin berbagi cinta suami dengan perempuan lain.

47 In a Muslim wedding, the bride's consent is given on her behalf by her guardian (usually her father).

48 'Ramli orangnya pendiam sehingga saya tidak memiliki seseorang untuk mencurahkan perasaan atau mendiskusikan masalah yang kami hadapi. Banyak masalah pernikahan kami yang tidak terselesaikan karena tidak adanya komunikasi. Saya mendapat gaji yang lebih tinggi ketimbang Ramli dan sayalah yang sebagian besar menopang kebutuhan rumah tangga kami. Ketidak bahagiaan saya berpuncak pada tahun 2001 ketika saya mengetahui bahwa Ramli menikah lagi dengan wanita lain, Mamah, secara diam-diam. Saya tidak bisa berbagi suami dengan wanita lain, jadi saya memilih bercerai.'

49 'Poligami merupakan jalan keluar dalam situasi darurat. Namun Islam bukanlah agama poligami. Islam adalah agama monogamy.'

50 'Saat saya menarik nafas, saya merasa kehilangan setengah dari nafas saya. Saat saya berjalan, saya merasa tidak seimbang, sampai suatu hari saat saya berjalan, saya hampir tertabrak mobil angkot di Dago. Saya merasa diperlakukan secara tidak adil. Namun saya terlalu gengsi untuk cemburu. Sejak saya mengetahui bahwa suami saya menikah lagi, saya ingin bersebadan dengan suami dan memilih pisah rumah. Saya tidak ingin ada giliran. Mendengar kata tersebut saja sudah terasa aneh.'

51 'Jika saya bukan istrimu dan melihat kamu duduk bersanding seperti itu, saya tidak akan sakit hati. Namun karena saya adalah istrimu, say amerasa sakit kepala dan sakit kepala saya ini membutuhkan obat.'

52 '"Ayah sudah ada yang mengurus, sehingga Ayah dan Ibu tidak lagi hidup bersama." Anak-anaknya bertanya, "Terus siapa yang mengurus Ibu?" Ayahnya menjawab bahwa, "Nanti juga ada yang akan mengurus Ibu".'

53 This encouragement of women to accept their husband's polygamous marriage by suggesting that the women will go to heaven also occurred in Malaysia (Ong, 2006: 40).

54 As discussed earlier, the vice-president's practice of polygamy in the era of President Megawati seems to encourage the proponents of polygamy to promote and practice polygamy.

55 As discussed in the Introduction, a wife's expected role in Indonesia is to serve her husband: for example, to serve his meals and to serve him sexually.

56 Fundamentalist thinkers, for instance, include Hasan Al-Bana, al-Mawdudi, Ali Syari'ati and Sayyid Qutb.
57 On the aim of marriage, Qur'anic verse ar-Ruum: 21 states: 'And among His Signs is this, that He created for you mates from among yourselves, that ye may dwell in tranquility with them, and He has put love and mercy between your (hearts): verily in that are Signs for those who reflect' (Ali, 1989: 1050).

5 Polygamous households

1 Dadi was a professor, with a number of sources of income from lecturing at several universities, giving speeches in seminars, book royalties, Qur'anic courses and from a firm that he ran.
2 Rina is the first wife of Indra, but her case is not discussed in this book.
3 'Saat itu, Hadi baru menerima mobil baru dari kantor yang kebanyakan dia gunakan bersama Nani sementara saya harus pergi sendiri pakai becak untuk memeriksa kehamilan, sekalipun saat hujan. Sedihnya, becaknya terjungkal. Bagaimana seorang suami yang berpoligami bisa sekhilaf itu? Dokter saya mengatakan bahwa karena serangan jantung saya, maka saya tidak dapat melahirkan secara normal. Saya harus menjalani oprasi sesar. Suami saya hanya tahu kondisi saya beberapa hari menjelang melahirkan. Setelah tahu kondisi kesehatan saya, dengan segan dia mau menemani saya pergi ke dokter. Dia juga membawa saya ke rumah sakit saat akan melahirkan. Namun dia meninggalkan saya dengan ibu saya di pintu ruang oprasi. Dia bilang mau ke kantornya.'
4 'Mungkin dia begitu karena terkadang kata-kata saya menyakitkan Indri. Sekarang ini saya tidak merasa sakit hati atau cemburu terhadap Indri. Mungkin karena saya merasa sudah terlalu banyak kehilangan emosi sehingga saya merasa kebal rasa.'
5 But Akbar told me that his roster was still based on the early agreement with Yanti: he spent one day with Iis and two days with Yanti. He intended to ask Yanti if he could instead spend two days with Iis and two days with Yanti.
6 'Saya percaya bahwa tidak mungkin Allah menurunkan suatu ayat kalau tidak membawa kebaikan atau solusi. Saya yakin bahwa jika ayat Al-Qur'an itu dijalankan secara ikhlas, pasti akan membawa hikmah kebaikan dunia dan akhirat.'
7 'Saya sudah berusaha untuk adil terhadap istri saya. Istri-istri saya akan memaafkan saya jika saya memang tidak adil … . Nabi sekalipun tidak dapat berbuat adil dalam hal cinta. Dia mencintai salah satu istrinya ketimbang yang lain. Saya memberi nafkah kepada istri saya berdasarkan kebutuhan mereka, tidak mesti dalam jumlah yang sama.'
8 'Ya, saya bisa menggunakan kesendirian saya untuk membaca buku, untuk belajar lebih banyak. Saya sering merasa rindu pada suami saya, tapi kan suami saya sedang bersama istrinya. Saya sering merasa cemburu, namun saya sadar mungkin Suhadi lebih merasa nyaman tinggal di rumah Mila karena semua bukunya ada di sana. Saya sering merasa iri dengan Mila namun kemudian saya menyadari bahwa Milalah yang waktu kebersamaannya dengan suami diambil oleh saya.'
9 *Ojek* is a motorcycle that carries public passenger.
10 The interview was in Sundanese, my first language. Eli expressed her anger using the rudest level of language, '*Ari sia ku aing disenangkeun, kalah ka nganyenyeri. Sia teh geus boga anak jeung batur. Sia teh teu seubeuh. Boga pamajikan teu geuring teu naha*' (Saya sudah membahagiakanmu, namun kamu menyakiti saya. Kamu punya anak dengan orang lain. Kamu tidak puas dengan hanya satu perempuan, sementara istrimu juga tidak sakit). This quotation implies Eli's acceptance of polygamy in a situation when a wife is sick and cannot 'serve' her husband sexually. It also implies rejection of polygamy in her situation because she thought that Yaya had no valid reason for it since Eli was not sick and could be a good wife who took care of him very well.
11 This annual rent for a house at that time (1996), in that area, can be categorized as expensive. Having this furniture at that time was also considered luxurious.

12 'Saya pernah mengontrog ke rumah Leli. Dia tinggal di rumah kontrakan yang mewah dan mahal, Rp. 2,500,000 per tahun. Di rumahnya ada 2 kasur Ligna yang mahal, TV besar dan kulkas. Saya iri pada apa yang ia miliki di rumahnya. Saya tidak punya perkakas semahal itu kecuali saya membelinya dengan mencicil dari uang tabungan saya karena saya tidak mau menuntut materi kepada Yaya. Saya tidak pernah makan di restoran mahal ataupun membeli baju mahal untuk bisa menabung. Eh malah Yaya menghamburkan uangnya untuk istri mudanya. Saya terkadang mengontrog ke rumah kontrakan Leli setiap tahu alamat mereka, namun Leli langsung pindah rumah setiap kali saya mengetahui alamatnya. Sekarang Leli dan Yaya hidup sangat miskin karena Yaya dipecat dari tempat kerjanya di sekolah swasta, mungkin karena dia menggunakan uang sekolah untuk kebutuhan pribadinya (korupsi).'

13 'Mungkin saya akan lebih bahagia jika saya hanya memiliki satu istri saja. Saya merasa bersalah karena telah beristri lagi saat punya uang banyak. Mengapa saya dulu tidak menginvestasikan uang saya agar bermanfaat buat istri dan anak-anak saya? Saya tidak tahu agama, jadi saya ingin beristri lagi.'

14 'Asyik ni ye udah dua, kurang dua lagi nih.'

15 'Sebelum menikah lagi, kita tidak pernah meminjam uang. Namun kemudian dia meminjam banyak uang untuk kesenangan istri mudanya. Karena itu, sekarang gajinya banyak dipotong untuk membayar utangnya. Gaji Yaya sebenarnya Rp. 1,400,000 namun saya hanya menerima Rp. 600,000 perbulan. Saya gunakan uang tersebut untuk membayar tagihan listrik dan air serta ongkos anak-anak saya. Kedua anak saya butuh ongkos Rp. 20,000 per hari.

'Sejak April 2004, saya hanya menerima Rp. 250,000 sangat sedikit sekali. Anak saya yang bungsu terpaksa harus cuti kuliah karena saya tidak punya uang, sekalipun untuk makan. Saya biasanya membeli beras 1kg untuk dua hari yang saya makan dengan garam. Saya sering tidak makan, paling-paling dua hari sekali karena yang penting bagi saya anak-anak bisa makan. Terkadang saya bantu-bantu tetangga dan mereka memberikan makanan. Ada juga saudara, yang dulu saat saya punya suka saya tolong, yang memberi beras. Pada hari lebaran Idul Fitri, saya tidak membeli apa-apa namun suami saya juga mengatakan bahwa dia juga tidak membeli apa-apa untuk istri keduanya juga anak-anaknya.'

16 'Anak-anak saya berterus terang pada saya bahwa mereka membutuhkan ayahnya hanya karena uangnya saja. Mereka juga sering mengurung diri di kamar saat ayah mereka di rumah. Ketika mereka tahu ayahnya pergi, mereka keluar dari kamar dan bertanya pada saya, misalnya, 'Papah kasih uang gak, saya ingin beli sesuatu.'

17 'Saya malu dengan perselingkuhan ayah saya. Pertamanya saya mendengar selentingan bahwa ayah saya punya istri dimana-mana. Saya tidak percaya, maka saya tidak mempedulikannya. Saya mengira selentingan tersebut disebarkan oleh orang-orang yang iri terhadap keluarga saya. Tapi, suatu hari, saya menemukan surat di kantor ayah saya. Surat tersebut berasal dari ayahnya Dina yang menyatakan bahwa mereka menolak lamaran ayah saya terhadap Dina, yang seusia dengan saya. Bagi saya, selingkuh dengan orang seusia saya sama saja dengan selingkuh dengan anaknya sendiri. Tapi dia tidak berpikir demikian.'

18 *Kosidah* is a kind of Muslim religious music.

19 'Saya percaya bahwa poligami itu dibolehkan dalam Islam dan saya bahagia bahwa ibu saya mengerti Islam (yang ditujukkan] dengan (sikapnya] yang tidak menolak poligami. Yang saya tidak tahu adalah apakah praktek poligami ayah saya berdasarkan aturan Tuhan atau tidak. Saya tidak menyukai sikap tetangga saya terhadap poligami, yang mereka tunjukkan dengan menghibur ibu saya dan menyatakan rasa kasihan terhadap ibu saya. Sikap seperti ini tidaklah Islami. Poligami dibolehkan dalam Islam dan saya menolak disyaratkannya adil dalam poligami karena tidak mungkin bagi seorang pria untuk bisa benar-benar adil terhadap istrinya, terutama dalam hal cinta dan hubungan sex. Saya juga percaya bahwa seorang suami tidak perlu meminta izin istri sebelum menikah lagi, karena shari'a tidak memintanya.'

20 'Tidak ada manfaatnya lagi membicarakan dia, karena dia tidak lagi peduli pada kita. Yang penting bagi kita sekarang adalah bagaimana supaya bisa bertahan hidup.'

6 Conclusion

1. See Mursalin (2007) on the idea that any law in Indonesia is legally binding for all Indonesian Muslims because parliament members have discussed it – which is equivalent with collective *ijtihad* in this modern era.
2. Since the 1990s, there has been an increasing number of IAIN/UIN graduates, both men and women, and Muslim feminists such as Amina Wadud, Riffat Hassan, Fatima Mernissi, Asghar Ali Engineer, Leila Ahmed and Asma Barlas have challenged literal and male-biased interpretations of the Qur'an.
3. I am aware that not all Middle Eastern scholars are conservative and in favor of a literal approach. Professor Quraish Shihab, who was educated in Egypt, and many other NU young *ulama* who were studying in the Middle East, are in favor of a contextual approach to the Qur'an. Similarly, not all western graduates are in favor of liberal and contextual approaches to the Qur'an.
4. Nasr Abu Zaid is a Professor of Islamic Studies at Leiden University and Professor of Islam and Humanism at the University of Humanistics in Utrecht, Netherlands.
5. The activities of P3M were then continued by Rahima, an NGO founded by young NU activists in 2000. It has become a common secret that Rahima was founded by some P3M activists in opposition to their male leader who took a second wife around that time, in order that they would still be able to continue their efforts in promoting women's rights.
6. The activities of P3M and Rahima are examples of how NU scholars, commonly labeled as 'traditionalists', have become more 'progressive' in their approach to Islam as compared to some Muhammadiyah male scholars, commonly labeled as 'modernist', who seem to have become more 'conservative'. This recent changing tendency of NU and Muhammadiyah scholars is also noted by Bowen (2004) and Doorn-Harder (2006). However, as Syamsiyatun (2008) noted, the young women's wing of the Muhammadiyah, *Nasyiatul Aisyiyah*, have tried to negotiate space within their fathers' organization in order that they can have women's representatives in Muhammadiyah to express their views and interests. But unlike the radical approach adopted by some Muslim feminists within NU circles, *Nasyiatul Aisyiyah* prefers to adopt what Syamsiyatun called a 'cultural evolutionary approach' or 'gradual, peaceful transformation from within' by providing mass education and raising awareness among women about unjust treatment, abuse and violence that may happen in marital or familial life.

References

Abdul Kodir, Faqihuddin (2001). *Fiqh Perempuan: Refleksi Kiai atas Wacana Agama dan Gender.* Yogyakarta: LKiS.
Abdul Kodir, Faqihuddin (2002). *Tubuh dan Seksualitas Perempuan dalam Islam.* Yogyakarta: LKiS.
Abdul Kodir, Faqihuddin (2004). *Bangga Menjadi Perempuan: Perbincangan dari Sisi Kodrat dalam Islam.* Yogyakarta: LKiS.
Abdul Kodir, Faqihuddin (2005a). *Memilih Monogami. Pembacaan Atas Al-Qur'an dan Hadits Nabi.* Yogyakarta: LKiS Pelangi Aksara.
Abdul Kodir, Faqihuddin (2005b). *Hadith and Gender Justice. Understanding the Prophetic Traditions.* Cirebon: Fahmina Institute.
Abdul-Samad, M.A. (1991). 'Modernism in Islam in Indonesia with special reference to Muhammadiyah', in M.C. Ricklefs (ed.), *Islam in the Indonesian Social Context.* Clayton: Monash University, pp. 57–68.
Abdurrahman (1992). *Kompilasi Hukum Islam di Indonesia.* Jakarta: Akademika Pressindo.
Abu-Dawud (2007). 'Book 12: Divorce (Kitab Al-Talaq)', *Partial Translation of Sunan Abu-Dawud,* USC-MSA Compendium of Muslim Texts (translator). Online. Available http://www.usc.edu/dept/MSA/fundamentals/hadithsunnah/abudawud/012.sat.html (accessed 13 January 2007).
Abu-Lughod, Lila (1991). 'Writing against culture', in Richard G. Fox (ed.), *Recapturing Anthropology: Working in the Present.* Santa Fe, N.M.: School of American Research Press: Distributed by the University of Washington Press, pp. 137–62.
Aedy, Hasan (2007). *Poligami Syariah dan Perjuangan Kaum Perempuan.* Bandung: Alfabeta.
Afshar, Haleh (1998). *Islam and Feminisms: An Iranian Case-Study.* New York: St. Martin's Press.
Agger, B. (1991). *A Critical Theory of Public Life: Knowledge, Discourse and Politics in an Age of Decline.* London and New York: The Falmer Press.
Ahmed, Leila (1992). *Women and Gender in Islam: Historical Roots of a Modern Debate.* New Haven: Yale University Press.
Ali, 'Abdullah Yusuf (1989). *The Meaning of the Holy Qur'an.* Beltsville, Maryland: Amana Publications.
Ali, Muhammad Daud (1994). 'Hukum Islam: Peradilan Agama dan Masalahnya', in Eddi Rudiana Arief *et al.* (eds), *Hukum Islam di Indonesia. Pemikiran dan Praktek* (2nd edn). Bandung: Remaja Rosdakarya, pp. 69–142.
Alimi, Yasir, *et al.* (1999). *Advokasi hak-hak perempuan: Membela hak mewujudkan perubahan.* Yogyakarta: LKiS.

Alimi, Yasir (2002). *Jenis kelamin Tuhan: Lintas Batas Tafsir Agama*. Yogyakarta: Yayasan Kajian dan Layanan Informasi untuk Kedaulatan Rakyat bekerjasama dengan Dewan Koordinasi Nasional Gerakan Pemuda Kebangkitan Bangsa.

Alimi, Yasir (2004). *Dekonstruksi Seksualitas Poskolonial: Dari Wacana Bangsa Hingga Wacana Agama*. Yogyakarta: LKiS.

Allan, Graham and Crow, Graham (2001). *Families, Households and Society*. New York: Palgrave.

Altman, Irwin and Ginat, Joseph (1996). *Polygamous Families in Contemporary Society*. New York: Cambridge University Press.

Amarudin, Didin (2007). *Menghapus Catatan Gelap Poligami: Membongkar Penyesatan Opini Buku 'Bahagiakan Diri Dengan Satu Istri'*. Jakarta: 'Adil.

Andaya, B. W. (2001). 'Southeast Asian studies: Gender', in Neil J. Smelser and Paul B. Baltes (eds), *International Encyclopedia of the Social & Behavioural Sciences* 22. Amsterdam; Oxford: Elsevier Science, pp. 14676–80.

An-Naim, Abdullahi (2000). 'Islamic Foundation for Women's Human Rights', in Zainah Anwar and Rashidah Abdullah (eds), *Islam, Reproductive Health and Women's Rights*. Kuala Lumpur: Sisters in Islam.

Anshari, Endang Saifuddin (1986). *Piagam Jakarta 22 Juni 1945*. Jakarta: Rajawali.

Antara (2006a). 'Aa Gym Kawin Lagi, Presiden Bertindak', 6 December 2006. Online. Available http://www.antara.co.id/seenws/?id=48028 (accessed 5 January 2007).

Antara (2006b). 'Meutia Hatta: Keliru Anggap Poligami Dilarang', 12 December 2006. Online. Available http://www.antara.co.id/seenws/?id=48525 (accessed 16 December 2006).

Aripurnami, Sita (1996). 'Feminist comment on the sinetron presentation of Indonesian women', in Laurie J. Sears (ed.), *Fantasizing the Feminine in Indonesia*. Durham and London: Duke University Press, pp. 249–58.

Armando, Ade (2004). 'Masih Soal Poligami', email (19 July 2004).

Armando, Ade (2004). 'Piala Poligami', email (19 July 2004).

'Ashmawy, Muhammad Sa'id (1998). *Against Islamic Extremism. The Writings of Muhammad Sa'id 'Ashmawy*. Gainesville: University Press of Florida.

Aura, (1999). 'Machicha Mochtar Tak Ingin Menuntut, Hanya Menggugah Hati Moerdiono', no. 04/TH III, March, p. 8.

The Australian (2006). 'Polygamy debate on Indonesian streets', *The Australian*, 22 December 2006. Online. Available http://www.theaustralian.news.com.au/story/0,20867,20965272-1702,00.html (accessed 3 June 2008).

Ave, J.B. (1959). 'Memandang masalah polygamy dari segi Anthropologi Budaya', in Solichin Salam (ed.), *Menindjau Masalah Polygami: Menghidangkan pendapat 200 sardjana dan tjerdik pandai Indonesia*. Djakarta: Tintamas, pp. 29–30.

Averroes (1995). *Bidāyat al-mujtahid wa-nihāyat al-muqtaṣid*. Cairo: Dār al-Salām.

Azra, Azyumardi (2002). 'The Making of Islamic Studies in Indonesia', in Fu'ad Jabali and Jamhari (eds), *Islam in Indonesia: Islamic Studies and Social Transformation*. Montreal and Jakarta: Indonesia-Canada Islamic Higher Education Project, pp. 96–102.

Azra, Azyumardi (2003). 'The Indonesian Marriage Law of 1974: An institutionalization of the Shari'a for social changes', in Arskal Salim and Azyumardi Azra (eds), *Shari'a and Politics in Modern Indonesia*. Singapore: Institite of Southeast Asian Studies, pp. 76–95.

Azra, Azyumardi (2005a). *Dari Harvard hingga Makkah*. Idris Thaha (ed.). Jakarta: Republika.

Azra, Azyumardi (2005b). 'The use and abuse of Qur'anic verses in contemporary Indonesian politics', in Abdullah Saeed (ed.), *Approaches to the Qur'an in Contemporary Indonesia*. Oxford: Oxford University Press, pp. 193–208.

Badan Pusat Statistik (2000). *Population of Indonesia: Results of the 2000 Population Census*. Jakarta: Badan Pusat Statistik.

Badran, Margot (1991). 'Competing agenda: Feminists, Islam and the State in 19th and 20th century Egypt', in Deniz Kandiyoti (ed.), *Women, Islam and the State*. Basingstoke and London: Macmillan, pp. 201–36.

Badran, Margot (1995). *Feminists, Islam, and Nation: Gender and the Making of Modern Egypt*. Princeton, NJ: Princeton University Press.

Barazangi, Nimat Hafez (2004). *Woman's Identity and the Qur'an: A New Reading*. Florida: University Press of Florida.

Barlas, Asma (2002). *'Believing women' in Islam: Unreading Patriarchal Interpretations of the Quran*. Austin, TX: University of Texas Press.

Barrett, Michele and McIntosh, Mary (1991). *The Anti-social Family*. London and New York: Verso.

Basya, Hilaly (2003). 'Dari Konsumerisme hingga Ekstasi Seksual', *Kompas*, 4 August 2003. Online. Available http://www.kompas.com/kompas-cetak/0308/04/swara/468996.htm (accessed 7 Novermber 2003).

Basyir, Abu Umar (2007). *Poligami. Anugrah yang Terzhalimi*. Solo: Rumah Dzikir.

Bataramunti, Ratna (2006). 'Justice for women? New anti-domestic violence law brings hope for women', *Inside Indonesia*, July–Sept. Online. Available http://insideindonesia.org/content/view/64/29/ (accessed 8 May 2008).

Bennett, Linda Rae (2005). *Women, Islam and Modernity. Single Women, Sexuality and Reproductive Health in Contemporary Indonesia*. London and New York: Routledge Curzon.

Berninghausen, Jutta and Kerstan, Birgit (1992). *Forging New Paths: Feminist Social Methodology and Rural Women in Java*. Translated by Barbara A. Reeves. London and New Jersey: Zed Books.

Bianpoen, Carla (2000). 'The Family Welfare Movement: A blessing or a burden?', in Mayling Oey-Gardiner and Carla Bianpoen (eds), *Indonesian Women: The Journey Continues*. Canberra: Australian National University. Research School of Pacific and Asian Studies, pp. 156–71.

Blackburn, Susan (1997). 'Western feminists observe Asian women: An example from the Dutch East Indies', in Jean Gelman Taylor (ed.), *Women Creating Indonesia: The First Fifty Years*. Clayton, Vic.: Monash Asia Institute, pp. 1–21.

Blackburn, Susan (1999). 'Women and citizenship in Indonesia', *Australian Journal of Political Science*, Canberra, 34 (July), 189–200.

Blackburn, Susan (2001). 'Gender relations in Indonesia: What women want', in Grayson Lloyd and Shannon Smith (eds), *Indonesia Today: Challenges of History*. Singapore: Institute of Southeast Asian Studies, pp. 270–82.

Blackburn, Susan (2004a). *Women and the State in Modern Indonesia*. Cambridge: Cambridge University Press.

Blackburn, Susan (2004b). 'Women's suffrage and democracy in Indonesia', in Louise Edwards and Mina Roces (eds), *Women's Suffrage in Asia: Gender, Nationalism and Democracy*. London: Routledge Curzon, pp. 79–105.

Blackburn, Susan and Bessell, Sharon (1997). 'Marriageable age: political debates on early marriage in twentieth-century Indonesia', *Indonesia*, No. 63 (April) pp. 107–41.

Blackwood, Evelyn (1995). 'Senior women, model mothers, and dutiful wives: Managing gender contradictions in a Minangkabau village', in Aihwa Ong and Michael G. Peletz (eds), *Bewitching Women, Pious Men: Gender and Body Politics in Southeast Asia.* Berkeley: University of California Press, pp. 124–58.

Blackwood, Evelyn (2000). *Webs of Power: Women, Kin, and Community in a Sumatran Village.* Lanham: Rowman & Littlefield.

Blackwood, Evelyn (2001). 'Representing women: The politics of Minangkabau adat writings', *Journal of Asian Studies* 60, 1: 125–49.

Blackwood, Evelyn (2005). 'Wedding bell blues: Marriage, missing men, and matrifocal follies', *American Ethnologist* 32, 1: 3–19.

Blackwood, Evelyn (2008). 'Not your average housewife: Minangkabau women rice farmers in West Sumatra', in Michele Ford and Lyn Parker (eds), *Women and Work in Indonesia.* London and New York: Routledge.

Boellstorff, Tom (2005). *The Gay Archipelago: Sexuality and Nation in Indonesia.* Princeton, NJ: Princeton University Press.

Boserup, Ester (1970). *Woman's Role in Economic Development.* London: George Allen and Unwin.

Bowen, John Richard (2003). *Islam, Law, and Equality in Indonesia: An Anthropology of Public Reasoning.* Cambridge and New York: Cambridge University Press.

BPS Bandung (2005). *Bandung Dalam Angka 2005.* Bandung: Badan Pusat Statistik Bandung Bandung.

BPS Bogor (2006). *Kota Bogor Dalam Angka. Bogor Municipality in Figures.* Bogor: Badan Pusat Statistik Bogor.

BPS Depok (2006). *Kota Depok Dalam Angka 2005.* Depok: Badan Pusat Statistik Depok.

BPS Jakarta (2006). *Jakarta Dalam Angka. Jakarta in Figures.* Jakarta: Badan Pusat Statistik Jakarta.

Brenner, Suzanne A. (1995). 'Why women rule the roost: Rethinking Javanese ideologies of gender and self-control', in Aihwa Ong and Michael G. Peletz (eds), *Bewitching Women, Pious Men: Gender and Body Politics in Southeast Asia.* Berkeley: University of California Press.

Brenner, Suzanne (1996). 'Reconstructing self and society: Javanese Muslim women and "the veil"', *American Ethnologist* 23, 4: 673–97.

Brenner, Suzanne A. (1998). *The Domestication of Desire: Women, Wealth, and Modernity in Java.* Princeton, NJ: Princeton University Press.

Brenner, Suzanne (1999). 'On the public intimacy of the New Order: images of women in the popular Indonesian print media', *Indonesia*, No. 67 (April), pp. 13–37.

Brenner, Suzanne (2005). 'Islam and gender politics in late New Order Indonesia', Andrew C. Willford and Kenneth M. George (eds), *Spirited Politics: Religion and Public Life in Contemporary Southeast Asia.* Ithaca: Southeast Asia Program, Cornell University, pp. 93–118.

Bretschneider, Peter (1995). *Polygyny: A Cross-Cultural Study.* Uppsala: [Uppsala University]; Stockholm: Almqvist & Wiksell.

Brown, Nathan J. (1997). 'Sharia and State in the modern Muslim Middle East', *International Journal of Middle East Studies* 29, 3 (Aug): 359–76.

Brunner, Edward M. (1961). 'Urbanization and ethnic identity in North Sumatra', *American Anthropologist* 63: 508–21.

Buchori, Binny and Soenarto, Ifa (2000). 'Dharma Wanita: an asset or a curse?' in Mayling Oey-Gardiner and Carla Bianpoen (eds), *Indonesian Women: The Journey Continues.* Canberra: Australian National University. Research School of Pacific and Asian Studies, pp. 139–55.

References

Budianta, Melani (2006). 'Decentralizing engagements: Women and the democratization process in Indonesia', *Signs* (Summer), pp. 915–22.

Budiman, Arief (2002). The 7th Roundtable Discussion, The University of Melbourne, September 14.

Bukhari (2006). *Translation of Sahih Bukhari, Book 62: Wedlock, Marriage (Nikaah)*. University of Southern California: USC-MSA Compendium of Muslim Texts. Online. Available http://www.usc.edu/dept/MSA/, (accessed 28 September 2006).

Buss, Doris and Herman, Didi (2003). *Globalizing Family Values: The Christian Right in International Politics*. Minneapolis: University of Minnesota Press.

Cairncross, John (1974). *After Polygamy was Made a Sin: The Social History of Christian Polygamy*. London: Routledge & Kegan Paul.

Cammack, Mark (1989) 'Islamic Law in Indonesia's New Order', *International and Comparative Law Quarterly* 38, 1: 53–73.

Cammack, Mark (2003). 'Indonesia's 1989 Religious Judicature Act. Islamization of Indonesia or Indonesianization of Islam?', in Arskal Salim and Azyumardi Azra (eds), *Shari'a and Politics in Modern Indonesia*. Singapore: Institite of Southeast Asian Studies, pp. 96–124.

Cammack, Mark *et al.* (1996). 'Legislating Social Change in an Islamic Society. Indonesia's Marriage Law', *American Journal of Comparative Law* 44: 45–73.

Candland, Christoper and Nurjanah, Siti (2004). 'Women's empowerment through Islamic organizations: the role of the Indonesia's Nahdlatul Ulama in transforming the Government's birth control program into a family welfare program'. Online. Available http://www.wfdd.org.uk/programmes/case_studies/nahdlatul_ulama.doc, (accessed 29 November 2006).

Carsten, Janet (2004). *After Kinship*. Cambridge and New York: Cambridge University Press.

Cek & Riceck (1999a). 'Menggugah Tanggung Jawab Moerdiono', 8–14 February, p. 3.

Cek & Riceck (1999b). 'Kontroversi Perkawinan Machicha-Moediono', 15–21 February, p. 9.

Centre for Intercultural Learning (2006). 'Country Insight. Indonesia'. Online. Available http://www.intercultures.ca/cil-cai/country_overview-en.asp?lvl=8&ISO=ID (accessed 13 January 2007).

City Population (2006). 'The Principal Agglomerations of the World'. Online. Available www.citypopulation.de/World.html (accessed 11 December 2006).

Collier, Jane and Yanagisako, Sylvia (eds) (1987). *Gender and Kinship: Essays Toward a Unified Analysis, Sylvia*. California: Stanford University Press.

Collier, Jane, Rosaldo, Michelle Z. and Yanagisako, Sylvia (1992). 'Is there a family? New anthropological views', in Barrie Thorne and Marilyn Yalom, *Rethinking the Family. Some Feminist Questions*. Boston: Northeastern University Press, pp. 31–48.

Collins, Patricia Hill (1992). 'Black women and motherhood', in Barrie Thorne and Marilyn Yalom, *Rethinking the Family:P Some Feminist Questions*. Boston: Northeastern University Press, pp. 215–45.

Cote, Joost (2005). 'Introduction', in *On feminism and Nationalism: Kartini's Letters to Stella Zeehandelaar 1899–1903*. Clayton, Vic.: Monash Asia Institute.

Darojah, Siti (2003). 'Poligami Award itu.', *Republika Online*, 28 July 2003. Online. Available http://www.republika.co.id/ASP/koran_detail.asp?id=133851&kat_id=6 accessed 27 August 2004).

Department of Economic and Social Affairs, UN (2004). 'The Convention on the Elimination

of All Forms of Discrimination against Women'. Online. Available http://www.un.org/womenwatch/daw/cedaw/cedaw.htm (accessed 22 June 2004).
Department of Information (1979). *The Indonesian Marriage Law*. Jakarta: Dept. of Information.
Dewantoro, Nugroho and Srihartini, Rinny (2006). 'Bisik-bisik Tetangga', *Tempo*, 11–17 December.
Djajadiningrat-Nieuwenhuis, Madelon (1992). 'Ibuism and Priyayization: Path to power?' in Elsbeth Locher-Scholten and Anke Niehof (eds), *Indonesian Women in Focus*. Leiden: KITLV Press, pp. 43–51.
Djamour, Judith (1965). *Malay Kinship and Marriage in Singapore*. London: Athlone Press.
Djohan, Bahder (1959). 'Polygami and monogami', in Solichin Salam (ed.), *Menindjau Masalah Polygami: Menghidangkan Pendapat 200 Sardjana Dan Tjerdik Pandai Indonesia*. Djakarta: Tintamas, pp. 18–22.
Djohan, Bahder (1977). *Di Tangan Wanita ... : Pidato, 1926*. Jakarta: Yayasan Idayu.
Dodik (2006). 'Syukuran Pernikahan Poligami yang "Aneh tapi Nyata"'. Online. Available http://www.mail-archive.com/fossei@yahoogroups.com/msg00267.html (accessed 8 October 2006).
Doi, 'Abdur Rahman I. (1989). *Woman in Shari'ah*. London: Ta-Ha Publisher.
Donzelot, Jacques (1980). *The Policing of Families*. London: Hutchinson.
Doorn-Harder, Pieternella van (2006). *Women Shaping Islam. Indonesian Women Reading the Qur'an*. Urbana and Chicago: University of Illinois Press.
Dube, Leela (1997). *Women and Kinship: Comparative Perspectives on Gender in South and South-East Asia*. New York: United Nations University Press.
Dzuhayatin, Siti Ruhaini, *et al.*, (2002). *Rekonstruksi Metodologis Wacana Kesetaraan Gender Dalam Islam*. Yogyakarta: PSW IAIN Sunan Kalijaga.
Echols, John M. and Shadily, Hassan (2003). *Kamus Indonesia-Inggris* (3rd edn). Jakarta: Gramedia.
Engineer, Asghar Ali (1992). *The Rights of Women in Islam*. London: C. Hurst & Co.
Engineer, Asghar Ali (2003). 'Is secularism dead in India?' *Secular Perspective*, March 16–31.
Era Muslim (2003). 'Poligami Award di RCTI, Pelecehan terhadap Syariah'. Online. Available http:www.google.com.au/search?q=cache:daLGOZZjVZ4J:www.eramuslim.com/berita (accessed 7 November 2003).
Esack, Farid (1997). *Quran, Liberation and Pluralism: An Islamic Perspective of Interreligious Solidarity Against Oppression*. Oxford: Oneworld.
Esposito, John L. (1982). *Women in Muslim Family Law*. New York: Syracuse University Press.
Faridl, Miftah (2007). *Poligami*. Bandung: Pustaka.
Faubion, James D. (1996). 'Kinship is dead: Long live kinship. A review article', *Society for Comparative Study of Society and History* 38: 67–91.
Federspiel, Howard (2003). 'Islamic Values, Law and Expectations in Contemporary Indonesia', in Arskal Salim and Azyumardi Azra (eds), *Shari'a and Politics in Modern Indonesia*. Singapore: Institite of Southeast Asian Studies, pp. 193–212.
Femina (2006). 'Homoseksual di sekitar kita', no. 21/XXXIV, 23–31 Mei.
Firth, Rosemary (1966). *Housekeeping Among Malay Peasants*. New York: Humanities Press.
Forbes, Mark (2006). 'Muslim evangelist sparks row over polygamy', *The Age*. Online. Available http://www.theage.com.au/news/world/muslim-evangelist-sparks-row-over-polygamy/2006/12/17/1166290413776.html (accessed 3 June 2008).

Freeman, Carla and Murdock, Donna F. (2001). 'Enduring traditions and new directions in feminist ethnography in the Caribbean and Latin America', *Feminist Studies* 27, 2 (Summer): 423–58.

Friedan, Betty (1998). *'It Changed My Life' Writings on the Women's Movement*. Cambridge, Massachusetts: Harvard University Press.

Gage-Brandon, Anastasia J. (1992). 'The polygyny-divorce relationship: a case study of Nigeria', *Journal of Marriage and the Family* 54, 2.

Gandhi-Lapian, Louisa M. (1979). 'The status of women in Indonesian Marriage Law', in Rounaq Jahan and Hanna Papanek (eds), *Women and Development: Perspectives from South and Southeast Asia*. Dacca: Bangladesh Institute of Law and International Affairs, pp. 71–94.

Geertz, Clifford (1956). *The Development of the Javanese Economy: A Socio-Cultural Approach*. Cambridge: Center for International Studies, Massachusetts Institute of Technology.

Geertz, Hildred (1961). *The Javanese Family: A Study of Kinship and Socialization*. USA: The Free Press of Glencoe.

Geertz, Hildred and Geertz, Clifford (1975). *Kinship in Bali*. Chicago, University of Chicago Press.

GeoHive (2006). 'GeoHive: Global Statistics. Population 2006·10·14'. Online. Available http://www.geohive.com/default1.aspx (accessed 15 October 2006).

Giddens, Anthony (1992). *The Transformation of Intimacy: Sexuality, Love and Eroticism in Modern Societies*. Cambridge: Polity Press; Oxford: Blackwell.

Gittins, Diana (1985). *The Family in Question. Changing Households and Familiar Ideologies*. Basingstoke and London: Macmillan.

Göle, Nilüfer (1996). *The Forbidden Modern: Civilization and Veiling*. Ann Arbor: University of Michigan Press.

Göle, Nilüfer (2000). 'Snapshots of Islamic modernities', *Daedalus*, 129, 1: 91–117.

Gonsoulin, Margaret (2005). 'The Islamic frontier: Islam and gender equity in Southeast Asia', *Hawwa: Journal of Women of the Middle East and the Islamic World* 3, 1 (March): 9–39.

Goode, William J. (1970). *World Revolution and Family Patterns*. New York: The Free Press.

Gouda, Frances (1995). *Dutch Culture Overseas: Colonial Practice in the Netherlands Indies, 1900–1942*. Amsterdam: Amsterdam University Press.

Grace, Jocelyn (2004). 'Sasak Women Negotiating Marriage, Polygyny and Divorce in Rural East Lombok', *Intersections: Gender, History and Culture in the Asian Context*, Issue 10, August.

Grossbard-Shechman, Shoshana (1993) *On the Economics of Marriage. A Theory of Marriage, Labor, and Divorce*. Boulder, San Francisco and Oxford: Westview Press.

Gusmian, Islah (2007). *Mengapa Nabi Muhammad berpoligami? Mengungkap kisah kehidupan rumah tangga nabi bersama 11 istrinya*. Yogyakarta: Pustaka Marwa.

Hafidz, Wardah, Taslim, Adrina and Aripurnami, Sita (1992). 'Family planning in Indonesia: The case for policy reorientation', *Inside Indonesia* 30 (March): 19–22.

Hakim, Rahma Nisa (2006) 'Dilema RUU Anti Pornografi dan Pornoaksi: Pemasungan kebebasan berekspresi ataukah solusi?', *Dukung RUU Anti Pornografi dan Pornoaksi*. Online. Available http://ruuappri.blogsome.com/2006/06/17/dilema-ruu-anti-pornografi/ (accessed 1 June 2008).

Hanifa, S. (1983). 'The Law of Marriage and Divorce in Indonesia', *Islamic and Comparative Law Quarterly* 3: 14–26.

Harding, S. (1987). 'Introduction: Is There a Feminist Methods?' in Sandra Harding (ed.), *Feminism and Methodology. Social Science Issues*. Indiana: Indiana University Press, pp. 1–14.

Hassan, Riffat (1999) 'Feminism in Islam', in Arvind Sharma and Katherine K. Young (eds), *Feminism and World Religions*. Albany: State University of New York Press, pp. 248–78.

Hassan, Riffat (2002) 'Islam', in Arvind Sharma and Katherine K. Young (eds), *Her Voice, Her Faith: Women Speak on World Religions*. Cambridge, MA: Westview Press, pp. 215–42.

Hatley, Barbara and Blackburn, Susan (2000). 'Representations of women's roles in household and society in Indonesian women's writing of the 1930s', in Juliette Koning *et al.* (eds), *Women and Households in Indonesia: Cultural Notions and Social Practices*. Richmond: Curzon Press, pp. 45–67.

Hazairin (1952). *Pergolakan Penjesuaian 'adat kepada Hukum Islam*. Jakarta: Bulan Bintang.

Heaton, Tim B. *et al.* (2001). 'Why is the divorce rate declining in Indonesia?' *Journal of Marriage and Family* 63, 2: 480–90.

Hekmat, Anwar (1997). *Women and the Koran: The Status of Women in Islam*. Amherst, NY: Prometheus Books.

Henry, Astrid (2004). *Not My Mother's Sister: Generational Conflict and Third-Wave Feminism*. Bloomington and Indianapolis: Indiana University Press.

Al-Hibri, Azizah (1982). *Women and Islam*. Oxford: Pergamon Press.

Hikmah (2003). 'Kontrovesi Seputar Poligami', 2 August 2003. Online. Available http://www.pikiran-rakyat.com/cetak/0803/02/hikmah/utama1.htm (accessed 7 November 2003).

Hilmy, Masdar (2006). 'Politics of negotiating boundaries: Shari'a-isation of PERDA and the future of pluralism in Indonesia', a speech delivered in the Open Discussion, University of Melbourne, 21 September 2006.

Hilmy, Ummu (2005). 'Poligami di kalangan buruh perempuan (Studi pada buruh industri dan buruh migran)', in Rochayah Machali (ed.), *Wacana Poligami di Indonesia*. Bandung: Mizan, pp. 112–36.

Hirschman, Charles (1994). 'Population and society in twentieth-century Southeast Asia', *Journal of Southeast Asian Studies* 25, 2 (September): 381–416.

Hirschman, Charles and Edwards, Jennifer (2006). 'Social change in Southeast Asia'. Online. Available http://www.soc.washington.edu/users/charles/pubs/8%20Hirschman%20and%20Edwards%20final_text.pdf (accessed 24 April 2006).

Hirschman, Charles and Teerawichitchainan, Bussarawan (2003). 'Cultural and socioeconomic influences on divorce during Modernization: Southeast Asia, 1940s to 1960s', *Population and Development Review* 29, 2 (June): 215–53.

Hobart, Mark (1991). 'The art of measuring mirages, or is there kinship in Bali?', in Frans Hüsken and Jeremy Kemp (eds), *Cognation and Social Organization in Southeast Asia*. Leiden: KITLV Press, pp. 33–53.

Hoesterey, James B. (Forthcoming) 'Marketing morality: The rise, fall and rebranding of Aa Gym', in Greg Fealy and Sally White (eds), *Expressing Islam: Religious Life and Politics*. Singapore: Institute of Southeast Asian Studies (ISEAS).

Hooker, M.B (1970). *Readings in Malay Adat Laws*. Singapore: Singapore University Press.

Hooker, M.B (1972). *Adat Laws in Modern Malaya: Land Tenure, Traditional Government, and Religion*. Kuala Lumpur and New York: Oxford University Press.

Hooker, M. B. (1978). *Adat Law in Modern Indonesia*. Kuala Lumpur and New York: Oxford University Press.
Hooker, Virginia (2000). *Writing a New Society: Social Change through the Novel in Malay*. St Leonards, NSW: Asian Studies Association of Australia in association with Allen & Unwin.
Hull, Terence H. (1994). 'Fertility decline in the New Order period: The evolution of population policy 1965–1990', in Hal Hill (ed.), *Indonesia's New Order: The Dinamics of Socio-economic Transformation*. NSW: Allen & Unwin, pp. 123–45.
Ichsan, Ahmad (1986). *Hukum Perkawinan bagi yang Beragama Islam*. Jakarta: Pradnya Paramita.
Ichtijanto (1994). 'Pengembangan Teori Berlakunya Hukum Islam di Indonesia', in Juhaya S. Praja (ed.), *Hukum Islam di Indonesia: Perkembangan dan Pembentukan* (2nd edn). Bandung: Remaja Rosdakarya, pp. 95–150.
Indonesia (1990). *Izin Perkawinan dan Perceraian bagi Pegawai Negeri Sipil*. Jakarta: Eko Jaya.
Indonesia Matters (2006). 'RUU APP Debate'. Online. Available http://www.indonesiamatters.com/416/ruu-app-debate/ (accessed 1 June 2008).
Ismail, Nurjannah (2003). *Perempuan dalam Pasungan. Bias Laki-laki dalam Penafsiran*. Yogyakarta: LKiS.
Iversen, Joan (1997). *The Antipolygamy Controversy in U.S. Women's Movement, 1880–1925: A Debate on the American Home*. New York: Garland.
Ja'afar, Haminah (1995). *Siapa Pencemar Poligami?* Jakarta: Pustaka Jaya.
Jacoby, Hanan G. (1995). The economics of Polygyny in Sub-Saharan Africa: Female productivity and the demand for wives in Cote d'Ivoire, *Journal of Political Economy* 103, 5: 938–71.
Jagger, Gill and Wright, Caroline (1999). 'Introduction: changing family values', in Gill Jagger and Caroline Wright (eds), *Changing Family Values*. London: Routledge, pp. 1–16.
Jagger, Gill and Wright, Caroline (eds) (1999). *Changing Family Values*. London: Routledge.
Jaspan, Helen and Hill, Lewis (1987). *The Child in the Family: A Study of Childbirth and Child-Rearing in Rural Central Java in the Late 1950s*. Hull: Centre for South-East Asian Studies, University of Hull.
Jawa Pos (2007). 'Bersyukur setelah Baca Suami Batal Kawin Lagi Ketika Buku Antipoligami Membikin Kader PKS "Terbelah"', *Jawa Pos*, 2 August 2007. Online. Available http://musadiqmarhaban.wordpress.com/2007/08/03/ketika-buku-antipoligami-membikin-kader-pks-terbelah/ (accessed 8 June 2008).
Jawad, Haifaa A. (1998). *The Rights of Women in Islam: An Authentic Approach*. Basingstoke: Macmillan and New York: St. Martin's Press.
Jay, Robert R. (1969). *Javanese Villagers: Social Relations in Rural Modjokuto*. Cambridge, MA: MIT Press.
Jennaway, Megan (2000). 'Female Agency and the Polygynous Household, North Bali', in Juliette Koning *et al*. (eds), *Women and Households in Indonesia: Cultural Notions and Social Practices*. Richmond: Curzon Press, pp. 142–62.
Jones, Gavin W. (1994). *Marriage and Divorce in Islamic South East Asia*. Kuala Lumpur: Oxford University Press.
Jones, Gavin W. (1995). 'Population and the Family in Southeast Asia', *Journal of Southeast Asian Studies* 26, 1 (March): 184–95.
Jones, Gavin W. (1997). 'Modernization and divorce: Contrasting trends in Islamic

Southeast Asia and the West', *Population and Development Review* 23, 1 (March): 95–114.
Jones, Gavin W. (2004). 'Not "when to marry" but "whether to marry": The changing context of marriage decisions in East and Southeast Asia', in Gavin W. Jones and Kamalini Ramdas (eds), *(Un)tying the Knot. Ideal and Reality in Asian Marriage*. National University of Singapore: Asia Research Institute (ARI), pp. 3–56.
Kamali, Mohammad Hashim (1999). 'Law and society: The interplay of revelation and reason in Shariah', in John L. Esposito (ed.), *The Oxford History of Islam*. Oxford and New York: Oxford University Press, pp. 107–53.
Kandiyoti, Deniz (1988). 'Bargaining with Patriarchy', *Gender & Society*, September, 274–90.
Kandiyoti, Deniz (1998). 'Gender, power and contestation: 'Rethinking bargaining with patriarchy', in Cecile Jackson and Ruth Pearson (eds), *Feminist Visions of Development: Gender Analysis and Policy*. London and New York: Routledge, pp. 135–49.
Karam, Azza M. (1998). *Women, Islamism and the State: Contemporary Feminisms in Egypt*. New York: St Martin's Press.
Kartini, Raden Adjeng (1992). *Letters from Kartini: An Indonesian Feminist, 1900–1904* (trans. Joost Coté). Clayton, Vic.: Monash Asia Institute, Monash University in association with Hyland House.
Katjasungkana, Nursyahbani (2004). 'From Kartini to Ayu Utami: One hundred years of women's struggle on marriage', in Gavin W. Jones and Kamalini Ramdas (eds), *(Un)tying the Knot: Ideal and Reality in Asian Marriage*. National University of Singapore: Asia Research Institute (ARI), pp. 154–70.
Katz, June S. and Katz, Ronald S. (1975). 'The new Indonesian Marriage Law: A mirror of Indonesia's political, cultural, and legal systems', *American Journal of Comparative Law* 23, 4: 653–81.
Katz, June S. and Katz, Ronald S. (1978). 'Legislating social change in a developing country: The new Indonesian Marriage Law revisited', *American Journal of Comparative Law* 26: 309–20.
Kemp, Jeremy and Húsken, Frans (1991). 'Cognatic kinship in Southeast Asia', in Frans Húsken and Jeremy Kemp (eds), *Cognation and Social Organization in Southeast Asia*. Leiden: KITLV Press, pp. 15–31.
Khan, Maulana Wahiduddin (1995a). *Woman between Islam and Western Society*. New Delhi: The Islamic Centre.
Khan, Maulana Wahiduddin (1995b). *Woman in Islamic Shari'ah*. New Delhi: The Islamic Centre.
Khan, Mazhar Ul Haq (1982). *Purdah and Polygamy*. Delhi: Amar Prakashan.
Kilbride, Philip (1994). *Plural Marriage for Our Times: A Reinvented Option?* London: Bergin & Garvey.
Kilbride, Philip (1997). 'African Polygamy and its Theological Lessons for America', in Frank A. Salamone and Walter Randolph Adams (eds), *Explorations in Anthropology and Theology*. Lanham, MD: University Press of America, pp. 139–55.
kiluva-ndunda, mutindi mumbua (2001). *Women's Agency and Educational Policy. The Experiences of the Women of Kilome, Kenya*. Albany: State University of New York Press.
Kipp, Rita Smith (1998). 'Emancipating each other: Dutch colonial missionaries' encounter with Karo women in Sumatra, 1900–1942', in Julia Clancy-Smith and Frances Gouda (eds), *Domesticating the Empire: Race, Gender, and Family Life in French and Dutch Colonialism*. Charlottesville, VA: University Press of Virginia, pp. 211–35.

Koentjaraningrat, R.M. (1957). *A Preliminary Description of the Javanese Kinship System*. Ann Arbor: University Microfilms International.

Koentjaraningrat, R.M. (1959). 'Polygami ditinjau dari segi anthropologi', in Solichin Salam (ed.), *Menindjau Masalah Polygami: Menghidangkan pendapat 200 Sardjana Dan Tjerdik Pandai Indonesia*. Djakarta: Tintamas, pp. 95–9.

Koentjaraningrat, R.M. (1967). 'Tjelapar: A village in South Central Java,' in R.M. Koentjaraningrat (ed.), *Villages in Indonesia*. New York: Cornell University Press, pp. 244–80.

Koentjaraningrat, R.M. (1978) 'Javanese', in Richard V. Weekes (ed.), *Muslim Peoples: A World Ethnographic Survey*. London: Greenwood Press.

Koentjaraningrat, R.M. (1985). *Javanese Culture*. Singapore and New York: Oxford University Press.

Kompas (1999). 'Nomor Urut Partai Politik Peserta Pemilu 1999', 6 March 1999. Online. Available http://www.kompas.com/kompas-cetak/9903/06/PARTAI/part15.htm (accessed 1 June 2003).

Kompas (2000a). 'PP 10 Seharusnya Tak Perlu Ada', Thursday, 14 September 2000. Online. Available http://www.kompas.com/kompas-cetak/0009/14/iptek/pp10.htm (accessed 8 November 2003).

Kompas (2000b). 'PP 10 Sebaiknya Disempurnakan Saja', Monday, 2 October 2000. Online. Available http://www.kompas.com/kompas-cetak/0010/02/iptek/seba10.htm (accessed 8 November 2003).

Koning, Juliette *et al.* (2000). *Women and Households in Indonesia: Cultural Notions and Social Practices* (eds). Richmond: Curzon Press.

KOWANI (Kongres Wanita Indonesia) (1978). *Sejarah Setengah Abad Pergerakan Wanita Indonesia*. Jakarta: Balai Pustaka.

Krulfeld, Ruth (1996). 'Sasak attitudes toward polygyny and the changing position of women in Sasak peasant villages', in Leela Dube, Eleanor Leacock and Shirley Ardener (eds), *Visibility and Power: Essays on Women in Society and Development*. Delhi: Oxford University Press.

Kunthie (2003). 'Puspo Wardoyo Melecehkan Wanita', *Republika Online*, 28 July 2003. Online. Available http://www.republika.co.id/sp_detail.asp?id=1203 (accessed 7 November 2003).

Lazreg, Marnia (1988). 'Feminism and difference: The perils of writing as a woman on women in Algeria', *Feminist Studies* 14, 1 (Spring 1988): 81–107.

Lazreg, Marnia (1994). *The Eloquence of Silence: Algerian Women in Question*. New York: Routledge.

LBH-APIK (2000). 'Sejarah UU No. 1 tahun 1974 tentang Perkawinan dan Pembakuan Peran Gender dalam Perspektif Perempuan', unpublished research report of LBH-APIK.

Lestari, Siti and Munti, Ratna Batara (2003). 'Poligami Sebagai Bentuk Nyata Diskriminasi dan Kekerasan Terhadap Perempuan', *Suara APIK untuk Kebebasan dan Keadilan* (23rd edn).

Lev, Daniel S. (1972). *Islamic Courts in Indonesia: A Study in the Political Bases of Legal Institutions*. Berkeley: University of California Press.

Lev, Daniel S. (1996). 'On the other hand?', in Laurie J. Sears (ed.), *Fantasizing the Feminine in Indonesia*. Durham and London: Duke University Press, pp. 191–202.

Living Islam (2003). 'Hadiths on the Formation of Human Life'. Online. Available http://www.livingislam.org/n/hfhl_e.html (accessed 27 January 2007).

Locher-Scholten, Elsbeth (2000). *Women and the Colonial State: Essays on Gender and Modernity in the Netherlands Indies 1900–1942*. Amsterdam: Amsterdam University Press.

Locher-Scholten, Elsbeth (2003). 'Morals, harmony, and national identity. "Companionate feminism" in colonial Indonesia in the 1930s', *Journal of Women's History* 14, 4 (Winter): 38–58.

Lubis, Nina Herlina (2000). *Tradisi dan Transformasi Sejarah Sunda*. Bandung: Humaniora Utama Press.

Maarif, Ahmad Syafii (1985). *Studi tentang Percaturan dalam Konstituante: Islam dan Masalah Kenegaraan*. Jakarta: LP3ES.

Machali, Rochayah (ed.) (2005). *Wacana Poligami di Indonesia*. Bandung: Mizan.

MacLeod, Arlene Elowe (1992). 'Hegemonic relations and gender resistance: The new veiling as accommodating protest in Cairo', *Signs* 17: 533–57.

Mahmood, Saba (2005). *Politics of Piety: The Islamic Revival and the Feminist Subject*. Princeton, NJ and Oxford: Princeton University Press.

Mahmood, Tahir (1972). *Family Law Reform in the Muslim World*. New Delhi: The Indian Law Institute.

Majelis Muda Muslim Bandung (M3B) (2006). 'Syukuran Pernikahan Poligami yang "Aneh tapi Nyata"'. Online. Available http://www.mail-archive.com/majelismuda@yahoogroups.com/msg01335.html (accessed 24 May 2006).

Maley, Barry (2001). *Family and Marriage in Australia*. New South Wales: The Centre for Independent Studies.

Mapes, Timothy (2003). 'Indonesian restaurateur puts polygamy on menu', *Wall Street Journal*, 24 November 2003. Online. Available http://www.polygamyinfo.com/intnalmedia%20plyg%2016wallsrtreet.htm (accessed 21 June 2004).

Marcos-Natsir, Lies (2000). 'Reproductive health and women's rights from an Islamic perspective: The experience of P3M Association', in Zainah Anwar and Rashidah Abdullah (eds), *Islam, Reproductive Health and Women's Rights*. Kuala Lumpur: Sisters in Islam.

Mardiana, Erna (2006). 'Di balik liputan poligami Aa', pbrunswick mailing list and jurnalisme@yahoogroups.com. Online posting. Available email: pbrunswick@yahoogroups.com (14 December 2006).

Martyn, Elizabeth (2005). *The Women's Movement in Post-Colonial Indonesia: Gender and Nation in a New Democracy*. London and New York: Routledge Curzon.

Mas'udi, Masdar F. (1997). *Islam dan hak-hak reproduksi Perempuan. Dialog Fiqih Pemberdayaan*. Bandung: Mizan.

Mawardi, Ahmad Imam (2003) 'The political backdrop of the enactment of the Compilation of Islamic Laws in Indonesia', in Arskal Salim and Azyumardi Azra (eds), *Shari'a and Politics in Modern Indonesia*. Singapore: Institite of Southeast Asian Studies, pp. 125–47.

Mawdudi, Sayyid Abul A'la (1989). *Towards Understanding the Qur'an Vol. II Surah 4–6* (English version of *Tafhim al-Qur'an*, trans. and ed. Zafar Ishaq Ansari). United Kingdom: The Islamic Foundation.

Mernissi, Fatima (1975). *Beyond the Veil: Male-Female Dynamics in a Modern Muslim Society*. Cambridge, MA: Schenkman Pub. Co.; New York: distributed solely by Halsted Press.

Mernissi, Fatima (1991). *Women and Islam: An Historical and Theological Enquiry*, trans. by Mary Jo Lakeland. Oxford: Blackwell.

Mernissi, Fatima (1994). *Dreams of Trespass: Tales of a Harem Girlhood*. Reading, MA: Addison-Wesley Pub. Co.

Mernissi, Fatima (1996). *Women's Rebellion & Islamic Memory*. Atlantic Highlands, NJ: Zed Books.

Mies, Maria (1982). *The Lace Makers of Narsapur: Indian Housewives Produce for the World Market*. London: Zed Press; Westport, CT: L. Hill, U.S.

Moghadam, Valentine (2003a). *Modernizing Women: Gender and Social Change in the Middle East.* Boulder, CO: L. Rienne.

Moghadam, Valentine (2003b). 'Globalizing the local: transnational feminism and Afghan women's rights'. Online. Available http://www.peuplesmonde.com/article.php3?id_article=20 (accessed 14 January 2007).

Mohanty, Chandra (1988). 'Under western eyes: Feminist scholarship and colonial discourses', *Feminist Review* 30: 61–88.

Mohanty, Chandra Talpade (1991). 'Introduction: Cartographies of struggle: Third World women and the politics of feminism', in Chandra Talpade Mohanty, Ann Russo and Lourdes Torres (eds), *Third World Women and the Politics of Feminism.* Bloomington: Indiana University Press, pp. 1–47.

Mulia, Musdah (1999). *Pandangan Islam tentang poligami.* Jakarta: Lembaga Kajian Agama & Jender, Solidaritas Perempuan, Asia Foundation.

Mulia, Musdah (2005). *Muslimah Reformis: Perempuan Pembaru Keagamaan.* Bandung: Mizan.

Mulia, Musdah (2006). *Islam and Violence Against Women: Promoting Gender Equality in Indonesia.* Jakarta: LKAJ.

Mulia, Musdah (2007). *Islam dan Inspirasi Kesetaraan Gender.* Yogyakarta: Kibar Press.

Mulia, Musdah (2008). *Menuju Kemandirian Politik Perempuan.* Yogyakarta: Kibar Press.

Mulkhan, Abdul Munir (2006). 'Politics of negotiating boundaries: Shari'a-isation of PERDA and the future of pluralism in Indonesia', a speech delivered in the Open Discussion, University of Melbourne, 21 September.

Munir, Lily Zakiyah (2002). '"He is your garments and you are his …": Religious precepts, interpretations, and power relations in marital sexuality among Javanese Muslim women', *SOJOURN* 1, 2 (2002): 191–220.

Mursalin, Supardi (2007). *Menolak Poligami. Studi tentang Undang-Undang perkawinan dan Hukum Islam.* Yogyakarta: Pustaka Pelajar.

Mustofa, Agus (2007). *Poligami Yuuk!? Benarkah Al Qur'an Menyuruh Berpoligami Karena Alasan Syahwat?* Surabaya: Padma Press.

Mustafa *et al.* (2006). 'Mental health aspects of Turkish women from polygamous versus monogamous families', *International Journal of Social Psychiatry* 52, 3: 214–20.

Muṭahharī, Murtaḍā (1981). *The Rights of Women in Islam.* Tehran, Iran: World Organization for Islamic Service.

An-Na'im, Abdullahi A. (ed.) (2002). *Islamic Family Law in a Changing World: A Global Resource Book.* London: Zed Books.

Nakashima, Ellen (2003). 'Debating polygamy's resurgence: Indonesians divided over meaning of Koran', *Washington Post*, 29 November.

Nasir, Jamal J. (1990). *The Status of Women under Islamic Law and under Modern Islamic Legislation.* London: Graham & Trotman.

Nasution, Khoiruddin (1996). *Riba & Poligami. Sebuah Studi atas Pemikiran Muhammad Abduh.* Yogyakarta: Pustaka Pelajar.

Nasution, Khoiruddin (2002). *Status wanita di Asia Tenggara: Studi terhadap perundang-undangan perkawinan Muslim kontemporer di Indonesia dan Malaysia.* Leiden: INIS.

Needham, Rodney (1971). 'Remarks on the analysis of kinship and marriage', in Rodney Needham (ed.), *Rethinking Kinship and Marriage.* London and New York: Tavistock Publications, pp. 1–34.

Nik Badli Shah, Nik Noriani bt (2004). 'Marriage, polygyny and divorce within the Malaysian Muslim community', in Gavin W. Jones and Kamalini Ramdas (eds), *(Un)tying*

the Knot: Ideal and Reality in Asian Marriage*. National University of Singapore: Asia Research Institute (ARI), pp. 117–32.
Noer, Deliar (1973). *The Modernist Muslim Movement in Indonesia 1900–1942*. Singapore, New York: Oxford University Press.
Noerdin, Edriana (2002). 'Customary institutions, *Syariah* law and the marginalisation of Indonesian women', in Kathryn Robinson and Sharon Bessell (eds), *Women in Indonesia. Gender, Equity and Development*. Singapore: Institute of Southeast Asian Studies, pp. 179–86.
Nurbowo and Mulyono, Apiko Joko (2003). *Indahnya Poligami. Pengalaman Keluarga Sakinah Puspo Wardoyo*. Jakarta: Senayan Abadi publishing.
Nurdin, Ali (2003). 'The Muslim women's movement in Indonesia: A study of Aisyiyah's organization, 1966–2001', unpublished MA thesis, University of New England, Australia.
Nuriyah, Sinta (2002). 'Islam Tidak Membolehkan Poligami', *Femina* no. 28/XXX, 11–17 Juli.
Ong, Aihwa (2006). *Neoliberalism as Exception: Mutations in Citizenship and Sovereignty*. Durham, NC: Duke University Press.
O'Shaughnessy, Kate (Forthcoming). *Gender, State and Social Power: Divorce in Comtemporary Indonesia*. London: Routledge.
Ostling, Richard N. and Ostling, Joan K. (1999). *Mormon America: The Power and the Promise*. New York: HarperSanFransisco.
Oyewumi, Oyeronke (2002). 'Conceptualizing gender: The eurocentric foundations of feminist concepts and the challenge of African epistemologies', *Jenda: A Journal of Culture and African Women Studies*. Online. Available http://jendajournal.com/vol2.1/oyewumi.htm, (accessed 30 June 2006).
Pahl, Jan (1980). 'Patterns of money management within marriage', *Journal of Social Science Policy* 9, 3: 313–35.
Parawansa, Khofifah Indar (2003). 'Berani, dong, ambil tindakan!', *Femina*.
Pearl, David (1990). 'Three decades of executive, legislative and judicial amendments to Islamic Family Law in Pakistan', in Chibli Mallat and Jane Connors (eds), *Islamic Family Law*. London: Graham & Trotman, pp. 321–37.
Pearl, David and Menski, Werner (1998). *Muslim Family Law*. London: Sweet & Maxwell.
Peck, David D. (2006). 'The Lord gave, and the Lord hath taken away: A history of Mormon polygamy', in C.K Robertson (ed.), *Religion and Sexuality*. New York: Peter Lang Publishing, pp. 77–94.
Peletz, Michael G. (1995). 'Neither reasonable nor responsible: contrasting representations of masculinity in a Malay society', in Aihwa Ong and Michael G. Peletz (eds), *Bewitching Women, Pious Men: Gender and Body Politics in Southeast Asia*. Berkeley: University of California Press, pp. 76–119.
Pengadilan Agama Bandung (2001). 'Laporan Tahunan Tahun 2001 Pengadilan Agama Tentang Perkara Yang Diterima', unpublished report.
Pengadilan Agama Bandung (2003). 'Laporan Tahunan Perkara Yang Diterima Pengadilan Agama Kls 1A Bandung Tahun 2003', unpublished report.
Pengadilan Agama Cimahi (2002). 'Laporan Tahunan 2002 Tentang Perkara Yang Diterima Pada Pengadilan Agama Cimahi Kls 1A', unpublished report.
Pengadilan Agama Cimahi (2003). 'Perkara Yang Diterima Tahun 2003 Pada Pengadilan Agama Cimahi', unpublished report.
Pickthall, Marmaduke (1979). *The Meaning of the Glorious Qur'an: Text and Explanatory Translation*. Delhi: Kutub Khana Ishayat-ul-Islam.

PMII UGM (2006). 'Aktivis Wanita Hizbut Tahrir Dukung Poligami, "Aa Gym" Palsu Tolak Poligami'. Online 22 December 2006. Available www.ahmad-s.web.ugm.ac.id/pmii_ugm.php?SlemanYK=Tulisan&file=article&sid=38 (accessed 1 June 2008).

Porter, Marilyn and Hasan, Tita Marlita (2003). 'Exploring perspectives in narrative research: an Indonesian case study', *Canadian Review of Sociology and Anthropology* 40, 2 (May): 153–70.

Poster, Mark (1978). *Critical Theory of the Family*. London: Pluto Press.

Praja, Juhaya S. (1994). 'Pengantar', in Juhaya S. Praja (ed.), *Hukum Islam di Indonesia. Perkembangan dan Pembentukan* (2nd edn). Bandung: Remaja Rosdakarya, pp. v–xxvi.

Prayitno, H. (2003). 'Masih Soal Poligami'. Online. Available http://www.republika.co.id/sp_detail.asp?id=1212 (accessed 7 November 2003).

Rahayu, Dewi (2003). 'Ada Apa di Balik "Poligami Award"?', *Pikiran Rakyat*, 29 August 2003. Online. Available http://www.pikiran-rakyat.com/cetak/0803/29/0802.htm (accessed 7 November 2003).

Rahman, Anita (2005). 'Perkawinan Poligami Ditinjau dari Perspektif Agama dan Perempuan', in Rochayah Machali (ed.), *Wacana Poligami di Indonesia*. Bandung: Mizan, pp. 74–94.

Rahman, Fazlur (1980). *Major Themes of the Qur'an*. Chicago: Bibiotheca Islamica.

Rahman, Fazlur (1982). *Islam & Modernity: Transformation of an Intellectual Tradition*. Chicago: University of Chicago Press.

Rapp, Rayna (1992). 'Family and class in contemporary America', in Barrie Thorne and Marilyn Yalom, *Rethinking the Family: Some Feminist Questions*. Boston: Northeastern University Press, pp. 49–70.

Reenen, Joke van (1996). *Central Pillars of the House: Sisters, Wives, and Mothers in a Rural Community in Minangkabau, West Sumatra*. Leiden, The Netherlands: Research School CNWS.

Reid, Anthony (1988). *Southeast Asia in the Age of Commerce 1450–1680. Volume One: The Lands below the Winds*. New Haven and London: Yale University Press.

Rene (2004). 'Iranian women protest over polygamy in Iran', *Persian Journal*, 4 May 2004. Online. Available: http://www.16beavergroup.org/mtarchive/archives/000958.php (accessed 1 June 2008).

Republik Indonesia (2006). *Undang-undang Republik Indonesia Nomor 23 Tahun 2004 tentang Penghapusan Kekerasan dalam Rumah Tangga*. Online. Available: http://www.komnasperempuan.or.id/public/UU%20No%2023%202004%20PKDRT-%20Indonesia.pdf (accessed 8 May 2008).

Reyneta, Vony (2003). 'Kebijakan Poligami: Kekerasan Negara terhadap Perempuan', *Journal Perempuan* 31: 7–17.

Ricklefs, M.C. (1991). 'Introduction: the coming of Islam to Indonesia', in M.C. Ricklefs (ed.), *Islam in the Indonesian Social Context*. Clayton: Monash University, pp. 1–6.

Rida, Muhammad Rashid (1973). *Tafsīr al-Qurān al-ḥakīm: Al-shahīr bi-tafsīr al-Manār*, Vol. 4 (ed.), Beirut: Darul Ma'rifah.

Ridhwan, Affandi (2000). 'Sambutan Ketua Dewan Dakwah Islamiyah Indonesia', in Ramlan Mardjoned and Lukman Fatullah Rais (eds), *Amandemen UUD 1945 tentang Piagam Jakarta*. Jakarta: Dewan Dakwah Islamiyah Indonesia, pp. xiii–xxii.

Ridwan, A. Cholil (2003). 'Mendukung Poligami Award'. Online. Available http://www.republika.co.id/sp_detail.asp?id=1194 (accessed 7 November 2003).

Rinaldo, Rachel (2006). 'Feminism in uncertain times: Islam, democratization, and women activists in Indonesia', Paper for 2006 Globalization Conference. Online.

Available http://cas.uchicago.edu/workshops/scg/conference/2006/Rachel_Rinaldo_ Globalization_Conference_2006.pdf (accessed 3 January 2007).

Robinson, Kathryn (2000). 'Indonesian women: From *Orde Baru* to *Reformasi*', in Louise Edwards and Mina Roces (eds), *Women in Asia: Tradition, Modernity and Globalization.* St. Leonards, NSW: Allen & Unwin, pp. 139–69.

Robinson, Kathryn (2001). 'Gender, Islam and culture in Indonesia', in Susan Blackburn (ed.), *Love, Sex and Power: Women in Southeast Asia*. Clayton, Vic.: Monash Asia Institute, pp. 17–30.

Rowbotham, Sheila (1992). *Women in Movement: Feminism and Social Action*. London and New York: Routledge.

Roy, Olivier (2002). *Globalised Islam: The Search for a New Ummah*. London: Hurst & Company.

Saeed, Abdullah (2002). 'Islamic Law and practice: a pragmatic view', a paper delivered in a seminar 'Islamic Law and the West: can secular laws and Shariah co-exist?' Melbourne Law School, University of Melbourne, 19 September.

Saeed, Abdullah (2006a). *Islamic Thought: An Introduction*. London and New York: Routledge.

Saeed, Abdullah (2006b). *Interpreting the Qur'an: Towards a Contemporary Approach.* New York: Routledge.

Said, Edward W. (1978). *Orientalism*. New York: Pantheon Books.

Sairin, Syafri (1982). *Javanese Trah: Kin-Based Social Organization.* Yogyakarta: Gadjah Mada University Press.

Salam, Solichin (ed.) (1959). *Menindjau Masalah Polygami: Menghidangkan pendapat 200 sardjana dan tjerdik pandai Indonesia*. Djakarta: Tintamas.

Salim, Arskal (2003). 'Epilogue: *Shari'a* in Indonesia's current transition', in Arskal Salim and Azyumardi Azra (eds), *Shari'a and Politics in Modern Indonesia*. Singapore: Institite of Southeast Asian Studies, pp. 213–32.

Salim, Arskal (2006). 'Islamising Indonesian Laws? Legal and political dissonance in Indonesian shari'a, 1945–2005', unpublished PhD Thesis, University of Melbourne.

Saptari, Ratna (2000). 'Women, family and household: tensions in culture and practice', in Juliette Koning *et al.* (eds), *Women and Households in Indonesia: Cultural Notions and Social Practices.* Richmond: Curzon Press, pp. 10–25.

Schacht, Joseph (1964). *An Introduction to Islamic Law*. Oxford: Clarendon Press.

Scheman, N. (1993). *Engenderings: Construction of Knowledge, Authority and Privilege.* New York: Routledge.

Schneider, David M. (1984). *A Critique of the Study of Kinship*. Ann Arbor: The University of Michigan Press.

Schoellman, Todd and Tertilt, Michele (2006). 'Marriage laws and growth in Sub-Saharan Africa', *American Economic Review* 96, 2.

Sears, Laurie J. (1996). 'Introduction: Fragile identities: Deconstructing women and Indonesia', in Laurie J. Sears (ed.), *Fantasizing the Feminine in Indonesia*. Durham and London: Duke University Press, pp. 1–44.

Sears, Laurie J. (ed.) (1996). *Fantasizing the Feminine in Indonesia*. Durham and London: Duke University Press.

Segal, Lynne (1995). 'A feminist looks at the family', in John Muncie *et al.* (eds), *Understanding the Family*. London: Sage Publications.

Segal, Lynne (1999). *Why Feminism? Gender, Psychology, Politics*. New York: Columbia University Press, pp. 295–316.

Sen, Krishna (1998). 'Indonesian women at work: reframing the subject', in Krishna Sen

and Maila Stivens (eds), *Gender and Power in Affluent Asia*. London and New York: Routledge.
Sen, Krishna (2000). 'The human rights of gendered citizens: Notes from Indonesia', in Anne-Marie Hilsdon *et al.* (eds), *Human Rights and Gender Politics: Asia-Pacific Perspectives*. London and New York: Routledge, pp. 107–23.
Shehadeh, Lamia Rustum (2003). *The Idea of Women in Fundamentalist Islam*. Gainesville, FL: University Press of Florida.
Smith, D.E. (1990). *The Conceptual Practices of Power. A Feminist Sociology of Knowledge.* Boston: Northeastern University Press.
Smith-Hefner, Nancy J. (2005). 'The new Muslim romance: Changing patterns of courtship and marriage among educated Javanese youth', *Journal of Southeast Asian Studies* 36, 3 (October): 441–59.
Soewondo, Nani (1977). 'The Indonesian Marriage Law and its implementing Regulation', *Archipel* 13: 283–94.
Soewondo, Nani (1986). 'Segi-segi Hukum Wanita dalam Keluarga dan Masyarakat', in BPHN [Badan Pembinaan Hukum Nasional] *Seminar Aspek-aspek Hukum Peranan Wanita*. Jakarta: Penerbit Binacipta.
Soewondo-Soerasno, Nani (1955). *Kedudukan Wanita Indonesia dalam Hukum dan Masyarakat*. Jakarta: Timun Mas.
Sofyan, Eko Hendrawan (2006a). 'Isu Nikahi Janda: Aa Gym Langsung Gelar Jumpa Pers', *Kompas Cyber Media*, 2 December 2006. Online. Available http://www.kompas.com/ver1/Hiburan/0612/02/145557.htm (accessed 5 January 2007).
Sofyan, Eko Hendrawan (2006b). 'Aa Gym Mengaku Nikahi Janda Beranak Tiga', *Kompas Cyber Media*, 2 December 2006. Online. Available http://www.kompas.com/ver1/Hiburan/0612/02/224716.htm (accessed 5 January 2007).
Spencer, Paul (1998). *The Pastoral Continuum: The Marginalization of Tradition in East Africa*. Oxford: Clarendon Press.
Stacey, Judith (1986). 'Are feminists afraid to leave home? The challenge of conservative pro-family feminism', in Juliet Mitchell and Ann Oakley (eds), *What is Feminism?* Oxford: Basil Blackwell, pp. 219–48.
Stivens, Maila (1985). 'The private life of the extended family: Family, kinship and class in a middle class suburb of Sydney', in Lenore Manderson (ed.), *Australian Ways: Anthropological Studies of an Industrialised Society*. Sydney: Allen & Unwin, 1985, pp. 15–32.
Stivens, Maila (1988). 'Sexual politics in Rembau: female autonomy, matriliny, and agrarian change in Negeri Sembilan, Malaysia', in Glen Chandler, Norma Sullivan and Jan Branson, *Development and Displacement: Women in Southeast Asia*. Clayton, Vic.: Centre of Southeast Asian Studies, pp. 79–114.
Stivens, Maila (1990). 'Thinking about gender, state and civil society in Indonesia', in Arief Budiman (ed.), *State and Civil Society in Indonesia*. Clayton, Vic.: Centre of Southeast Asian Studies, Monash University.
Stivens, Maila (1991). 'The Evolution of Kinship Relations in Rembau, Negeri Sembilan, Malaysia', in Frans Hüsken and Jeremy Kemp (eds), *Cognation and Social Organization in Southeast Asia*. Leiden: KITLV Press, pp. 71–88.
Stivens, Maila (1991). 'Why gender matters in Southeast Asian politics', in Maila Stivens (ed.), *Why Gender Matters in Southeast Asian Politics*. Clayton, Vic.: Centre for Southeast Asian Studies, Monash University.
Stivens, Maila (1996). *Matriliny and Modernity: Sexual Politics and Social Change in Rural Malaysia*. St. Leonards, NSW: Allen & Unwin.

Stivens, Maila (2000). 'Introduction: gender politics and the reimagining of human rights in the Asia-Pacific', in Anne-Marie Hilsdon *et al.* (eds), *Human Rights and Gender Politics: Asia-Pacific Perspectives*. London and New York: Routledge, pp. 1–36.

Stivens, Maila (2003a). 'Kinship and State in Southeast Asia, East Asia, Australia, and the Pacific', in Suad Joseph *et al.* (eds), *Encyclopedia of Women & Islamic Cultures, Vol. 2*. Leiden: Boston: Brill, pp. 351–4.

Stivens, Maila (2003b). '(Re)framing women's rights claims in Malaysia', in Virginia Hooker and Norani Othman (eds), *Malaysia: Islam, Society and Politics*. Singapore: Institute of Southeast Asian Studies.

Stivens, Maila (2006). '"Family values" and Islamic revival: Gender, rights and state moral projects in Malaysia', *Women's Studies International Forum* 29, 4 (July–August): 354–67.

Stoler, Ann (1977). 'Class structure and female autonomy in rural Java', in Wellesley Editorial Committee, *Women and National Development: The Complexities of Change*. Chicago and London: The University of Chicago Press, pp. 74–89.

Stone, Lawrence (1977). *The Family, Sex and Marriage in England 1500–1800*. New York: Harper & Row.

Stone, Linda (2006). *Kinship and Gender: An Introduction*. Boulder, CO: Westview Press.

Strange, Heather (1981). *Rural Malay Women in Tradition and Transition*. New York: Praeger Publishers.

Strathern, Marilyn (1992). *After Nature: English Kinship in the Late Twentieth Century*. Cambridge: Cambridge University Press.

Strathern, Marilyn (2005). *Kinship, Law and the Unexpected: Relatives are Always a Surprise*. New York: Cambridge University Press.

Suara Merdeka (2003). 'Poligami Award Kontra Gerakan Perempuan', 30 July 2003. Online. Available http://www.google.com.au/search?q=cache:aeJK_qWGjfEJ:www.suaramerdeka.com/harian//0307/30/kot17.htm (accessed 7 November 2003).

Suara Merdeka CyberNews (2003). 'Sosok Puspo Wardoyo. Pria Mampu Wajib Berpoligami'. Online. Available http://www.suaramerdeka.com/cybernews/lelaki/sosok/sosok-lelaki01.html (accessed 27 August 2004).

Suara Merdeka (2004). 'Poligami Sebabkan Hak anak Terabaikan', 7 February 2004. Online. Available http://www.suaramerdeka.com/harian/0402/07/dar26.html (accessed 23 August 2004).

Suardiman, Siti Partini (2001). *Perempuan Kepala Rumah Tangga*. Yogyakarta: Jendela.

Suastra, I. Made (1996) *Kinship and Address Terms: A Preliminary Study of the Balinese Case*. La Trobe University: Asian Studies Papers-Research Series.

Subandrio, Hurustiati (1959). 'Pandangan ringkas disekitar [sic!] "Apakah Prija Polygam?"' in Solichin Salam (ed.), *Menindjau Masalah Polygami: Menghidangkan pendapat 200 sardjana dan tjerdik pandai Indonesia*. Djakarta: Tintamas, pp. 25–8.

Subhan, Zaitunah (1999). *Tafsir Kebencian: Studi Bias Jender dalam Tafsir al-Qur'an*. Yogyakarta: LKiS.

Sullivan, Norma (1983). 'Indonesian women in development: State theory and urban kampong practice', in Lenore Manderson (ed.), *Women's Work and Women's Roles: Economics and Everyday Life in Indonesia, Malaysia and Singapore*. Canberra: Australian National University: distributed by ANU Press, pp. 147–71.

Sullivan, Norma (1991). 'Gender and politics in Indonesia', in Maila Stivens (ed.), *Why Gender Matters in Southeast Asian Politics*. Clayton, Vic.: Centre for Southeast Asian Studies, Monash University, pp. 61–86.

Sullivan, Norma (1994). *Masters and Managers: A Study of Gender Relations in Urban Java*. NSW: Allen & Unwin.
Sumiarni, Endang (2004). *Kajian hukum perkawinan yang berkeadilan jender*. Hessel N.S. Tangkilisan (ed.). Yogyakarta: Wonderful Publishing Company.
Suminto, H. Aqib (1985). *Politik Islam Hindia Belanda*. Jakarta: LP3ES
Sunindyo, Saraswati (1996). 'Murder, gender, and the media: Sexualizing politics and violence', in Laurie J. Sears (ed.), *Fantasizing the Feminine in Indonesia*. Durham and London: Duke University Press, pp. 120–39.
Suny, Ismail (1994). 'Kedudukan Hukum Islam dalam Sistem Ketatanegaraan Indonesia', in Juhaya S. Praja (ed.), *Hukum Islam di Indonesia. Perkembangan dan Pembentukan* (2nd edn). Bandung: Remaja Rosdakarya, pp. 73–82.
Surjadi, A. (1974). *Masyarakat Sunda: Budaya dan Problema*. Bandung: Alumni.
Suryakusuma, Julia I. (1996). 'The State and sexuality in New Order Indonesia', in Laurie J. Sears (ed.), *Fantasizing the Feminine in Indonesia*. Durham and London: Duke University Press, pp. 92–119.
Suryakusuma, Julia I. (2004). *Sex, Power and Nation*. Jakarta: Metafor Publishing.
Suryono, Eko (2002). 'Kiat Sukses Poligami Islami. Pengalaman Puspo Wardoyo dan Empat Istrinya', seminar material.
Suryono, Eko (2003). *Kiat Sukses Beristri Banyak: Pengalaman Puspo Wardoyo bersama 4 Istri*. Solo: Bumi Wacana.
Syahrani, Riduan (1986). *Perkawinan dan Perceraian bagi Pegawai Negeri Sipil*. Jakarta: Media Sarana Press.
Syamsiyatun, Siti (2008). 'Women negotiating feminism and Islamism: The experiences of Nasyiatul Aisyiyah, 1985–2005', in Susan Blackburn, Bianca J. Smith and Siti Syamsiyatun (eds), *Indonesian Islam in a New Era: How Women Negotiate their Muslim Identities*. Clayton, Vic.: Monash University Press.
Tabari, Muhammad Ibn Jarir (1903). *Jami al-Bayan fi Tafsir Al-Qur'an*. Egypt: Al-Maymaniyah.
Takariawan, Cahyadi (2007). *Bahagiakan diri dengan satu istri*. Solo: Era Intermedia.
Taylor, E.N. (1970). 'Aspects of customary inheritance in Negri Sembilan', in M.B Hooker (ed.), *Readings in Malay Adat Laws*. Singapore: Singapore University Press.
Taylor, Jean Gelman (1997). 'Introduction', in Jean Gelman Taylor (ed.), *Women Creating Indonesia: The First Fifty Years*. Clayton, Vic.: Monash Asia Institute, pp. vii-xxv.
Tempo (2006). 'Poligami Masuk Istana', 11–17 December 2006.
Therborn, Göran (2004). *Between Sex and Power: Family in the World, 1900–2000*. London and New York: Routledge.
Thomas, Lynn Louis (1977). *Kinship Categories in a Minangkabau Village*. Ann Arbor: University Microfilms.
Thorne, Barrie (1992). 'Feminism and the family: Two decades of thought', in Barrie Thorne and Marilyn Yalom, *Rethinking the Family: Some Feminist Questions*. Boston: Northeastern University Press, pp. 3–30.
Thorne, Barrie and Yalom, Marilyn (eds), (1992). *Rethinking the Family. Some Feminist Questions*. Boston: Northeastern University Press.
Tibi, Bassam (2002). *The Challenge of Fundamentalism: Political Islam and the New World Disorder*. Berkeley, CA: University of California Press.
Tim Detikcom (2006). Aa Gym Menikah Lagi, Ucapan Selamat Mengalir. Online. Available http://www.detiknews.com/indexfr.php?url=http://www.detiknews.com/index.php/detik.read/tahun/2006/bulan/11/tgl/30/time/183414/%0c/714726/idkanal/10 (accessed 1 December 2006).

Tiwon, Sylvia (1996). 'Models and maniacs: Articulating the female in Indonesia', in Laurie J. Sears (ed.), *Fantasizing the Feminine in Indonesia*. Durham and London: Duke University Press, pp. 47–70.

Tjahyani, Rika (2003). 'Suara Hati Anak Korban Poligami', *Femina*.

Tohidi, Nayereh (2006) '"Islamic feminism": negotiating patriarchy and modernity in Iran', in Ibrahim M. Abu-Rabie (ed.), *The Blackwell Companion to Contemporary Islamic Thought*. Maiden, MA; Oxford, UK: Blackwell Publication, pp. 624–43.

Tomasic, Roman (1985). *The Sociology of law*. London: Sage.

Ucok (2003). 'Tentang Poligami. Sebuah Kesaksian', 6 October 2003. Online. Available http://www.kompas.com/kompas-cetak/0310/06/swara/566287.htm (accessed 7 November 2003).

Umar, Nasaruddin (1999a). *Argumen Kesetaraan Jender. Perspektif Al-Qur'an*. Jakarta: Paramadina.

Umar, Nasaruddin (1999b). 'Kodrat Perempuan dalam Perspectif Al-Quran', in Lily Zakiyah Munir (ed.), *Memposisikan Kodrat. Perempuan dan Perubahan dalam Perspektif Islam*. Bandung: Mizan, pp. 91–110.

Umar, Nasaruddin (2002a). *Qur'an untuk Perempuan*. Jakarta: Jaringan Islam Liberal dan Teater Utan Kayu.

Umar, Nasaruddin (2002b). 'Metode Penelitian Berperspektif Gender tentang Literatur Islam', in Siti Ruhaini Dzuhayatin *et al.* (eds). *Rekonstruksi metodologis wacana kesetaraan gender dalam Islam*. Yogyakarta: PSW IAIN Sunan Kalijaga.

Umar, Nasaruddin *et al.* (2004). *Membangun Kultur Ramah Perempuan. Reinterpretasi dan Aktualisasi Pesan Kitab Suci*. Jakarta: Restu Ilahi.

Unicef (2007). 'Convention on the Rights of the Child'. Online. Available http://www.unicef.org/crc/ (accessed 5 January 2007).

Utami, Sukowati (2006). 'Haruskah UU Perkawinan direvisi?', *Forum*, 11–17 December.

Vanaik, Achin (1992). 'Reflections on Communalism and Nationalism in India', *New Left Review I/196*. Online. Available http://www.newleftreview.net/?page=article&view=1692 (accessed 12 October 2006).

VanEvery, Jo (1999). 'From modern nuclear family households to postmodern diversity? The sociological construction of "families"', in Gill Jagger and Caroline Wright (eds), *Changing Family Values*. London: Routledge, pp. 165–84.

Visweswaran, Kamala (1997). 'Histories of feminist ethnography', *Annual Review of Anthropology*, 26, pp. 591–621.

Vreede-de Stuers, Cora (1960). *The Indonesian Woman: Struggles and Achievements*. The Netherlands: Mouton.

Wadud, Amina (1999). *Qur'an and Woman: Rereading the Sacred Text from a Woman's Perspective*. New York: Oxford University Press.

Wadud, Amina (2006). *Inside the Gender Jihad: Women's Reform in Islam*. Oxford: Oneworld.

Wadud-Mushsin, Amina (1992). *Qur'an and Woman*. Kuala Lumpur: Penerbit Fajar Bakti.

Walby, Sylvia (1997). *Gender Transformations*. London and New York: Routledge.

Warta Kota Bandung (2006a). 'Pengajian Aa Gym Mulai Sepi', *Warta Kota Bandung*. Online. Available http://www.kompas.com/ver1/Hiburan/0612/08/073640.htm (accessed 5 January 2007).

Warta Kota Bandung (2006b). 'Beredar SMS Boikot Aa Gym', *Warta Kota Bandung*. Online. Available http://www.kompas.com/ver1/Hiburan/0612/07/075746.htm (accessed 5 January 2007).

Weston, Kath (1992). 'The politics of gay families', in Barrie Thorne and Marilyn Yalom,

Rethinking the Family: Some Feminist Questions. Boston: Northeastern University Press, pp. 119–39.

Whitehead, Ann (1981) '"I am hungry, mum": the politics of domestic budgeting', in Kate Young, Carol Wolkowitz and Roslyn McCullagh (eds), *Of Marriage and the Market: Women's Subordination in International Perspective*. London: CSE Books, pp. 88–111.

Widayatun (1991). 'Women's status and child survival in West Java, Indonesia', *Asia-Pacific Journal* 6, 1: 3–24.

Wieringa, Saskia (1995). 'The politicization of gender relations in Indonesia: the Indonesian women's movement and Gerwani until the New Order state', unpublished PhD thesis, the University of Amsterdam.

Wita (2003). 'Poligami Award'. Online. Available http://www.republika.co.id/sp_detail.asp?id=1209 (accessed 7 November 2003).

Wiyana, Dwi, Agustina, Widiarsi and Bardiyah (2006). 'Setelah Kejutan Poligami Aa Gym', *Tempo* 11–16 December.

Wolf, Diane L. (1992). *Factory Daughters: Gender, Household Dynamics, and Rural Industrialization in Java*. Berkeley: University of California Press.

Wolters, Willem (1991). 'The political economy of kinship and marriage strategies in Java and Central Luzon', in Frans Hüsken and Jeremy Kemp (eds), *Cognation and Social Organization in Southeast Asia*. Leiden: KITLV Press.

Yakan, Fathī (2002). *'Revolusi' Hasan al-Banna: gerakan Ikhwanul Muslimin dari Sayid Quthb sampai Rasyid Al-Ghannusyi*. Bandung: Harakah.

Yenni (2003). 'Terima Poligami Award', 27 May 2003. Online. Available http://www.mail-archive.com/rantau-net@rantaunet.com/msg16766.html (accessed 27 August 2004).

Yoddumnern-Attig, Bencha (2002). 'Conjugal and parental roles: A behavioral look into the past and present', *Women's Studies Center* 2, 6: 69.

Younce, William C. (2001). *Indonesia: Issues, Historical Background and Bibliography* (ed.). New York: Nova Science Publishers.

Yunus, Mahmud (1956). *Hukum Perkawinan dalam Islam Menurut Mazhab Syafi'i, Hanafi, Maliki dan Hanbali*. Jakarta: Pustaka Mahmudiah.

al-Zamakhsharī, Abī al-Qāsim Jār Allāh Maḥmūd ibn 'Umar ibn Muḥammad (1995). *Tafsir al-Kashshāf 'an ḥaqā'iq ghawāmiḍ al-tanzīl wa-'uyūn al-aqāwīl fī wujūh al-ta'wīl Vol. 1*. Beirūt: Dār al-Kutub al-'Ilmīyah.

Zinn, Maxine Baca (1992). 'Family, race and poverty in the eighties', in Barrie Thorne and Marilyn Yalom, *Rethinking the Family: Some Feminist Questions*. Boston: Northeastern University Press, pp. 71–90.

al-Zuḥaylī, Wahbah (1991). *al-Tafsīr al-munīr fī al-'aqīdah wa-al-sharī'ah wa-al-manhaj*. Beirūt, Lubnān: Dār al-Fikr al-Mu'āṣir; Dimashq, Sūrīyah: Dār al-Fikr.

Index

Aa Gym 9, 65, 76, 175, 181, 188, 190, 192, 193, 194
Abangan 29, 159
Abduh, Muhammad 42, 44, 48, 149, 162, 186
Abu Zaid, Nasr 151, 173
agency 3, 10, 34, 80, 81, 104, 113, 155, 182–3
 agent 3, 27, 158
Aisyiyah 5, 46–8, 146, 154, 162, 173, 187, 192
 Nasyiatul 154, 173, 192
Ali, Mukti 150
An-Naim, Abdullahi 41, 175, 186
arbitrary divorce 47–8, 50
Aripurnami, Sita 36–7, 175, 180
'Ashmawy, Muhammad Sa'id 39–41, 161, 175
autonomy 10, 24–6, 28, 30–1, 36, 113, 190–1
Azra, Azyumardi 1–2, 7, 21, 50, 52, 57, 150–1, 162, 175, 178–9, 185, 189

Blackburn, Susan 2–3, 22–4, 28–9, 35, 47, 54, 154, 160, 176, 181, 189, 192

CEDAW 152, 179
Chinese 22, 49, 52, 138, 162
Christian 24, 34, 46, 52–4, 85, 106, 156, 162, 178
Compilation of Muslim Family Law (KHI) 3–4, 6, 45, 76, 90, 185
confidentiality 18
conservative 7, 9, 12, 27, 37, 121, 148–9, 151, 156, 159, 165, 173, 190
Contextualist 43–5, 74, 80, 103, 112, 147
Counter Legal Draft of the Compilation (CLD KHI) 45, 76
Bogor 2, 13–17, 53, 118, 120, 134, 177

Depok 2–3, 14–17, 118, 120, 123, 133–4, 177
Dharma Wanita 6, 35, 58, 59–61, 63, 156, 177
 Panca 6, 156
Djohan, Bahder 42, 48
double movement 43, 149

feminism 4, 11–12, 33–4, 155–7, 160, 174, 178, 181, 183–90, 192–3
 companionate 4
 western 4, 11, 35, 155, 160
 Muslim 11
Fiqh 3, 8–9, 11, 40–2, 56, 77, 100, 108, 150, 153, 157, 161–3, 174
fitnah (social anarchy and chaos) 27
Flower of Aceh 134
Front Pembela Islam 7
fundamentalist 7–8, 27–8, 34, 112, 171, 190

Golkar 7, 53–4, 61

Hadith 34, 65, 68, 72, 74, 160–1, 164, 174, 184
Hatta, Meutia 76, 175
Hemas, Gusti Kanjeng Ratu 75
Heterosexual 5, 35, 57, 159–60
Hijab 82, 94, 165
Hizbut Tahrir 7, 126, 141, 156, 188
Hudud 42

IAIN/UIN 150–1, 153, 173, 179, 193
Ibuism 24, 35–6, 158, 179
'iddah 110
ijtihad 3, 42, 150, 161, 173
Islamic Studies 11, 39, 45, 65, 75, 98, 105, 150–1, 173, 175
Islamism 6, 9, 31, 183, 192

Islamized 2, 4, 10, 157

Jamaah Islamiyah 7
janda 29, 110, 159, 170, 190
jilbab 31, 95, 119, 165, 167

Kartini 30, 33, 46–8, 146, 160, 162, 178, 183
Katjasungkana, Nursyahbani 57, 61, 183
keluarga maslahah 5, 147
keluarga sakinah 5, 147, 187
kiayi 65–7, 69, 76, 117–18, 121, 125, 127–8, 133–4, 141–4, 146, 157
kinship
  bilateral 23–4, 29–30
  cognatic 23, 183
  matrilineal 23, 158
  patrilineal 23, 29–30, 158

LBH APIK 13–14, 35, 45, 54, 57, 64, 72, 79, 110, 154, 184
LKAJ (*Lembaga Kajian Agama dan Jender*) 45, 154, 186

Madjid, Nucholish 150
mahar 43, 75, 95, 97, 101, 109, 161, 163
Majlis Mujahidin Indonesia 7
marriage
  early 31–2, 38, 56, 176
  child 3, 47, 50–1
  forced 3, 47, 50, 148
  free-choice 32, 38, 128
  registration 4, 48–9, 55, 60–1, 85, 122–3, 128, 130, 143, 148
Mas'udi, Masdar 9, 153, 181, 185
Marcos, Lies 153, 185
maslahat 149
Mas'ud, Abdurrahman 151, 162, 174
matrifocal 25–6, 158, 177
  matrifocality 25
matrilocal 24, 29
Megawati 6, 64, 170
Mernissi, Fatima 9, 44, 161, 173, 185
Ministry of Religious Affairs (MORA) 50, 146, 151
Mitra Perempuan 35
modernity 7, 32, 49, 76, 177, 184, 188–90, 193
Moerdiono 60–61, 175, 178
Monogamous 2, 5, 14, 21, 44, 49, 75, 106, 147, 152, 186
Muhammadiyah 42, 45–6, 74, 146–7, 154, 157, 173–4
Mulia, Siti Musdah 9, 45, 76, 151, 154, 157, 186

Nasution, Harun 150
New Order 24, 32, 35–7, 52, 58, 60, 63, 92–3, 95, 149, 155–6, 159–60, 163, 177–8, 182, 192, 194
Nitisastro, Widjojo 5
NU (*Nahdlatul Ulama*) 5, 157, 163, 178
  Muslimat 5, 46, 154
  Fatayat 154
Nuriyah, Sinta 63, 187

Parawansa, Khafifah Indar 63, 187
Partai Bulan Bintang 7, 63
patriarchal 9, 60, 75, 143, 176
  system 26, 34
patrilocal 29
pesantren 11, 76, 136, 150, 153, 157
PKK (Pembinaan Kesejahteraan Keluarga) 6, 35
PKS (Partai Keadilan Sejahtera/Prosperous Justice Party) 7, 10, 112, 119, 148, 182
Polygamy Award 6, 13–14, 65–73, 75, 77
pornography 7–8
PP 10 3, 58–64, 76–7, 88, 90, 130, 163, 176, 184
priyayi 26, 29
Puan Amal Hayati 154

Rahima 154, 173
Rahman, Anita 2
Rahman, Fazlur 43, 149, 188
Religious Court 1, 21, 32–3, 53, 56, 60, 85, 94–5, 122, 148, 163
Revivalism 31, 57
Rifka Annisa 35, 45, 72
RUU APP 7, 182

Saeed, Abdullah 3, 4, 6, 42, 155, 161–2, 176, 189
santri 29, 45, 159
secular 3, 7, 19, 30, 40, 45–6, 49, 51–5, 58, 85, 106, 108, 128, 148–9, 155–6, 163, 179, 189
  law 4
Semitextualist 42, 153
sexuality 25, 27, 34, 36, 63, 96, 111–12, 155, 176, 177, 180, 186–7, 192
shari'a 6–9, 19, 38–42, 45–6, 53, 65, 70–3, 77, 108, 111–12, 123, 141, 147–8, 156, 160–1, 164, 172, 175, 177–9, 181, 183, 185–6, 189, 194
Sisters in Islam (SIS) 153, 156, 175, 185
Soeharto
  post- 1–2, 5–6, 8, 11, 19, 31, 40, 45, 57, 63–4, 78, 84, 109, 149

Soekarno 11, 51, 148
Soewondo, Nani 47–9, 51–2, 54–6, 163, 191
standpoint feminist 12, 157
stigma 28–9, 32, 105, 108, 110, 143, 150, 159
sunnah 9, 39–41, 65, 70, 73, 147, 160–1, 164, 174
Suryakusuma, Julia 2, 5, 25, 35–6, 58–61, 63, 156, 158, 160, 192

Takariawan, Cahyadi 9–10, 48, 192
tafsir (Qur'anic exegesis) 8–9, 11, 41–2, 150, 161–2, 175, 188, 191–2, 194
taklik-talak 50, 162
Textualist 42–3, 45, 47, 80–1, 112, 141, 147, 153, 155

Ulfah, Maria 49–50, 54

Undang-undang Penghapusan Kekerasan dalam Rumah Tangga 8, 100
uxorilocal 23

violence
  domestic 8, 13–14, 34–5, 61, 100, 152, 169, 176
virilocal 23

Wadud, Amina 9, 40, 44–5, 149, 173, 193
Wardoyo, Puspo 6, 9, 64–75, 98, 113, 120, 123, 125, 144, 164, 184, 187, 191–2
westernization 7, 46

Yasanti 35, 45
Yudoyono, Soesilo Bambang 76

zina 9, 32, 38–9, 42, 62, 65, 74, 99, 109, 147, 164–5

eBooks – at www.eBookstore.tandf.co.uk

A library at your fingertips!

eBooks are electronic versions of printed books. You can store them on your PC/laptop or browse them online.

They have advantages for anyone needing rapid access to a wide variety of published, copyright information.

eBooks can help your research by enabling you to bookmark chapters, annotate text and use instant searches to find specific words or phrases. Several eBook files would fit on even a small laptop or PDA.

NEW: Save money by eSubscribing: cheap, online access to any eBook for as long as you need it.

Annual subscription packages

We now offer special low-cost bulk subscriptions to packages of eBooks in certain subject areas. These are available to libraries or to individuals.

For more information please contact webmaster.ebooks@tandf.co.uk

We're continually developing the eBook concept, so keep up to date by visiting the website.

www.eBookstore.tandf.co.uk